ACADEMIC PLANNING

The Heart and Soul of the Academic Strategic Plan

Daniel James Rowlcy
Herbert Sherman

University Press of America,® Inc.
Lanham · Boulder · New York · Toronto · Oxford

™
⊖ The paper used in this publication meets the minimum
requirements of American National Standard for Information
Sciences—Permanence of Paper for Printed Library Materials,
ANSI Z39.48—1984

✿ Contents ✿

Preface

Part One: What Should We Teach

Part Two: How Should We Teach

Higher education is being challenged today, perhaps as never before. The demands of educational consumers and the general public for improved performance and accountability increase almost daily as the academy finds itself under more and more scrutiny and criticism. The emergence of for profit universities, universities without walls, e-learning, and university consortiums are changing the postsecondary educational landscape and toppling the image of the university as an ivory-covered, secluded tower. For some in the modern college or university, they see these challenges as intrusions that are most unwelcome. For others, they have seen the changes coming and have already begun working on changing their programs to respond better to the needs and demands of the modern student, as well as to the critiques of those beyond the campus. For still others, they welcome these changes and see them as an important opportunity to create programs and services that will carry their campuses well into the future. And for the most innovative and proactive, they are already on the cutting-edge of life-long learning and have already reshaped their campus community.

At the heart of all this activity is the relevance of the academic plan. Certainly, everyone inside the academy and outside its hallowed walls would agree that the academic offerings of every college and university should be relevant, current, of high quality, able to add to the welfare of society, and useful to students as they prepare for their personal and professional lives after graduation. What people don't tend to agree on, however, is what should be the driving force in determining the characteristics and tenets of academic offerings? Should that driving force be the faculties of our colleges and universities – those who have become experts in their fields, those who research and discover new knowledge, and those who know the curriculum well and should be able to disseminate it accurately and competently? Or, should the driving force be educational consumers and society itself – those who are building the Information Age and need new knowledge bases to support it, those who engage in their own commercial research projects and are responsible for creating new theory bases and paradigms, and those who want the academy to be more responsive to societal needs and ills. When the rhetoric is high, neither faction seems to be receptive to new ideas or compromise. However, when the academic community and its stakeholders begin to work together to create academic programs that they both can be proud of, then everyone can benefit.

This book looks at the process of academic planning as the primary activity that sets academic programming on a college or university campus. Academic planning involves matching campus strengths and distinctive competencies to societal needs in such a way that the best resources of the campus come into play in supporting existing services and programs or in creating new ones. In partnership with external stakeholders, internal stakeholders of the academic community devise the academic plan to meet existing demand, but also to help create a basis for meeting future demand. As such, then, it is appropriate that the academic planning process be tied to the strategic planning process of the campus.

As we have discussed in three previous books, *Strategic Change in Colleges and Universities* (Rowley, Lujan, and Dolence, 1997), *Strategic Choices for the Academy* (Rowley, Lujan, and Dolence, 1998), and *From Strategy to Change* (Rowley and Sherman, 2001) the use of strategic planning in today's colleges and universities is not only more and more common, it is essential. For the health and well-being of the campus, strategic planning provides a proven method of using its resources to maximize its opportunities, as it seeks to form a better fit with its important stakeholders beyond the campus. Yet, it is often surprising to discover that many college and university strategic plans address a wide variety of campus issues, but tend to give only lip service to the strategic plan or ignore it all together. The reason for this may be that strategic planning is far often more associated with administrative activities than it is with academic activities. The administrative function of the campus seems a more natural place to do strategic planning than it would be in the faculty senate or the curriculum committee. Academic planning is often seen as tied to administrative planning only through regional accreditation self-studies and is the sole purview of the college or university faculties. Here it is only impacted by faculty expertise under the protections of academic freedom. In other words, it is not uncommon to see both planning activities not only as separate, but as necessarily so.

This is a mistake. The academic plan must be the heart and sole of the strategic plan, and vice versa. Any campus that has a stellar strategic plan, but a poor academic plan is certain to fall on hard times. Further, any campus that has a stellar academic plan, but a poor strategic plan is also certain to perform poorly. It is crucial that both plans evolve together; that the strategic portion of the planning process looks to establish sound guidelines for operating the campus while advising (and being advised by) the academic planning process as they develop together. This involves cooperation at a level that is uncomfortable to some because it means that people other than pure academics may well have a say in the academic program mix and its methods. It also means that faculty leaders and other academics may well have a say in the administrative direction of the campus. For those who don't share power well, these eventualities are a severe threat. However, for those campuses that learn to share power and use their own particular resource bases to improve the overall standing of the campus and its academic programs, the potential benefits for everyone involved are enormous.

We have focused this book on the academic planning side of the equation because we believe that the field of strategic planning needs to better understand and incorporate the academic program within its boundary set. In doing so, we ask two major questions: 1) what should we teach, and 2) how should we teach it? In addressing these questions, we do so within a strategic and holistic concept. From the strategic point of view, we examine the opportunities and threats of the academic program to determine how they can better fit with the demands and conditions of the environment. From a holistic point of view, we view the constituents who are involved with the academic process, particularly the student (learner), faculty members, administrators, and service providers and how the academic program must encompass all facets of student life in order to be most effective. What the reader will see is that we do not view academic programming narrowly – we do not view it only as courses, classes, and roads to academic degrees. Certainly these are important factors and we treat them as significant, but we also present the case that if education is to be useful to a learner, then the college or university has to know a great amount of information about the learner so that it can best provide the environment, services, and education that will best benefit both the campus and the learner.

In Part One, we investigate the question, what should we teach. In Chapter One, The Learning Environment: Academic Planning in the 21st Century, we provide a broad introduction to academic planning and tie its development and implementation to the strategic planning process of the campus. We discuss the modern era and also what is different from previous eras and how this impacts academic planning. In Chapter Two, Academic Planning and the Changing Learning Environment of the 21st Century, we look at the nature of knowledge today – how it has changed as we have moved from the Industrial Age as the driving force behind higher education to an Information Age that has new demands and needs from the general knowledge base. In Chapter Three, The Academic Plan and the Campus Community, we set the parameters of academic planning to include nearly every phase of campus operations, especially those that have the ability to impact the learner and his/her learning process. Then, in Chapter Four, The Academic Community and the Academic Plan, we continue the discussion begun in the precious chapter by examining the role of campus faculty members in contributing to the institution's academic plan. Here, we also discuss the planning process and the elements of the academic plan. In Chapter Five, Knowledge, Learning, and Academic Disciplines, we look more carefully at the knowledge centers that form the disciplines and discuss the changes that many disciplines reflect and how these changes impact the campus academic plan and the process that creates it. With these basics in hand, Chapter Six, What the Academic Plan Should Look Like, gives a more practical guide for putting the academic plan together by discussing processes and elements involved in constructing a comprehensive academic plan for the campus. The chapter does this in a highly applied manner, using some of the basic elements of the strategic planning process to suggest analysis and evaluation techniques to help a campus best understand what academic programs and services make the most amount of sense for its resource base and the whole of its current and potential body of learners. Finally, in Chapter Seven, How to do Academic Program Planning, we move to the specific and more narrow topic of academic programs, the plans that affect them in the future, who should be involved, and how the process should come together to cement the curriculum base of the various faculties of the campus and the work they do.

In Part Two, we examine the issues involved with the question, how should we teach. We begin in Chapter Eight, So What's Wrong with the Lecture? by examining the pros and cons of the preferred method of educational instruction, the lecture. It's not simply the preferred method of many instructors and professors; it may also be the only method they know. Fortunately, many new methods for transferring knowledge to learners are now readily available and we develop these in the next several chapters. In Chapter Nine, Pedagogical Alternatives, we outline the pros and cons for several popular alternatives, or at least augmentation methods of teaching course materials. The chapter then concentrates on a discussion of Problem Based Learning (PBL) and examines it as a new philosophy as well as different method of learning that is gaining popularity and seems a nice fit with 21st Century learners in the Information Age. Chapter Ten, Moving the Paradigm from Teaching to Learning, presents a series of discussions about the art and science of teaching, looking at the motivations of the instructor and the learner in a classroom setting and drawing conclusions about tying teaching philosophies to the overall academic plan. Then, in Chapter Eleven, Tying It All Together in a Strategic Context, we discuss the methods of tying the academic plan together with the strategic plan and how the finished products might look. Finally, in Chapter Twelve, The New Paradigm Revisited: Learner-Focused Education, we finalize our discussion on learner-centered academic planning and then discuss several methods of implementing the academic and campus strategic plans.

This book attempts to combine a wide variety of campus activities that have seldom been combined before, into a single, coherent, planning approach. Pure academics may be uncomfortable with the strategic planning application we use, while the pure administrator may be a bit put off by the notion of having to combine the strategic plan of the campus with its academic community. Yet, both communities aspire to the same goals – serving learners, societal communities, and the academic profession as effectively as possible. The inability to work together may come from a tradition that has separated the academic portion of the college or university from the administration portion. The entire notion of shared governance tends to imply two different campus operations working along side of each other, not necessarily with each other. The world of the 21st Century, however, has introduced new paradigms and norms, and has challenged the academy to move ahead or pay the consequences. By seeing campus planning as a holistic event, combining strategic planning, operations planning, and academic planning into a single effort, today's colleges and universities will find new economies, new opportunities, and new rewards. We hope that those who read this book will keep this goal in mind. The academy has always been a precious resource to society, and if it can plan properly, it will continue to be so in the future.

Daniel James Rowley, Ph.D.
Greeley, Colorado

Herbert Sherman, Ph.D.
Southampton, New York

ೞ Part One ೲ

What Should We Teach?

ೲ Chapter One ೞ

The Learning Environment: Academic Planning in the 21st Century

It was a bright, shiny morning a week before the fall semester began. The faculty of ABC University had gathered for the annual freshmen convocation, a ceremony to welcome new students into the folds of the academy. This year, unlike years in the past, the president had asked the members of the faculty to attend an afternoon meeting where he would address them about the state of the university. Many rumors were floating around that morning, from the president's retirement to closing of several less popular academic programs. The university had been losing enrollment for several years, despite several innovations and personnel changes in admissions. The faculty members, normally quite chipper and boisterous about the prospects of meeting new students and filled with the excitement of getting back into the classroom, were somber and contemplative.

The after-ceremony reception went quite well, with faculty members losing a bit of their solemnity once they had a chance to mingle with the freshmen class. Many of them made positive comments about the students to their colleagues and the college admissions personnel, a very good sign for student retention. As the faculty members entered the main lecture hall for the President's State of the University address, they quieted down and waited in anticipation.

The president began his opening remarks with a series of statistics: enrollment was down by 10% over the last two years while competitor universities were increasing by 3% per annum; total revenues were declining while scholarships increased (tuition discounting), and the university was experiencing a negative cash flow. The picture the president was painting was an economically grim one, and the faculty became restless in their seats. They had heard this all before, and knew that the president had more on his mind.

"We need to increase our enrollment," the president announced to the faculty. "In order to do so, we need new academic programs and I need you, the faculty of this university, to be creative in developing new curricula that will attract new students to our

1

university. So let's put our heads together, be innovative, and work as a team to offer students exciting new courses, majors and degrees. I expect each and every department to submit a proposal for new program development to the University Academic Vice President for analysis and approval." The members of the faculty were so stunned that it took them a while to realize that the president had abruptly ended his speech and walked off the stage.

The event we describe in opening this chapter presents a situation that is not too uncommon on many college and university campuses today. The need to up-date a curriculum base and make certain that the academic programs, which mark the mission and direction of each campus, are of the highest quality, underscore the importance of challenging the status quo, revisiting discipline importance and viability, and becoming willing to reengineer programs that do not fit the needs of a fast-paced society. But what is the best way of addressing this challenge? There are so many directions to go, so many different options to examine, and so much to catalogue in terms of current campus academic strengths and weaknesses.

Clearly, there is a need for an organized method of proceeding that will objectively evaluate the current state of affairs, determine a good fit between what a campus provides in its academic program offerings and the emerging needs of society, and can suggest relevant options for going forward. We believe that strategic planning is precisely that method.

Most organizations in all sectors of the economy understand the importance of strategic management, and they have come to view it as a practice designed to keep them viable. More specifically, while business organizations have been practicing strategic planning and strategic management over the past few decades, these practices have also become more common in many other types of organizations including today's colleges and universities. Yet, as we have suggested previously (Rowley and Sherman, 2002; Rowley, Lujan, and Dolence, 1998; and Rowley, Lujan, and Dolence, 1997), the practice of strategic planning in colleges and universities is necessarily different from strategic planning in business and other types of organizations. The biggest single reason that this is true may be found in the existence of and the nature of the academic program.

One of the unique characteristics that is found in colleges and universities is what has developed over centuries is the principle of shared governance. In such a system, an odd mix to outside observers, campus administrators and members of the faculty divide management responsibilities so that administrators oversee the business side of the campus, while academics oversee the academic side. In practice, this can be a cumbersome system at times with faculties and administrators often at odds over how to best use the scarce resources of the institution. Yet, when the system works well, it is also a system that is responsible for helping the academy develop into the crucially important locus of research and learning that it is today.

Several institutions of higher education have turned to strategic planning as one method of helping them organize better to address the challenges they face in today's world of growing population and declining resources. However, when one looks at many of these college or university strategic plans, it is not always apparent as to what the precise role of the academic program is. It is also unclear as to how academic planning fits within the overall tenets and constructs of the campus strategic plan (Long, 1980). The reason for this is that the process of strategic planning is not particularly well understood on many college or university campuses, and many plans that do go forward tend to utilize the more traditional business model (very hierarchical and not especially democratic in nature) instead of a model that recognized the importance of characteristics such as shared governance. This is a mistake, because in the traditional business planning mode, the process is typically top-down, economically-oriented, and concerned with creating a strategic competitive advantage. Since the writings of Chandler (1962), the idea that strategy should dictate structure has been a given of the strategic planning process. As a consequence the use of these methods has not been well received in many institutions of higher education.

For many academics, the idea that an overall strategy should be able to dictate the structure of the campus (academic program mix and emphases) can be viewed as a serious threat. It also explains why many faculty members and faculty senates around the country often engage in political behaviors designed to disrupt or even kill the strategic planning process. The business strategic planning process is necessarily non-collegial and can appear somewhat dehumanizing, which helps one understand much of the resistance that can exist to strategic planning initiatives on college and university campuses. We believe, however, that strategic planning in academia is a different type of process from the more traditional business process; it is also one that should engage and incorporate academic planning as one of the (if not the) major element of the plan. Keller (1983); Rowley, Lujan, and Dolence (1997); and others have strongly suggested that not only is strategic planning in the academy a different process than one sees in business, they have also emphasized the need for participation in the process. They have incorporated the values of shared governance into the process and have encouraged strategic planners in the academy to design strategic planning methods that combine fiscal and growth opportunities with this important element of campus life rather than displace the academic direction of the campus to second-string behind what many may perceive as more pressing administrative concerns.

In this book, we develop the importance of academic planning as a central tenet of the college or university strategic plan. We present a model for active cooperation between the administrative and academic portions of the planning process and develop a system of operation that not only marries the academic planning process to the central strategic planning process, but also addresses the important connection between academic planning and the rapidly changing environments of the 21st century.

The types of questions one needs to ask when beginning to consider how best to combine the strategic plan and the academic plan rely heavily on the nature of the academic direction the college or university has chosen to follow.   Specifically, in developing a companionable academic plan, academic planners need to ask two questions: 1) what should we teach; and 2) how should we teach it? The answers to these two questions will have a dramatic effect on the nature of the accompanying strategic plan. To address these differing issues, we have divided this book into two parts, each one dealing with one of these two questions regarding the academic planning component. Throughout the book, however, we combine the activities of strategic planning with academic planning to demonstrate the interconnectedness of all aspects of both types.

The Importance of the Academic Plan

The academic plan defines the curriculum of a campus and its potential impact on a variety of learning communities within it. It develops over time and results from the collective wisdom, make-up, discipline interests, and research of the academic faculty members of the institution. It also reflects several emergent realities:

1. The growth and change of traditional programs that have characterized campus academic departments from the day the campus opened,
2. The growth of new programs coming from the natural development of the major disciplines as they constantly redefine themselves,
3. The distribution of institutional resources to support the emergent academic program base, and
4. The organizational structure which has been constructed to reflect academic needs of the campus and to a large extent, the administrative structure that supports them.

What Is and What Isn't Academic Planning

So then, what is academic planning, how is the plan devised? Long (1980) suggests that academic planning is an outgrowth of traditional planning and is "open, rational, and effective.... in the great measure an evolutionary stage in efforts to develop a grand strategy by which universities and colleges may respond to the current and forecasted flattening enrollment and resource growth curves" (pg. 29). Anketell (1996) states that an institution's academic plan is "an identification of program strengths, areas of expertise, and selected priorities where the institution wants to focus its attention and resources" (pg. 117). These definitions also identify why it is so important that the academic plan must be connected to the institutional strategic plan. They also suggest an openness and willingness to change that may not always be present in many institutional academic planning activities.

Academic planning needs to focus on two things: one, the need for, and shape of education in the college or university's service area; and two, the ability of its current resource base to adequately provide for these needs. This process must be objective, and the reality of potential change must be embraced. The prevailing objective of academic planning should be to either match current academic strengths with needed academic opportunities (including teaching, research, and service) or to begin a process of resource reallocation and/or accumulation to better serve needed academic opportunities. This is an externally-driven process.

Academic planning cannot be an exclusively internally-motivated process where faculty members, departments, schools, and colleges try to validate their current academic interests. It cannot be simply an ivory tower experience where members of the academic community plan to continue their present courses of research, teaching, and service because they are comfortable with what they are doing and don't believe outside influences should interfere with their parochial agendas.

This is not to suggest that academic planning is, or should be a threat to academic freedom. The academy has always reflected and responded to the needs of society, and to the potential for addressing those needs through an unchallenged research environment and freedom of expression. Academic freedom comes with responsibility. If an academic (or group of academics) seek the protection of academic freedom to prevent change or to thwart campus changes that will make the campus more viable and responsive to society, then they are misusing the concept.

One might ask, what is the difference between academic planning and program review? Aren't they the same, or are they different? The answer is that program review should be a significant part of academic planning, as we will describe further in Chapter Five, but it is not the only part. As we develop our views on academic planning, we will describe how it is a campus-wide event (as opposed to a single departmental or unit event), which is ongoing (as opposed to occurring once every 5, 7, or 10 years), and both holistic and part of the overall campus planning activities (as opposed to concentrating on the health of a single unit or department). So while program planning is clearly important, it's not all that must happen in academic planning.

The Holistic Academic Plan (Total Quality Management)

The modern academy needs to be about quality and excellence. While these terms are often misused, their importance cannot be ignored. Colleges and universities partner with society in general to provide needed and emergent knowledge bases. While the academy is about knowledge discovery and delivery, society is about improving the quality of life for all its citizens and has traditionally valued the academy as a major partner and inventor of improved quality-of-life activities.

Academic planning defines academic programs in a way that supports this central relationship between a college or university and its service area, or societal niche. It seeks to understand how its various disciplines can effectively work to explain society's ills or expand its opportunities. The decisions that academic planners make in defining and then redefining the academic plan need to be couched in this understanding of mutual dependence. So it is important that faculty members view academic freedom as both an important element of knowledge discovery, but also as somewhat tempered by the marketing realities of providing the services society needs. In failing to do so, they may have to live with the consequences of society's withholding necessary and valuable resources.

Further, academic planning impacts the student's total college experience: work, play, day-to-day living, and learning. As Ankatel (1996) and Anderes (1996) have suggested, academic planning needs to involve not only a wider-world perspective in terms of program decisions; it must also work within the campus environment to impact all other areas of student and other stakeholder well-being. Unsafe student housing, improperly balanced meal services, unsafe campus areas and personal problems do not seem to be a consideration of an academic planning process. Yet, they are. The academic environment is only one aspect of student life, and the other aspects of a learner's environment can and do impact the ability of the academic plan to be effective. For example, September 11, 2001 was a horrible day. The tragedy of New York was felt by all. Many institutions of higher education did not shut down, even for the day, and statements such as, "We can't let the terrorists win – we must conduct business as usual," was common. Nonetheless, one of the authors of this book recalls walking into a classroom and seeing the faces of students in shock over what had happened. The lesson plans for that day seemed pretty silly, and we spent our time together just talking, letting each other say how we felt.

The point of this short example is that until our students are ready to learn, we can shove academics at them all we want and it won't do any good. Thankfully, we are not talking about the September 11th event as common, but there are many things in a campus environment that do impact students, instructors, and administrators within the learning process. Improving campus safety can reduce anxiety and improve learning. Adding study groups to dorm settings can improve academic involvement and peer tutoring. Holding classes at times that allow our working students a more convenient schedule can improve their participation, retention, and graduation rates. All in all, academic planning is part of a holistic campus environment and must be developed as such.

The issue of quality is also complex. Standards of quality range with the populations defining it. One professor's high quality research may not seem so to a grant agency which rescinds funding. Another instructor's high quality lecture puts the class to sleep. Still another professor, an inspiring and captivating instructor, hasn't updated his content for 20 years. Again, there appears the potential for conflict between what an academic and his consumers consider quality. Who's right? The hard answer is whatever best contributes to the effective learning environment and serves the clientele to which it is targeted.

Who Does Academic Planning and Why

While we believe that the academic component of any campus should lead the academic process, it must not do so in a vacuum. A holistic approach will lead to a much more effective academic plan.

Though the process should be led by the Office of Academic Affairs, it is also important to include other members of the campus community in the process, and this has additional benefits. As we suggested above, if it would be desirable to provide opportunities for peer counseling in the dorms, then people from the Office of Facilities and Student Life should be involved. If safety is an issue, the process should include members of the campus security force. In many cases, academic planning will also be an issue that may need to involve a campus president or chancellor, and the governing board should modify and perhaps approve the finished plans.

Effective academic planning is a campus-wide activity. Naturally, primary responsibility should lie with the institutional faculty; every faculty member should be involved to some degree. Academic managers such as department chairs, deans, academic vice presidents (or academic vice chancellors), and provosts should all take part in the process. These are the people who best understand what their disciplines are and ought to be. Academic managers provide structure, resources, and timelines to help assure that academic planning activities proceed and progress.

The Relationship to Strategic Planning Model

From the organizational point of view, one would think that there should be no separation between the strategic plan of the college or university and its academic planning process. Yet, when one examines most higher education strategic plans, it is often difficult to see where academic programs fit as well as the planning required to create and operate them. We believe this is one reason that many faculty members are suspicious of strategic planning, and why they tend not to see how it ought to involve them.

Thus, it is a major mistake not to combine strategic planning with academic planning. Remembering that the central activity of any college or university campus is related to academics, it is crucial that the strategic plan mirror the academic direction that the college or university should or can follow.

The Strategic Plan Should Enact the Academic Plan

Without a strategic plan in place, every campus runs on traditional ideas that have grown over time. These emanate from the growth of the institution. As programs develop, as enrollment numbers rise, as different leaders (both administrative and academic) impact the nuances of the campus culture, and as the campus responds to undeniable external funding and regulatory pressures, the state of the campus emerges without purposeful development. The problem with the emergent college or university is that it reflects the past, which may not reflect a course of activities that fit well with the needs of society. Keller (1983); Shirley (1988); Morrison, Renfro, and Boucher (1984); and Rowley, Lujan, and Dolence (1997), have all shown that strategic planning is the method available to contemporary colleges and universities to create structures congruent with the developing needs and demands of society.

As campuses develop their strategic plans, they need to challenge the current developed structure to determine whether the offerings of the campus fit the developing strategic plan and the needs of the relevant stakeholders. Of course, there is an obvious choice here -- should the academic offerings of the campus match the strategic plan, or should the strategic plan match the academic programs in place? Further, is there enough flexibility in either to allow for an easy fit?

The answer to these questions lies in the processes each campus creates for its strategic and academic plan. If these two planning processes are separate, it is unlikely that the needed fit will exist. If, on the other hand, these two planning processes are related and intertwined, the fit should be much more natural.

How Administrative and Academic Planning Fit in the Model

The first steps of any sound strategic planning process involve the analyses of both the external and internal environments. While many colleges and universities allow this to be primarily an administrative assessment, it should include both administrative and academic perspectives. The administrative perspective of the external environment should identify and analyze the financial, political, legal, cultural, and societal elements that will identify both opportunities and threats outside the campus; these will either nourish or constrain specific strategic alternatives for the campus. Meanwhile, administrative analysis of the internal environment should identify resources, resource use patterns, and structures that promote or inhibit the institution's ability to take maximum advantage of present and potential opportunities, while explaining the institution's ability to thwart external threats.

On the academic side, external analysis should focus on the state of the various disciplines the campus presently supports. Academic planners need to understand whether certain disciplines are growing, stable, or in decline. From this, the viability of continuing to support disciplines at the current level can be determined. Also, as we become more and more encased in the Information Age, it is important to see if there are new discipline bases that might be important additions to the campus. Internally, the academic planners need to examine how well the campus serves learners applying the disciplines. This is an analysis of how well instructors teach, how well learners learn, how current pedagogical methods affect the discipline and the best methods available to transfer learning effectively.

These perspectives are necessary *prior to* the next step of the strategic planning process. By forming both an objective administrative view of the college or university service area and an objective academic view of the discipline base the institution offers, planners can begin to examine what the institution currently does and what it should be doing. Further, as Anketell suggests, the academic plan "should serve as the foundation for an integrative planning process" (pg. 117). As planning progresses, then, administrative and academic planners can each begin to plan for their own areas of responsibility, but in close contact with each other so that the final plan is a logical and well-orchestrated consensus of both areas.

How the Academic Plan Reflects the College Campus and its Learning Communities

The basic approach we provide above highlights the importance of academic planning in several ways. Among other considerations is the fact that the campus learning community is not a singular community. There are several different learning communities on a campus vary and they are based on the differing needs and directions of differing learners. They tend to reflect differing backgrounds and expectations relative to the institution. As a result, learning communities are defined from the students' perspectives, which is an interesting challenge to both the academic plan and the strategic plan. For example, a typical adult non-traditional student probably has no interest in the college's housing authority and is looking for evening and weekend classes to the exclusion of most other campus and/or academic services. On the other hand, a more typical traditional just-out-of-high-school resident student may be very concerned with comfortable dorm space and how to choose a major, but may have no interest in attending a weekend course (which would probably interfere with the student's social life or need to work at a part-time job). Differing learning communities require their colleges or universities develop differing academic opportunities and support services. This requires the campus to develop different academic and support service resource bases to best serve the needs of differing populations of learners on their campuses. Further, this brief example demonstrates that issues such as these impact both the academic and the strategic planning processes, and adequate solutions will be a combination of both academic accommodation as well as campus service accommodation that are harmonic and coordinated.

The specific learning community of which each learner becomes a part is based upon his /her experiences and needs. Weick's (1979) classic definition of organization helps provide further understanding about how this impacts colleges and universities and their planning priorities. In his work, Weick stated that in successfully managing organizations, one must recognize that all individuals are unique based on personal needs and drives that delineate individual perceptions and define motivations, desires, and their resulting behavioral activities. These perspectives meld within the organization, and define its nature. Individual needs that find a comfortable level of accommodation in a communal setting create an organization, and in the case of colleges and universities, academic planners and strategic planners need to understand those needs, motivations, and desires as they create programs and services to best meet those requirements. This organized approach is important in beginning to understand that there is not a single campus or a single student body that requires the existence of a single academic plan or unilateral strategic planning process.

As an example of the challenges to a multi-dimensioned academic and campus service approach, the registration process at Southampton College has traditionally been advisor-driven. Under this system, most students cannot register for classes unless they obtain the signature of their advisor on their registration form. This practice has created a situation in which each student must interact with a knowledgeable person to help assure that he/she signs up for important classes, is in line for a timely graduation, and can find help for other campus life problems. For most students, then, the advisor is an important resource in their academic lives. However, the college has changed its policies on registration in order to accommodate its non-traditional adult learners. For this particular group of students, the college allows adult students more flexibility in registering for classes by allowing online and telephone registration to occur without the signature of an academic advisor. In a very real way, however, this policy has potentially devalued the role of the advisor for adult students who can avoid the inconvenience of seeking out an advisor, but who also may not benefit from the important advising services available from the institution. In situations such as this, academic planning combined with strategic planning should identify ways that assist all members of its several learning communities to better understanding the entire range of programs and services to better to enhance the overall learning experience.

One of the important uses of the academic plan, then, is that it helps define the overall academic and support needs of its body of learners and then to combine the learning community with the communities of faculties and departments, college administration, and support staff activities. The academic plan should then incorporate the needs of the learning communities to form a set of useful formal and informal learning systems which also creates the shared culture of the institution. The academic plan provides a common language, a collective set of norms and values, and a shared vision as to the nature of learning at the institution. From this perspective, individual colleges and universities define their mission and values -- smaller colleges and universities can concentrate on personalized service and small classes, while virtual universities can strive to excel in the quality of their instructional delivery systems as well as their flexibility.

The Format of this Book

This book will develop and expand the basic ideas we have presented in this chapter. The book is divided the book into two parts: the first discusses academic planning and how institutions might go about doing it. The second part defines several best practices available for delivering effective education.

Part One looks at several of the issues regarding what we teach in the academy. This is a sensitive area because it coincides with two different elements that could potentially clash. One element is the faculties of our contemporary colleges and universities and their rights regarding academic freedom. The other element is societal demand and what society expects the academy to furnish learners to help add to the quality of life and improve our general knowledge base. Of course, neither element can have exclusive decision-making control, but finding the right balance between provider-driven education and consumer-driven learning is a major challenge to the academic process. In this section, we also expand upon academic planning, suggesting that academic planning isn't simply about research, teaching, and service. It is also about supporting a learning environment for students, taking into account their social and living needs while they are involved in achieving their higher educational goals. This is not a normal part of academic planning, but we strongly argue that it should be.

Part Two looks at the options modern educations have in terms of how they present knowledge in the Information Age. The lecture method is standard and wide-spread, but it may not be the most effective way of learning in today's world. This section develops a variety of choices, and suggests that the modern college or university instructor can choose methods of delivering knowledge that can create a better fit between course and learner. Finally, this section pulls together the aspects of academic planning with strategic planning and discusses how both should be formulated and implemented together.

In several chapters, we have chosen to use a question and answer model. Each chapter begins by identifying several major questions which affect the central themes. A great deal of effort goes to identifying the content of administrative and academic plans and trying to provide a logical and coherent manner of addressing these issues. Here, we seek to create linkages between administrative and academic operations that make logical sense and provide for greater areas of cooperation and understanding in the accomplishment of higher levels of academic excellence.

We then formulate a response to each question, including relevant research and logical discussion. Using this format, we hope to present material that academic planners and strategic planners can use in developing and coordinating their academic planning efforts. We also hope this method will prove useful in creating an overall unified academic plan for the college or university that logically connects all areas of the campus and provides an environment where high quality research, learning, and service will thrive.

Academic Planning and the Changing Learning Environment of the 21st Century

"What do you mean that this robot won't work? Of course it will work. I designed it myself, tested it on the class's computer simulator, now all we have to do is build the prototype and test it in the training area!" Jonathan was furious at his teammates and stormed out of the room before they even had a chance to respond to his accusations. What did they know about designing robots anyway!

Jonathan never thought that an engineering class would be anything like this. He figured that engineering would be a great major for him since he enjoyed mathematics and working on computers and had always been fascinated with building things. More importantly, he was a bit of a loner, not exactly the outgoing, party-type of person, and did not really enjoy hanging out in groups. The engineers he had met through family contacts seemed to be just like him, individualists who worked alone.

Yet here he was in Mechanical Engineering 101, working with a group of three other students, taking part in NASA's Langley Research Center's annual robotics competition. Each year, NASA kicks off the robotics competition by supplying a project problem and a kit of parts to teams of students. Each team has six weeks to organize, design, build, program, and test its project for competition. In this year's game, "Attack Bots" are to be designed that can disable an opponent robot through a variety of methods including high speed crashes, spinning blades, hydraulic lifts, armor piercing spears, etc.. The event has become known as the super-bowl of engineering and the ultimate mind sport.

Jonathan felt that he could have done this project alone. In fact, he wanted to do this unaided, but his teacher insisted that each student be part of a student team and share in the responsibility of building the attack robot. Now he had to work with his so-called teammates and try to explain to them why his robot design was just what they needed to at least win the regional competition. Yet every time he proposed his design, one of his teammates would find something else wrong with it. None of them had come up with better alternatives, in fact, not one of them had proposed a design of their own at all – it appears that all they could do was nitpick his ideas.

15

Jonathan made a decision. He would go and talk with the instructor and insist that he be allowed to do this project on his own. However, if the instructor insisted that his teammates had to be involved in the project, then he would compromise only if the instructor made them build the robot that Jonathan had designed. As he was walking to his professor's office, he found himself wondering exactly what he was supposed to be learning in this class and this group project. Designing robots was fun (if you left out the group stuff) but what did this project have to do with solving real-world problems Jonathan would have to deal with down the road?

Many universities, their administrators, and their faculties at the beginning of the 21st century are facing challenges that they have never faced before. As suggested in the introductory scenario, faculty members are now being asked to do more than teach, research, and serve on committees. They are being asked to become proactive in developing new academic programs and curricula that are more market-driven in nature (VanWagoner, 2001) as opposed to discipline-driven. They are also being asked or told to share in the responsibilities of marketing campus programs, tasks with which they may have neither the inclination nor training.

At the same time, accrediting bodies are holding college administrators more accountable for the quality of education produced within their institutions and to prove the quality through outcomes assessment. These and other regulatory bodies (if a public institution, these include the funding branches of state governments) are also questioning the relevancy of the curricula to potential students, and the efficient operation of their institutions by their boards. In such an environment, faculty members are also demanding greater information, such as student cost/revenue ratios by program, admissions marketing strategies, and college allocation of resources, as well as greater campus management authority, given the university's request for greater faculty participation in the more operational aspects of the organization. Through the tenets of shared governance, not only do campus faculties determine the process and content of the academic plan of the university, they now push for being including in the decision-making activities of the entire operation of the university, to the chagrin of many administrators.

The Changing Environment of Higher Education

Whether administration or faculty members like it or not, social and technological forces have changed postsecondary education and turned it into a hypercompetitive marketplace - an industry with more supply than demand. Gone are the days where the college or university could count on a steady stream of traditional, daytime students while allowing the two-year institutions to service the nontraditional, adult evening students. In fact, as Klein, Scott and Clark have suggested, "strategy based on the traditional/ nontraditional concepts was not working - useful segmentation of the higher education market is multidimensional" (2001, pg. 9). Keller has also stated that, "These changes suggest that planners must be prepared to enter a third stage of higher education planning. This third stage of academic planning will most likely derive from increased advocacy by planners for structural change and the adoption of innovative forms of postsecondary education created by institutions outside the traditional colleges and universities" (1999, pg.1).

Proprietary, nontraditional, and virtual universities have arisen both because there were emerging market opportunities, but also because there were unmet needs of students -- whether those needs were based on the content of what needed to be learned or the method of delivering the learning. Rowley and Sherman have suggested that these new breeds of universities can potentially negatively impacted classical, more traditional colleges and universities (2001), as demonstrated by the success of such nontraditional colleges as the University of Phoenix, Union Institute and University, Walden University, and Excelsior College (formerly Regents College) and the decline of many smaller traditional liberal arts colleges and universities.

As noted by Rowley, Lujan and Dolence (1998), the nature of work in the Information Age, denoted by the transformation of data into marketable information, has created a less formally structured, employee-centered workplace. Douglas McGregor's (1960) vision of the Theory Y worker, the worker who believes that work is fun and is capable of self-direction, has come to fruition with the introduction of such working arrangements as flextime, telecommuting, and job-sharing.

This emergent workforce is demanding the same type of treatment from educational institutions as they are now receiving from their employers and other service providers. To paraphrase an old Burger King advertisement, they want education their way. This has changed the time-honored role of higher education from being a creator, repository and provider of knowledge to a facilitator of learning. Higher education is being asked to move from being the sole proprietor of learning to becoming a partner in the learning process. Perhaps the center of the world of knowledge management is shifting somewhat away from the campus and towards those who help learners more directly obtain needed knowledge bases, especially in technology.

Higher Education as a Commodity

Kotler and Fox suggest that a fairly radical notion of education has emerged in the last few decades in reaction to the changing desires and requests of students, education as merely a product of the marketplace, a consumable good (1995). From this perspective, one can view attending college as an investment in human capital, and one that might understand better from an economic analysis correlating years of schooling, types and quantities of degrees, and cost with future earnings. Obtaining a college degree should have a positive return on investment, a return that is higher than any of the other alternatives available to the potential student such as going to work, joining the military, and volunteerism, including debt management and opportunity costs (Kiker, 1971). Kotler and Fox also stated that, "Today's consumer is looking for a strong return on educational investment. The question being asked is, 'With my academic background, my financial means and personal goals, where can I get the education that will be best for me?'" (pg. 43).

This viewpoint suggests that education has become just another article of trade in the market, an exchange of services for resources, and is subject to the invisible hand of the marketplace and the whims of the consumer. Birnbaum has stated that, "The tendency [is] to turn education into a commodity whose components can be bought and sold to the highest bidder" (2000, pg. 241), and Lewis and Smith have suggested that "(the public) is buying instruction and higher education is selling research" (1994, pg.2).

Given the notion that education is a commodity purchased by tax dollars, accountability for utilization of public resources has become an important public issue. Public institutions, and even private institutions utilizing public sources for funding student financial aide and research, have had to begin to demonstrate their effectiveness and efficiency as noted by the Spring 2002 special issue of *Planning for Higher Education* on cost and productivity models. Furthermore, a congressional mandate in the 1998 Amendments to the Higher

Education Act of 1965 required that the National Center for Education Statistics collect and analyze national data on revenues, costs, and prices across a board category of higher education institutions (Cunningham and Merisotis, 2002). Outcomes assessment, once considered a fad that many faculty members and administrators thought would just go away, has become part and parcel to a college's operation, as mandated by regional and state education accrediting bodies and specialized accrediting bodies alike (International Assembly for Collegiate Business Education, 2002).

Birnbaum has further stated that, "Given the transactional nature of education and the need for accountability, many critics of higher education have asked, 'Why can't a college be more like a business?'" (2000, pg. xiii), and have inevitably tried to mold higher education institutions into images that are more business-like in nature. These critics have somewhat succeeded. College administrators, who at least had always been accountable to their Board of Trustees, are finding that other stakeholders who include government agencies, donors, alumni, students and their parents, and lending institutions want performance information indicating that the institution is achieving their objectives (Mathews, 1993). College and university administrators find they need to break the mold of the traditional bureaucracy and become much more customer-driven and responsive. Higgerson and Rehwaldt have concluded that, "Their success hinges on communication - both personal and institutional - within the context of financial, political and personnel issues" (1993, pg. xxvii). For example, few students are going to tolerate waiting on long lines for registration. If the campus can not provide timely services, students will take their business, and their tuition revenue, elsewhere.

As peripheral consumers, parents and students also want to know much more about campus life, student social and recreational activities, housing, campus safety, job prospects, and financial aide. Most colleges and universities have created offices of institutional research to collect and develop a steady stream of data for these important stakeholders so that they can adequately address these new concerns. Kotler and Fox (1995) have found that, more and more, colleges and universities are moving away from the notion that marketing is unnecessary (colleges select students) to marketing as sales (students select colleges) and have even started to discount their tuition through selective scholarships and creating attractive promotional packages. A different level of organizational professionalism and expertise is now required throughout college administration and academics in order for a campus to operate effectively in a highly competitive economy.

The roles of faculty members have had to change right along with those of administrators. The current environment asks faculty members to work with administration on what was historically management, not academic issues. Academic meetings that traditionally have dealt with discussions of curriculum and research are periodically being replaced, at least in the experience of one of the authors of this book, by discussions that address more administrative issues such as student enrollment, faculty/student class ratios, expenditures on adjunct faculty and full-time faculty overload, promotion of academic programs, grant writing, and donor management. Members of the faculty are not being asked to reduce their teaching, research and service load to accommodate these management issues – rather, this is now considered part of their job and commitment to the institution to partake in such discussions.

From another perspective, however, if higher education is becoming more like a market-driven economic institution, then the faculty members, as well as staff members, can also be expected to act in their own best interest. In many places, it is made abundantly clear to the faculty that their jobs hang in the balance when it comes to the institution's ability to attract students, grants, and donors – not only administrator's jobs but their own jobs as well. Tenure, the security blanket of the academic community, means little if the entire educational institution closed.

Second, important internal and external governance stakeholders are putting pressure on campus faculties to demonstrate their effectiveness in their more traditional roles as well. Colleges and universities cannot afford to tenure and promote mediocre faculty if the market rewards enhancing customer value. It is important that students perceive that they are obtaining a quality education, particularly in light of the ever-increasing tuition amounts they pay. Middaugh, (2002) concluded that besides high levels of performance in the classroom, today's faculty members are being asked to also account for the relevancy of their research, and college service – not in terms of traditional measures of performance (teaching evaluations, publications, number of grants, committee membership and participation) but in terms of actual time spent on those activities and demonstrated outcomes. He also stated that, "External pressure on colleges and universities for full disclosure about what faculty do and how productive they are is not likely to disappear," (pg. 39) and in order to better manage faculty time distribution, many faculty contracts now specify such operational requirements as the number of days and hours faculty must be present in their office and/or on-campus, college committee participation, and academic advising (Long Island University & Southampton College Federation of Teachers, 2000). If it is true that the market place is going to hold colleges and universities directly accountable, then the institution is going to contractually hold the members of the faculty accountable as well.

The Commodity Revolt

Many members of the faculty and administrators bemoan their changing role from knowledge seeker and disseminator to service provider, especially in terms of the status and function of higher education in society. Many faculty members feel that their colleges or universities have prostituted their institutions and believe that their admissions offices have sunk to the status of door-to-door salespersons.

Certain faculty and administrators resist this particular transformation of higher education, and understandably so (Hawkins, 1999). Many bristle when students are referred to as either customers, consumers or even clients and many abhor the notion that students see higher education as merely an instrument to career development, or worse, an immediate path to a job or promotion. Knowledge, according to these faculty members, should be appreciated for knowledge's sake and education should serve a broader purpose then merely job and career training. Higher education should be insulated from market pressures, similar to regulated monopolies, given its vital role in society.

Further, many members of the faculty feel that viewing students as customers alludes to a level of student entitlement that goes beyond the noble opportunity to learn. Students now, as consumers, have the right to challenge grades and grading techniques, question the content and instructional method of courses and instructors, and may demand extra credit and/or additional time to complete course requirements. At least one of the authors had heard students say "I paid my tuition, I deserve _____ (to pass, a good grade, a diploma, etc.)." The focus of student-faculty discussions has shifted somewhat from course content (let's talk about XYZ) to course outcomes (tell us how to get a good grade in your class) and the dialogue between instructor and student often centers on quantitative course results rather than what is to be learned.

The notion of being held accountable to external stakeholders regarding what they teach and how they research is a fairly contemptuous concept for college faculty members. They deem themselves as professionals guided by the principles of their disciplines and are already being continuously being evaluated by their discipline colleagues in their research and their instruction is regularly examined through peer review and student evaluations. This is the norm for their disciplines and other outsiders could not possibly understand the nuances associated with evaluation of work within a particular discipline. Faculty members resent any notion that there is value in the bean-counting approach to productivity. Middaugh (2001) found that, "It is not unusual for professors in English, history, modern languages, political science, and philosophy, for example, to come to campus only two or three days a week. The rest of the time professors spend writing at home or conducting research in libraries, archives, and museums - both local and afar" (pg. 11). Many faculty members believe that quantitative measures of how they allocate their time cannot possibly capture their true productivity. And to some degree, they are right.

Many faculty members also feel that market-driven accountability has gone too far, in particular, some reject the notion that outcomes assessment is a valid method for evaluating what they perceive as learning for life. Simply, the value of college education cannot be measured through attitudinal surveys, content examinations, and certainly not through quantitative measures of higher education return on investment (Southampton College of Long Island University Middle States Decennial Self-Study, 2002).

Many faculty members see colleges and universities as the last bastions of human and intellectual development. The Southampton College Undergraduate & Graduate Bulletin states that their faculty members are "dedicated to educating students to realize their full potential and make a positive contribution to the world we live in" (2001-2003, pg. 5). There is an innate incongruity of applying business techniques and its inherent values of profit-maximization and means-end chains to a culture that values learning, the search for truth (not profit), and human dignity. Birnbaum (2000) stated that, "There can never be a management system that supports in equal measure all the goals to which higher education is committed," (pg. 228) and that "words and phrases such as *personal growth, intellectual development, the scholarly community, humanism, improving society*, and *liberal education* (p.204)" are alien concepts in a purely economic transaction. For these types of faculty members, the culture of business rationality, the bottom line, clashes with university tradition and values and it would be both undesirable, as well as near impossible, to change the culture of higher education to fit these business models (Miles and Snow, 1984).

Higher Education as a Community (Both Real and Virtual)

An emerging perspective of higher education, one that combines the traditional values of the college or university to provide education and the market-driven demands for value from educational institutions, is to view higher education as a community, a social network of administrators, faculty, and students dedicated to creating and nurturing a learning environment. The shifts in educational paradigms from provider to commodity and then to community also suggests a shift in the balance of power, first from faculty and administration to student and then to shared power (Keith and Keith, 1994) as suggested in Figure 2.1, below.

Figure 2.1
Three Paradigms of Higher Education

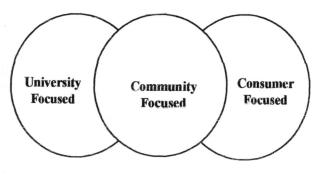

Traditional Approach → Collaborative Approach ← Market Approach

(Faculty Driven) (Faculty Mentor /Student Centered) (Student Driven)

Today's colleges and universities, according to Ehrlich (1997), need to actualize John Dewey's vision of democracy and education – a pedagogy that is increasingly infusing undergraduate education is one that consists of community-service learning, problem-based learning, and collaborative learning. This pedagogy has two common elements: education as a social and socializing function, as well as a shift in emphasis from teaching to learning; and a change in the faculty member's role from teacher to coach. However, in order to accomplish such a shift, colleges and universities need to create an egalitarian community of learners, where the student becomes the teacher and the teacher becomes just another student (Ackoff, 1994).

Kushner (1994) suggests a community approach to higher education through a model of quality education that is based on lasting principles of excellence, dignity, and connectedness. Here, excellence is surpassing one's personal best while also achieving dignity by choosing actions and participating in activities that contribute to self-esteem and self-respect. Further, the learning experience benefits from the connectedness of drawing people together, rather than separating, segregating, or discriminating against them. It also benefits by including others in decision making. Kushner conceptualized such a supportive environment as having four cornerstones that represent fundamental human needs: to live, to love, to learn, to leave a legacy. Kushner broadened the definition of the traditional academic community to encompass what Senator Hillary Clinton of New York referred to when she stated that it takes a village to raise a child; the community should not only nurture the intellect of the learner but should nurture the whole human being.

In going further and defining a community of learners, Haworth and Conrad (1997) focused on the interactive roles of students, faculty, and administrators and proposed five clusters of academic program attributes: (1) diverse and engaged participants-- faculty, students, and leaders; (2) a participatory culture, which is defined as requiring a shared view of program direction, a community of learners, and a risk-taking environment; (3) interactive teaching and learning, encompassing critical dialogue, integrative learning, mentoring, cooperative peer learning, and out-of-class activities; (4) connected program requirements, which includes breadth and depth of course work, a professional residency requirement such as university research and teaching assistantships, and a culminating program activity; and (5) adequate resources that provide support for students, for faculty, and of the basic institutional infrastructure. As comprehensive as this operational definition may be, it is unfortunately inadequate in capturing the philosophical underpinnings of the learning community, more specifically the role of learning in an individual's life and society in general.

The modern agenda for higher education, according to Queeney (1996), is to create a society in which lifetime learning is encouraged, valued, and rewarded and how a community of learners can be created and sustained. The principles she sets forth to guide this agenda include: the value of learning both to society as a whole and the individual, universal equity of access, enhancement of the natural propensity for learning, acknowledgment that a lifetime learning society will be consumer-driven, the importance of arts and cultural studies, the unique commission of public higher education institutions, and the ability to identify learning needs.

Higher education can neither remain the ivory tower, the recluse existing only for knowledge and knowledge sake, nor the diploma mill, the organization one attends to be legitimized by for the workforce. Each learner has differing educational needs and a one size fits all philosophy about educational programs and related services will not give rise to a learning community. Colleges and universities must be flexible, adaptive and caring in order to provide for the long-term needs of the learner. Ironically, the institution must become what Senge (1990) and others have called a learning organization, an organization which supports continuous learning and acknowledges the differences between early career, mid-career and post-career needs (Wick and Leon, 1993) and allows the learner to take an active rather than passive role in the learning process.

Argyris's (1982) best exemplified this concept of passive versus active learning in describing single-loop and double-loop learning. Single loop learning is the development of knowledge and expertise by students in a particular subject by following the path, or curriculum the course instructor has developed. Using this method, students must continuously find and avail themselves of new experts in the field they wish to study and to follow a predetermined learning plan. They seldom learn new material on their own and normally require constant support and guidance. In single loop learning, the student is the empty vessel that is filled with the water of knowledge by academic institution. The student is assumed to have minimal or no prior knowledge and the faculty member's task is to fill the container until it is full.

Double-loop learning takes the opposite approach. Here, the instructors first instruct and assist students to learn how to learn – that is, teach the students the basic skills necessary for self-instruction and self-enlightenment. Once students have the requisite skills for knowledge acquisition, they are then encouraged to pursue their interests as they see fit. Students create their own learning program and may even opt out of taking courses (or learning modules) within which they have demonstrated competency (Boyatzis, 1982). Prior knowledge is not discounted. In this approach, students consult faculty members as experts on a as needed basis. The faculty member's larger role is to produce a culture and learning environment that supports self-develop. In double-loop learning, the student is the gatherer of the water of knowledge and creates his or her own vessels to fill.

Technology and the New Distribution Channels of Learning

Technology and new ways of accessing learning are yet additional components planners must grapple with in developing the tenets of the modern academic plan. In viewing the ever-increasing importance of technology in the classroom, Swope (1994) stated that, "Higher education will be enhanced and challenged by new technologies that will reduce delivery costs for the educational product and increase its effectiveness. In order to accommodate the future, it is necessary for universities to respect their stakeholders and treat them with dignity, provide a value-added education, create a value-added community, and encourage scholarship judged according to new criteria. The university must be seamless, consisting of a community of learners made up of students, faculty, staff, and administrators" (pg.17).

The community model of higher education is strongly supported by communication and information technologies that allows for asynchronous as well as synchronous modes of learning. Students and faculty members alike can interact both within and outside of the framework of the traditional classroom setting using numerous means of communication and data transmission methods including e-mail, chat rooms, search engines, on-line libraries and journals, and other interactive multimedia that allowed for knowledge exploration, acquisition, and dissemination to occur twenty-four hours a day, seven days a week (Chamberlin, 2001). Along with the growth and proliferation of electronic communication in higher education, is the rise of virtual classrooms. Virtual classrooms exist because of technologies such as electronic mail, list-servers, chat rooms, and World Wide Web pages (Powers and Mitchell, 1997).

As Rowley, Lujan and Dolence first noted (1998) and then as Rowley and Sherman (2001) further elaborated upon, there is a new breed of colleges and universities that has emerged within the last two decades. They are based upon alternative learning distribution networks, most predominately those driven by the employment of information technology. Colleges such as Western Governors University, Open University and the University of Phoenix have created virtual universities while other universities such as Walden University, Nova Southeastern, and Union Institute and University are more hybrid in character, with varying degrees of use of distant instructional technology, distance hard copy, and face-to-face instruction. Meanwhile, more traditional universities such as Columbia University and M.I.T. have also joined the new breed of universities in hyperspace by offering their version of the click and mortar approach to instruction. The concept of community (especially college community) has therefore been redefined through both paper and digital forms of distance learning.

Misanchuk et al. (2000) indicated that shifts from traditional classroom education to computer-mediated distance learning poses enormous challenges to instructors and learners since it redefines the learning environment. The concept of the classroom is one where students meet to interact with other learners and the instructor no longer exists. Learners lack a natural social outlet to engage with other learners thus leading to feelings of isolation. The instructor must consciously strengthen the feeling of community amongst the learners by utilizing instructional and non-instructional strategies that have students interacting at the levels of discussion, cooperation and collaboration.

Powers and Mitchell (1997) in analyzing data from list-servers and e-mail messages, student journals and time logs, transcripts of chat sessions, and a group interview from a virtual graduate class found four significant themes related to the virtual learning community: student peer support; student-to-student interaction; faculty-to-student interaction; and time demands of the course. A definitive community of learners emerged despite the physical distance of the learners from each other and the lack of face-to-face contact. Students were able to develop rapport and provide support to one another and were able to develop and maintain interactions that may not have been attainable in a regular classroom situation.

Powers and Mitchell also discovered that the faculty-student relationship also manifested itself differently. Although the instructor remained the head of the class during synchronous chat sessions, during asynchronous communication, the instructor became less of a purveyor of information and more an unobtrusive part of the community of learners. Further, although students felt that the course was more time-demanding because of the format, an analysis of the time logs revealed that students has spent additional time surfing the Internet collecting and validating data and that their general perception of the course was more a function of perceived useful time in front of the computer completing their assignments. From the analysis of student performance and perceptions in this particular class, it seems apparent that as virtual classrooms become more prolific, the classroom community of learners can continue to flourish with proper design and faculty training.

Yet, there are some downsides to the wholesale use of technology. Sonwalker (2001) cautions that success in a pedagogically-driven instructional design for on-line education is a function of the learning style of the student as well as the teaching style of the instructor. Teacher-centered techniques are varied and can include on-line text, graphics and audio while more student-centered approaches tend to include video, animation, and computer simulation. This is quite a choice and not all methods speak equally well to all learners. Teacher-centered methods tend to be single media, unidirectional while student-centered procedures tend to be more multimedia and interactive. According to Sherman (1984), multimedia, two-way transmissions of information can lead to greater task and social system certainty. In the case of a classroom setting, such methods can lead to greater learning and a stronger sense of community on the part of the students. The challenge in the development of a virtual learning community also involves overcoming the resistance of the faculty to using new technology as well as the ability of the institution to garner the resources necessary to obtain the needed hardware/software and train the faculty, and match technology to optimal student learning experiences.

A Student-Centered Approach to Academic Planning in Higher Education

With the growing acceptance of the idea that learning should be a collaborative effort, it is also important to examine how higher education develops its academic plan from a human systems perspective. In utilizing the human systems approach, planners identify key factors in the development and implementation of an academic plan that address the needs of the learner and also allow the institution to develop an organizational design that will best service those needs. However, in developing a humanistic, student-centered approach to academic planning it is helpful to understand the traditional approach to academic planning in higher education as well as the rational systems perspective from which it emerges as suggested in Figure 2.2.

Figure 2.2
The Rational Management Systems Approach to Higher Education

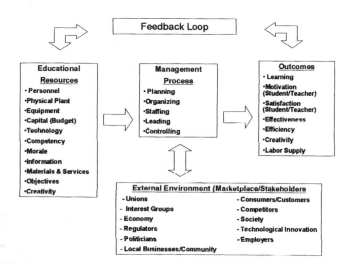

Lewis and Smith (1994) have suggested that higher education should be viewed from a process management or rational systems perspective. In such a system, the college or university acquires inputs (educational resources), which it then transforms through the activities of the faculty and administration (academic and management processes) into outputs (learning, knowledge, and service). These activities occur within the unique context of the institution's particular external environment. However, in such a model, the institution regards the student as a consumer and the market conditions and the resource base of the institution create a dependency relationship between the student and the college or university. Further, Rowley and Sherman (2001) have suggested that the relationship is further defined by the consciously-chosen orientation of the institution as being either provider- or consumer-driven. Academic planning, under the rational model, will tend to be either mission-driven or customer-driven.

A mission-driven university creates a series of academic and research programs based upon an internally generated academic mission. This is a defender approach to the market. Rowley and Sherman have suggested that, "Defender organizations tend to ignore changes in the marketplace that do not directly impact their operation and tend to be laggards in new product development" (p. 97). These institutions focus on either continuous academic program improvement to create centers of academic excellence or on continuous improvement of student and administrative support services in order to create better and more efficient service. Such academic institutions have a very high student application reject ratio based upon either their superb reputation, such as Harvard University, specialized programs with limited space, such as Cooper Union, or low cost relative to perceived competitors, such as state-funded colleges and universities like Rutgers (New Jersey) or University of Texas at Austin. As long as these institutions maintain the integrity of their current academic programs and/or their low cost advantage, they can continue to enjoy their market position.

Customer-driven colleges and universities, that one can classify as reactors, "respond only when forced to by environmental pressures" (Rowley and Sherman, 2001, p. 100) or by budget deficits and have no consistent and integrated academic plan. At best, their academic planning consists of being what marketers would call industry laggards; they adopt academic programs only after there is clearly demonstrated long-term market demand. At worst, these colleges and universities become academic fad followers. They jump at every perceived opportunity to attract students, whether or not they have the in-house expertise and resources to deliver a quality program. These institutions tend to have very high student acceptance rates (or may even have open enrollment), have very liberal transfer credit policies, and/or heavily discount tuition. Students learn to play "let's make a deal" with these institutions in terms of both funding their education and crafting their academic programs.

Academic planning is defined via the rational model in one of two ways:
1. The traditional or provider/defender approach -- deciding on the substance of the creation, storage and dissemination of knowledge (focusing on curriculum, research and library/digital storage).
2. The commodity or customer driven/reactor approach -- deciding on the substance of curriculum, research and library/digital storage based upon shifting market demands.

Towards a Humanist Model of Higher Education

The rational model described above has several limitations:
1.   Students are external to the education process. Knowledge is treated either as a sacred trust to be given to the privileged few, or as a

consumable good to be sold to the highest bidder. The needs of the student as a human being, however, are not being addressed.
2.   Academic planning is either totally deliberate (purposive) and rational or imposed by the market. However, as Mintzberg (1987) has suggested, academic planning (or planning in general) tends to be more emergent. It is a combination of intended and unintended strategies which account for numerous stakeholders' interests.

Looking at an alternative model of the systems approach to higher education we described above allows us to account for the limitations of the rational approach. This new model is designed, in part, "to provide academic planners with the tools to perform core functions and activities that facilitate the transformation of higher education institutions from provider-centered cultures and organizations to learner-centered franchises" (Nedwek, 1996, pg. iv) and places the learner and his or her interests within the system's core as suggested in Figure 2.3 below.

Figure 2.3
The Humanist Management Systems Approach to Higher Education

Learner Background	Day-to-Day Living	Stakeholders
Socio-demographics Life Style/Religion Career Aspirations Academic Abilities & Aptitudes	Play (Learner) Work Spirituality Learning	Family Friends (home) Friends (on-campus) Employer Creditors Fellow Students

University Stakeholders (internal) – Academic Planning
Faculty   Academic Staff   Administrative Staff   Trustees Academic Programs   Administrative Services   Other Learner Services

University Stakeholders (external) – Strategic Planning
Competitors   Regulators   Economy   Technology   Society   Donors/Alumni Mission   Goals   Competitive Position   Distintive Competencies

In the learning community, those individuals directly and indirectly connected to the learner, are an integral part of this humanist or social system since the focus of the system is not only on the tasks and goals of the system but the interaction and sentiment of those involved in the learning process (Homans, 1950). The educational system is presented less as a set of interconnected subsystems and rather more as a series of building blocks which are necessary in order to construct a learner community.

The base of the system is comprised of the university's external stakeholders and the external forces that push and pull the organization (Lewin, 1951). The organization creates a strategic plan to define for itself and for its external stakeholders the institution's mission, goals, competitive position and distinctive competencies. External governing bodies that fund and regulate their operations may dictate (and if not, certainly influence) the mission and goals of public institutions of higher education.

The middle layer of the system consists of the university's internal stakeholders, such as faculty, administrators, and the Board of Trustees, who enact academic and administrative services through the academic plan. The academic plan acts as both a buffer (Thompson, 1967) and a bridge (Pfeffer and Salancik, 1978) between the external environment and the university's strategic plan and the learner. We will describe he relationship between the academic plan and the strategic plan are described in greater detail in Chapter 11.

The top of the system centers on the learner and the aspects of the learner's life during this period of learning (work, play, day-to-day living, learning, and spirituality). The wings connected to the learner, his or her background and his or her stakeholders, define the world of the learner. An effective academic plan must address many of these aspects of the learner's life, translating learner needs into organizational structures, work processes, and service delivery that adequately support the learning process. Unlike the rational systems approach, where academic planning processes educational inputs via interaction with the external environment, the humanist systems approach utilizes academic planning as the means of addressing learner requirements within the context of the college while mediating externalities. We will discuss the relationship between the academic plan, the learner, and society more thoroughly in the next chapter.

The humanist approach to higher education challenges the definition of academic planning as defined by the rational approach. Academic planning through the humanist perspective is the creation of a learning community based upon the needs of the learner and the mission of the institution.

℘ Chapter Three ℘

The Academic Plan and the Campus Community

"The central question of academic planning: in the 21ˢᵗ Century, what is the role of the campus community?"

     Jonathan's parents were worried – they were worried sick. They had not heard from Jonathan in over two weeks and it was very unlike him not to call or e-mail them, even if it were just to say, "Hi." They knew that every parent worried about their first child's freshman year in college, especially if the child was living away from home for the first time. They had talked to several of their friends who already had children in college and had heard horror stories. This did not make them feel any better. Should they call or e-mail Jonathan? They didn't want him to feel like they didn't trust him or that he was still a baby. Yet, they did want to know that everything was alright. Perhaps they could call someone at the college to check up on him ... .

     Jonathan was having the time of his life living away from home. His roommates were pretty cool and did their own thing (one was a jock, the other a party animal) while Jonathan enjoyed surfing the net and listening to death metal. They still took time out to hang with each other at night, including during study time. Classes were okay and he was finally getting used to living in an urban environment; there wasn't as much open space as his rural home town but there was plenty to do. More importantly, he had no parents to bug him about stupid things like cleaning his room and making his bed, and no younger siblings to get underfoot or want to tag along with him and his friends. He missed all that at first but found that as the days turned into weeks, and weeks into months, that he needed less and less contact with the folks back home. In fact, the last phone call from his mother nearly drove him crazy with her insistent questioning. When were his parents going to let him live his own life?

     Dr. Peters was Jonathan's freshman advisor. She conducted a course called College 101: Introduction to College which all of her advisees attended. It was about two months into the semester, what Dr. Peters jokingly called the "blue period" since either some of her advisees or their significant others (parents, siblings, boy/girl friends) would experience separation anxiety. Dr. Peters had just heard from one of her advisee's parents, Jonathan, who were worried since they had not heard from him in over two weeks. Jonathan had had a few problems adjusting to college life at first, especially dealing with such

33

issues as clean laundry and finding his way around campus, but he seemed to have settled down very quickly and even looked as if he was starting to enjoy college life.   Dr. Peters shrugged her shoulders and figured it was about time to have her little role reversal exercise in class – that's the one where students enact the role of the anxious parents and other students try to either calm the parents down or purposely unnerve them.   The debriefing sessions usually led to some interesting insights for the students about their relationships with their parents and some good tips on how to manage the relationship from a distance.   In the interim, Dr. Peters decided to fire off a short e-mail to Jonathan about the call she received from his parents.   It would be purely factual in nature (not accusatory) and would request no action on his part.

The Academic Community Revisited

The scenario above is not unusual for a first year college student living away from home and his or her parents, as many faculty, students, parents, and administrators might attest.   Faculty who teach freshmen courses, along with resident assistants, academic advisors, college psychological counselors, and campus ministers, have certainly come across this type of situation and we would hazard a guess that they will continue to do so.

Some faculty members, and perhaps even some administrators, who ascribe to the traditional approach to higher education might read the above case and remark that Jonathan's personal life, including being away from home, has little to no bearing on what occurs in their classrooms, their research laboratories, their libraries, and even their offices.   For them, any activities that are outside the confines of knowledge discovery, acquisition, storage, and dissemination are not a part of the academic community and have no bearing or relevancy in academic planning.

As we discussed in Chapter One, the traditional approach is being challenged by a changing higher education environment and, more importantly, by a paradigm-shift from a provider-driven academic community to a collaborative, learner-centered approach.   Further, the academic community is discovering the importance of meeting the needs of the life-long learner, and conforming to the mission of the college or university.

The issue of academic mission is changing, and now includes

the understanding a broader role that the institution plays both in its local community and society in general (Harvard University, Office of the President, 1993). Such an understanding broadens our early definition of academic planning from the *creation of a learning community based upon the needs of the learner and the mission of the institution* to include the needs of society as well. If this is the case then we need to ask three basic questions about the academic community:

1. What do students want and need from our academic community, and why?
2. What does the academy want and need from our academic community, and why?
3. What does society want and need from our academic community, and why?

Students and the Academic Community

The academic plan is a multifaceted document, resulting from a multifaceted process. In its simplest form, the academic plan marries the programs of the institution to the needs of the learners. However, the complexities of the college or university academic programs, combined with the complexities of what comprises a single student, let alone an entire student body, presents a challenge of paramount importance in bringing it all together. On another note, it is a mistake for a campus to try to be all things to all people. No campus has the resources to do this, and the mere attempt to do so often leads to disaster. The key to success, then, is to support those programs that the campus can effectively support and attract only those learners whose motivations and needs fit within the academic offerings of the institution. This is then an issue of choices for both the institution and the learner. In refining the process, it is important to gain a deeper understanding of not only the colleges' or universities' program base, but gain an insight as to what learners they can best serve.

Students, as we described earlier, do not come to an academic institution either as empty vessels, or with blinders on. Student bring their own experiences, motivation, background, and personal network to the academic community as well as a knowledge of the higher education market – not perfect knowledge per se but certainly enough knowledge to make a fairly satisfactory choice, one good enough to meet his or her educational needs (Simon, 1976). Students are distinct individuals who demands that higher education meet their needs.

In Chapter One, we described the humanistic approach to higher education as centering on the student. The top portion of the humanistic model (see Figure 3.1) directly addresses those issues which we will elaborate upon below.

Figure 3.1
The Learner

Learner Background	Day-to-Day Living	Stakeholders
Socio-demographics Life Style/Religion Career Aspirations Academic Abilities & Aptitudes	Play (Learner) Work Spirituality Learning	Family Friends (home) Friends (on-campus Employer Creditors Fellow Students

Looking Within the Learner – Motivation

Central to the learning process is the motivation that drives the students to learn, their rationale for attending the university. Their grounds for pursuing an education may include such noble reasons as the pursuit of knowledge, self-discovery or community service, or they might be more pragmatic such as developing a career, obtaining a job or advancing a promotion. Regardless of the particular motivator at work, for students to want to learn they have to have an unmet desire, a specific need translated into a certain set of actions or drive, and they must be self-directed towards a goal which will satisfy those specific needs. Of course, motivation is also a function of other factors such as the students' expectation of reaching desired goals, the desirability of those goals (is this really what I want to learn?), and the consequences or rewards associated with obtaining those goals (what do I get if I learn this?) (Luthans, 1998).

Much of this personal, internal process is unclear even to the student and, as a result, the student may appear aimless, distant, and uninvolved. Some parents may find this disheartening, as may be also true for significant others, and employers who send their child/spouse/employee to college and then not be able to see that their college student is embarking on a clear path. Further, where real problems exist, learning will not occur unless there is a clear connection for the student between effort (working hard), performance (demonstrated learning) and outcomes (rewards) (Pinder, 1984).

It is also not surprising to find that some students choose particular courses of study because of the promise of post-graduation rewards they believe are associated with the completion of the study of that topic.   For example, in times of high unemployment, many students will find business education highly desirable because there is a perception that this degree will help assure better job opportunities. However, some of these same students may find that they have inordinate difficulty learning this material because they are not suited to business disciplines or find that the business learning environment is unsupportive to their particular needs and interests.   The academic plan should provide mechanisms for students to test their own needs and interests and find an academic path that makes the most amount of sense for current capabilities and academic preparation.   The plan should address both the learners' ability to learn and the academic community's ability to support the learning process, given the institution's mission and the type of learners the institution attracts.

A case in point – both authors are business professors and can attest to the fact that they have worked with students who would like to be business majors but do not have the quantitative skills necessary to succeed in certain higher level finance and quantitative methods courses.   However, each of their institutions deals with this problem quite differently.   One of the author's institutions   created several preparatory quantitative programs (B.A. in Business Administration, B.A. in Liberal Studies with a concentration in Business) in order to better prepare the potential business learner. This approach fit with the institution's consumer orientation, and its need to attract and retain a particular type of pre-professional student.   The other author's institution has set very high standards for their business majors – the program is accredited by the American Assembly of Collegiate Schools of Business or AACSB. This institution believes that in order to afford its students the best opportunities in the marketplace that they must graduate students who possess superior business acumen. They have used high program admissions standards and extensive student advising to help support it goals for its graduating seniors. Part of the initiation procedure is to work directly with business learners and underscore the importance of developing quantitative, qualitative, and analysis skills. This school also provides tutoring services for those students who need help to improve their skills and meet the program admissions and graduation requirements.

Student Needs as a Factor

Motivation in students comes from the satisfaction of a variety of needs. Further, those needs are unique to each learner. Understanding motivation and how the academic experience can help students satisfy needs is another important aspect of the planning process. Though needs are different, it is possible to categorize them by the type of internal process that drives them. The most basic theory of human motivation, Maslow's Hierarchy of Needs Theory offers a helpful vehicle for describing the differing types of needs of the learner. Nowacki (1977) found this a useful model for helping understand student motivations related to learning in higher education when he explored and correlated Maslow's Hierarchy to the various departments within Student Affairs in an effort to show how Student Affairs can satisfy those needs. In our discussion here, we have broadened Nowacki's application of Maslow's model to include the entire academic community, and address all of the needs of the learner relative to his or her college experience.

Maslow suggested that there were five different levels of human need. Starting with the most basic, primary motives (unlearned and physiologically based), these needs include securing physical welfare and personal safety. There are good examples of this particular need on a college campus. For example, referring back to our resident student in the case at the beginning of this chapter, one can see that for many such students, basic needs might include knowing where the student's next meal is coming from and feeling comfortable being away from home for the first time.

The second type of needs include secondary motives, and are both learned and psychological in nature. They include affiliation or belonging, self-esteem and self-actualization. Again looking back at Jonathan, while he was reducing his affiliation with his family and friends, he formed new affiliations with his roommates as well as with other fellow classmates. Because he was able to cope well with living on his own, he was able to increase his self-esteem. By definition, self-actualization needs represent the culmination of all of the other needs and the ability of the individual to transform their perception of self into reality (Luthans, 1998). Many faculty and administrators would argue that this is the ultimate purpose of higher education, especially those working in liberal arts institutions, and when Jonathan graduates with honors and moves on to a preferred job, he will have achieved some level of self-actualization. As the overall academic experience encompasses all of these areas of a student's life and study on campus, the academic plan should be connected to each area and demonstrate concern for helping students satisfy their needs and become motivated to obtain higher levels of academic achievement.

Please note that we are presenting Maslow's theory here in a slightly modified fashion in that we don't necessarily see motivation as a hierarchy. The theory states that individuals concentrate on satisfying lower level needs before they can become motivated by the potential of achieving higher level needs. Research evidence contradicts the hierarchical nature of human needs by developing data that strongly suggest that multiple needs can exist simultaneously, and that these needs may turn into motivational drives (Bowditch and Buono, 2001). For our purposes in examining the role of student motivation in the learning process, we envision needs as enmeshed together, as depicted in the forming of a series of concentric experiences as Figure 3.2 depicts. Here, the larger external rings represent those needs that are satisfied through external stimuli or resources (i.e. housing, campus security) and the internal rings represent those needs satisfied through personal growth and development. This approach to motivation also fuses the concept of locus of control as defined by Rotter (1990) with needs theory. As individuals begin to view their lives from being controlled by externalities (forces they cannot control) to being controlled by themselves (internal locus), they are then moving from lower level needs to higher level needs, according to Maslow.

The challenge for creating effective academic plans within the larger academic community is to provide an environment where learners, based upon their individualized needs, can be motivated to satisfy those needs, take control of their lives, and master their academic goals. They take responsibility for their education. Understandably, various learners have diverse needs and differing loci of control and academic plans, and the larger academic community must be flexible to accommodate as many of those differences as possible and improve the learners' ability to manage their own education. This is not to suggest that learners want faculty members and administrators to disappear or get out of their way. On the contrary, recent research has indicated that 75% of the students want some form of academic leadership, guidance and advice (Goral, 2001). All this suggests that it is useful for higher educational institutions to better understand the variety needs of their students, and determine the range of the advising, campus-life, and academic services they offer their learners. Clearly, however, no single institution can be all things to all people.

Figure 3.2
Modified Maslow's Hierarchy of Needs

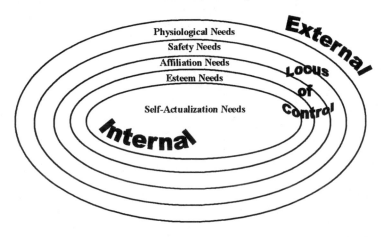

Although it is important that academic planners focus on students' various needs, different campuses will tend to focus on certain areas, while other campuses will focus on different ones. One academic strategy for certain higher institutions may be to cater to only certain types of learners in certain stages of learning development and to create specialized programs which address those. For example, Union Institute and University provides bachelors' and doctoral students a non-traditional approach to higher education, and was "designed for adults who have the desire to assume a significant measure of personal responsibility for planning and executing their degree programs" (http://www.tui.edu/About/ index.html). Berkeley College in New York serves a more traditional, profession minded student population by providing a structured educational environment which prepares "men and women for careers in business ... (through) small classes, individualized advisement and counseling ..." (http://www.berkeleycollege.edu/Overview/BerkeleyWay.htm) including formal internships as part of the degree program.

Where college and universities have missions that emphasize meeting the diverse needs of their learners, then it is important that they understand and provide services that address those needs as they develop of their academic plan and their strategic plan. This seems very apropos for teaching institutions, community colleges, proprietary colleges and even public institutions, whose mission directly addresses the primacy role of the learner. What, then, is the proper approach for other academic institutions whose missions are research-driven, religious-based, or corporate-based?

McKee, Kiser and Lea (1999) addressed this issue very succinctly for research institutions. They observed that "the primary focus of most university research programs is not revenue but the critical nature of the relationship among the research, education, and public service missions of the university. Since a strong research program attracts and helps retain [top-quality] faculty ... [who] attract top-quality students ... faculty, students and research are intertwined in institutional competitiveness" (pg. 158-9). The suggestion is then, interestingly enough, that for research institutions to be successful, they should address the needs of their learners in the same way as any other type of higher educational institution.

This same conclusion can be drawn for religious and corporate universities. Dominican College of Blauvelt's mission is "in the tradition of its Dominican founders, [the college]fosters the active, shared pursuit of truth and embodies an ideal of education rooted in the values of reflective understanding and compassionate involvement" (http://www.dc.edu/mission.shtml). However, "Motorola University South Asia's mission is to anticipate and meet the training needs of the corporation and community to enhance individual competence, improve organization performance and achieve competitive advantage" (http://sg.motorola.com/inside/mu/ aboutus.htm). Both missions clearly include the learner (although Dominican more tacitly when referring to "shared pursuit") and focus on providing a value-added to the learner through pursuit of knowledge or increased competency.

Learner Demographics as a Factor

Another important factor that helps academic planners better understand their learners is that of their students' demographics. Here is where they can begin to understand many of their students' learning preconditions, those features that students bring with them to the institution which affect the type of learning learners are seeking. These factors also often explain the student's ability to learn and why they respond they way they do to the institution's programs and services. From a marketing perspective, individual student's background will also help determine whether the student is a prospect for the institution. A student's economic demographics may also be used in order to segment the institution's market. Also, small private colleges may choose to segment their market by a student's ability to pay while state colleges may do so by residency qualifications (Kotler and Fox, 1995).

In today's sensitive social and political environments, the socio and psycho-demographics of learners play a critical role in determining the type of administrative and academic services/ programs that a college or university needs to provides. The Educational Resources Information Center's (ERIC) online database has identified one hundred and fifty seven articles describing the impact of student background on various aspects of the student academic experience which can be helpful to academic planners in specific geographic and societal locations. These includie community college transfer rates (Bradburn and Hurst, 2001); the desire to finish college (Allen, 1999); tuition/price sensitivity (Hu and Hossler, 1998); library instruction (Moore-Jansen, 1997); student performance and satisfaction (Harris and Nettles, 1991); and student effort and involvement in college activities (Davis and Murrel, 1993).

Psychographics, or life style, is also an important factor in creating academic and student support services, especially in the area of student assimilation and socialization. In one study, Yao (1983) observed that Chinese students from Taiwan, Hong Kong, and other parts of Asia who pursue higher education in the United States had to adjust to a different life style and value system, as well as to a new language and new learning methods.

Student's career aspirations and academic ability impact the student's capacity to learn since the student's career aspirations should fit the academic program he or she is pursuing (will my education land me the job/career I want?) and the student must possess the requisite skills in order to successfully complete the program (can I do the work that is required?). These factors impact the student's choice of an educational institution based upon the institution's academic programs and standards as well as the college's selection of prospective students.

Looking Beyond the Learner – Institutional Stakeholders as a Factor

Another factor that also complicates a thorough understanding of the learner is that of the existence of other stakeholders, people beyond the learners who make claims on the campus. Sturdivant and Vernon-Wortzel (1990) have identified that "Stakeholders consist of any individual or group who feel that they have a stake in the consequences of management's decisions and who have the power to influence current and future decisions" (pg. 59). Ihlanfeldt (1980), in describing the college-choice process, noted that the college-bound student's decision was influenced by numerous parties not affiliated with the colleges. These parties included the student's friends, other peers, parents, high school personnel and college alumni. Although Ihlanfeldt's observation concerned traditional college students and their initial decision to attend a college, his point is that learners bring their world with them into their higher educational experience.

For the purposes of our discussion, we broaden the list of stakeholders to include employers, creditors, on-campus friends and fellow students in order to provide a wider range of possible influences on the learner. Adult learners certainly have a dissimilar influence from their more traditional counterparts, and undoubtedly significant others such as children, elderly parents, and employers need to be accounted for by colleges and universities in the formulation and implementation of academic programs and services. These stakeholders indirectly influence the institution's academic and student support operations. For example, fast-track, evening, weekend, and on-line courses and programs have been developed for adult learners who have work and family obligations which do not allow them to attend during regular class time.

It is also important to convey the fact that these stakeholders may make direct demands on the institution. For example, if stakeholders are paying for the learner's education they may require documentation of said learning. Besides the fact that the documentation cannot be provided without the learner's consent, the college's registrar is going to have to develop a system for sharing this information. A good example of potential problems caused by stakeholder involvement has occurred at one author's college where an employer has contracted with the institution to provide on-site education. The employer has agreed to pay for their employees' tuition but only after the course grades have been posted; a poor grade, 'C' or lower, will result in the employee paying their own tuition. The college has agreed to hold off their billing, which normally occurs at the beginning of the semester of employees until that date. This has caused some real headaches for the business office since the student billing system is not sophisticated enough to discern which bills to hold and which bills to send; they have had to go through all the college's bills by hand and manually remove bills.

The Academic Community as a Facilitator of Learner Activities

Based on the multifaceted behaviors of the learner, the institution's role in supporting those behaviors is multifaceted as well as suggested in Figure 3.3 below.

Figure 3.3
The Multiple Roles of the Academic Community

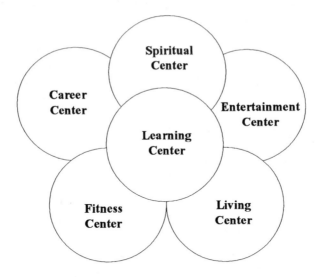

Looking at the Activities of the Learner

The motivation and needs of the learner, his or her demographic background, and the learner's stakeholders comprise the forces that push and pull the learner and lead to the behaviors exhibited by the learner along the model suggested by Lewin (1951). These behaviors can be categorized in terms of work, play, learning, spirituality, and day-to-day living, and are enacted to satisfy the needs of the learner. Again, each learner will exhibit a different set of behaviors which may occur within or without the academic community. For example, even in more traditional colleges and universities, the residential student is involved in many more activities on-campus (such as attending concerts, eating and sleeping in the dorm system, playing sports, exercising, doing laundry) than his or her commuter counterpart. The services each campus provides will take this mix of activities into account along with the stated mission of the institution, its resource bases, in order to best assist learners to achieve their goals as comfortably as possible. We will address these issues in more detain in the next section.

The Academic Community as a Role Set

Throughout this chapter, we have portrayed the academic community, in the forefront of the model, as being a system of interacting and overlapping roles or role set, as suggested by Katz and Kahn (1966), where learning is the primary role of the academic community. The fact that the roles are both interacting and overlapping indicate that there are connections between each of the roles and that these connections may lead to both role conflict and role ambiguity based upon the looseness or tightness of the connections (Weick, 1979; Brown, 1983). Based on this definition of the academic community, it is then evident that at least part of the purpose of academic planning is to:

1. Define the roles of the academic community relative to the mission of the institution.
2. Define their interfaces
3. Create a fit between the roles so as to maximize operating efficiency and institutional goal attainment (Miles and Snow, 1984).

The academic community as an interlocking role set is subject to short term, mid-term and long-term forces: what we have called change at the subsystem level (Rowley and Sherman, 2001). These changes are due to changes in the academic community's external environment and/or caused by administrators intervening in the system. Short term forces have a cause-and -effect impact on the roles, and may affect one or numerous roles simultaneously.

For example, an increase in student applications may lead to the administration is accepting a higher number of residential students. Given the college's physical capacity to absorb more students, this will positively or negatively impact those services that residential students utilize such as housing and food services, student activities, availability of exercise equipment and health services, personal counseling, and faculty/student ratios.

Also note that a domino effect may occur given the relative connectivity of each role or center. As in the last example, increased enrollment may cause student activities to run out of their allocated physical space, and for its new planned activities they may have to compete with other centers for program space.

Mid-term forces refer to the relative alignment of the roles of the academic community – how well the roles fit together. Most colleges and universities do not have a perfect fit of their roles due to the changing internal and external forces affecting their academic communities. For example, the use of new technology, especially information technology, may not be universal across differing centers of the campus. Student registration may occur within a virtual environment, yet learning may be predominately synchronous and face-to-face.

Role misalignment is natural and expected and as Rowley and Sherman (2001) suggested, "most misalignments will realign themselves through the path of least resistance" (pg. 212). Academic planning must analyze the current state of the academic community vis-à-vis role alignment and take deliberate measures to ensure corresponding roles.

These are long-term forces that identify driving roles or roles of the academic community and the comparative adaptability of those roles. In an academic community one would expect, by definition that learning would be the driving role of the college or university. That is why we have placed the learning center or role within the core of the academic community. But there may be other driving roles which equal or, at times, even outweigh those of the learning center, most notably sports. Kersterrer and Kovich (1997) report that spectator appeal for intercollegiate athletics has increased dramatically within the last decade, especially in women's sports. Attendance at NCAA games rose from four million to five million from 1991 to 1995, with revenues increasing over 20% from 1993 to 1995.

Clearly, higher education is realizing the value of sports as both a non-instructional revenue enhancer and a student recruitment device. The importance of the sports program, and its impact on the other centers of the university, need to be discussed and analyzed by college administrators and faculty to determine how sports should fit overall into the academic community in light of student demands for those programs. This analysis needs to include the relative flexibility of all of the roles regarding sports. Questions such as, "are faculty willing to work with athletic administrators in monitoring student athletes' academic performance?", and "do we have the health facilities needed to train quality athletes?" need to be asked and answered.

The Community as a Learning Center

The most traditional role of the academic community, as described in Chapter One, is that of a learning center. It is the most fundamental role of the academic community, and appropriately, we have placed it in the center of the academic community. The learning center consists of academic learners, programs, faculty, administrators, staff, facilities, and equipment dedicated to the creation, dissemination and storage of both raw data and knowledge.– in more traditional terms research, instruction, and library services.

This broad-based definition of the learning center also includes what has been historically categorized as either nontraditional or noncredit learning, and includes off-campus programs, lecture series, and even high school acceleration programs. No matter in what context, location or mode learning occurs, that activity is considered part of the learning center or role.

The Community as a Career/Employment Center

Some faculty members may at times be displeased by the notion that the academic community should facilitate the activities surrounding the ability of a learner to get a job. Some may think that the proper role of the academy is to discover, analyze, and disseminate knowledge and that using its resources to do anything else (including finding their students jobs) is simply wrong. Yet, on many campuses, certain learners are less interested in gaining knowledge for knowledge's sake and more interested in gaining knowledge for financial sake. Further, with the growing need for knowledge workers in the Information Age (Rowley, Lujan, and Dolence, 1998) and the academy's historic strength in producing learned individuals, it should come as no surprise that many individuals see higher education as the institution for increasing their value in the job market and see the role of colleges as providing marketable knowledge. So, while some campuses separate the activities of learning from that of supporting employment opportunities, many other campuses are integrating them into student life and academic life through their academic plans.

Besides providing what might be called technical information about the subject matter with which a job might deal, the learner also expects the college or university to provide knowledge and support in the areas of job placement and career development. The learner looks forward to receiving information about specific career opportunities and services that assist the learner in matching his or her skills with specific types of jobs, and wants assistance from the university in the job search process.

Last, learners may see the academic community as a possible venue for employment. The learner may in fact work for the college while obtaining educational services. Such work may include work-study programs, teaching and/or research assistantships, residential aides, adjuncts, and regular administrative/ staff/faculty positions.

The Community as an Entertainment Center

Jonathan, the character at the case in the beginning of the chapter, seems to be having fun while he was living away from home while attending college. Whether the fun was related to surfing the net, attending a concert or sporting event, joining a club or fraternity, or even attending class and hearing a guest lecturer, Jonathan wanted to enjoy himself. To help complete the collegiate experience it is important that the academic community provides numerous entertainment outlets for the learner, beyond the typical popular entertainment venues, whether it is entertainment in the classroom (Trout, 1997; Kreps, 1998), the library and its website (Smith, 2000), the radio station website (McClung, 2001), the bookstore (Stronsnider, 1997), collegiate sports (Atwell, 2001; Selingo, 1998), or college fundraisers (Harris, 1998). These help complete the learner's experience.

The Community as a Fitness Center

Both of the authors, when they attended college as undergraduates, remember taking athletic courses as a required part of the curriculum. Many academic curriculums have, within the past thirty years, dropped their physical education requirements, although within the last two decades Americans have both become more health conscious and out of shape (Cobb et al., 2000). Physical education programs, instead of limiting programs to the needs of physical education majors, are once again becoming an important part of the academic program and serve the health, fitness, and wellness needs of everyone (Cardinal, 1990a). Yet, physical health is only part of the concern here. Cardinal (1990b) broadens the definition of fitness to include total wellness of the individual (intellectual, physical, emotional, social, occupational, and spiritual) and described The Body Shop wellness program at Eastern Washington University as a demonstration model for total wellness. Universities and colleges, both private and public, are including fitness centers as ways of increasing their student enrollment levels (Fickes, 1999) since students are demanding better access and facilities to support their exercise regimens. Physical exercise, whether through organized intercollegiate sports and/or fitness programs or through individual endeavor, needs to be available to the learner.

The Community as a Spiritual Center

Spirituality, or religion, is significant in the academic community. Love and Talbot (1999) argue that spirituality and spiritual development have been conspicuously absent from student development theories and ignored by many student affairs professionals while Tisdell (2001) noted that until very recently, with the exception of adult religious education, spirituality had been given little attention in mainstream academic adult education.

Separation of church and state is still an issue at public colleges and universities, while many private institutions still have church sponsorship. Spirituality, however, is a much broader issue than religion. Many colleges and universities have chosen not to include any issues related to spirituality within their programs, and perhaps this is a mistake. This relative unwillingness to engage in discussions or programs involving human spirituality in higher education may be changing due to a number of factors. These include parents who concerned about excessive drinking and promiscuous sex, the widespread fascination with spirituality in the general culture, and social scientists' realization that it is impossible to understand American politics, race relations, volunteerism, and law without a fuller appreciation of religion's role in shaping social institutions (Wolfe, 2002). The importance of spirituality in learning cannot be understated. Further, Dalton (2001) suggested that college students typically make a spiritual quest in their learning and development in college and that their spirituality influences expectations and preparation for work and community life beyond college. He considers spiritual development as a form of deeper learning that has been neglected in higher education and believes that community service is a means of encouraging spiritual growth among students. A committed life of moral and civic responsibility will result from a higher education that integrates spirituality with intellectual and personal development.

The subject of spirituality is currently a theme in workplace and human resource development literature (Ashar and Lane-Maher, 2002). Most recent discussions in adult and higher education specifically focus on the role of spirituality in teaching and learning. Attending to spirituality in learning does not necessarily mean that one needs to discuss it directly in classes or learning activities, although there may be occasions for drawing it into course content. Given the connection between adult learning and adult development, discussions of spiritual development are relevant to concerns in adult education (Tisdell, 2001).

Rogers and Dantley (2001) noted that professionals in higher education are beginning to acknowledge the significance of the spiritual dimension in students' lives, but they have been slow to address the same issue in the work lives of faculty, administrators, support staff, and student affairs professionals. Student affairs leadership, informed by spiritual intelligence, can create campus environments that support and enhance the sense of wholeness, connection, and community for students, faculty, and staff. Spirituality is not only a concern for the student but for the faculty and staff as well. Huebner (1995) challenged educators to embrace the spiritual aspects of life in their image of education, suggesting the importance of including spirituality in one's approach to life and letting that sense of life infuse one's teaching.

Astin and Astin (1999) reported that a three year project sponsored by the Fetzer Institute had more than 80 scholars, students, and educational leaders participate in an extended series of dialogues about issues of spirituality, authenticity, meaning, wholeness, and self-renewal in higher education. These dialogues explored issues related to achieving a greater sense of community, spirituality, and shared purpose in higher education. They further explored the causes of the divisions and fragmentation experienced by many academics in their institutional and personal lives i.e. what it means to be authentic, both in the classroom and in dealings with students, and what disconnections higher education is experiencing within and in relation to the larger society. It is evident that the academic community, and the academic plan, must account for and allow learners to express their spirituality in a mode that is inclusive, open and tolerant.

The Community as a Living Center (or Home)

At one time or another in their academic careers, both of the authors have been accused by their friends and family of spending most if not all of their time within the confines of the academic community. Unfortunately, there is more to this accusation than either of us would care to admit. However, we note this fact to support the notion that the academic community is a living center, a place where people do spend an inordinate amount of their time, and peoples' physical needs also have to be accommodated in order to facilitate learning.

In devising his explanation of motivation and needs-satisfaction behaviors, Herzberg (1968) noted that living, learning, and working conditions are what he referred to as hygiene factors -- factors that, when overlooked or left unfulfilled, can lead to dissatisfaction which can in turn negatively impact learning. Part of the modern campus, then, makes provisions for helping students deal more effectively with their lives as they work toward graduation. The more traditional method of dealing with a learner's living needs has been to address issues involving food services, residence halls, parking, transportation, student unions, bookstores, security, and other physical plant issues. The quality of student life is important and research has demonstrated that learner perception of these conditions can impact college selection (Kotler and Fox, 1995), orientation (Allen, 1984), and student retention (Olagunju, 1981). Further, adult students' needs differ from their traditional counterparts especially in the need for additional non-standard administrative support and non-traditional food services (Davila, 1985).

In the last few decades, higher education has explored the concept of the living-learning center, a residential service that combines recreational and dormitory facilities and sometimes groups students into micro learning communities (Fisher and Andrews, 1976) as well as other integrative models. In 1998, the Association of College and University Housing Officers-International (ACUHO-I) suggested that there are ways in which campus residential programs could become strategic partners in student learning. It proposed partnerships between campus housing professionals and faculty colleagues, and presented a number of archetypes for consideration including residential colleges, living-learning centers, specialized residential programs directly connected to specific academic programs; theme housing which allows students with special interests to live together; academic residential programs, which provide academic support services and programs within the residential setting; residential learning centers, in which students who live together also attend class together; freshman year experience, which offers specialized housing configurations to maximize academic services to first-year students; and use of technology such as residential computer labs, in-room networks, and in-house cable televisions channels (Residential College Task Force, 1998).

Of course, in the current approaches to adult education, university extension sites, virtual classrooms, distance learning, college exchange programs, and travel courses, the living center may expand off-campus and encompass a learner's home, place of work, or even his or her vacation location. This boundaryless university requires that the learner also take an active role in the creation of a comfortable learning environment having a separate study room which includes a computer with fast access to the internet. Regardless of the location of the living center, colleges and universities will face new challenges in assisting their learners, both traditional and nontraditional, in creating a living center that meets the learners' needs.

The discussion we have presented here may seem unusual for an analysis of academic planning, since we have introduced a wide variety of activities that go beyond the classroom in defining elements that academic planners need to consider in developing the overall plan. Many members of the faculty might feel that the activities beyond the classroom are extraneous to the issues of academics. In terms of course material and curriculum development, this is mostly true. Yet, the point we have tried to make here is that learning does not only occur in the classroom. It also does not just happen in the study and research activities learners engage in as they prepare for classes. Learning also occurs within the living environment of learners, and if academics are truly interested in maximizing the learning experience, then they need to be willing to open up the academic planning process to include those environments. An understanding of the overall learning environment will help academic planners better formulate their plans to best fit with its most important environment – that of the learner.

The Academic Community and the Academic Plan

One of the members of the English Department was walking around campus when one of her most promising undergraduate students approached her. "Good morning Dr. Johnson, I had hoped to catch you before you left for the day. I was wondering if you could do me a big favor. I have been asked by my industrial psychology professor to interview a faculty member about his or her work and to find out why one would want to become a teacher. I have interviewed two professors already and would really appreciate your comments."

Dr. Sykes was quite flattered by this request and immediately launched into a soliloquy about the virtues of being a college professor. These qualities included being self-directed, the joy of teaching, time off to purse research and course development, and community service. Dr. Sykes continued heaping laureates on the education profession until the student asked about the negative aspects of the job.

"Of course," continued Dr. Sykes "one of the worst parts of the job is certainly attending committee meetings. These tend to have little meaning, waste much time and energy, and also have a propensity to become circular; little is accomplished for many people in a large amount of time. Second, giving students grades is a very difficult process. Without getting into detail, grades rarely reflect the performance of a student and students tend to become fixated on the grade for a course rather than the learning they have derived from the course. I cannot abide grade disputes and find any conversation pertaining to a student's grade demeaning."

"I can understand that" responded the student. "What I cannot understand, however, is the little time that faculty actually spend in the classroom. My research on this campus has indicated that the average faculty workload is two courses per semester, six hours per week, and that many of the faculty receive research offload which may in fact reduce their teaching to as little as one course per year. Some faculty members do not teach students at all! Faculty, from my observation, seem to be either involved in their research, away at conferences, seminars, or consulting projects, writing journal articles or publishing books, and have very little interaction with students. Professor Sykes in the political science department has labeled college

educators as scam artists[1] since they earn a prorated salary of over $100,000 per year yet do not have half the responsibilities or work half of the hours of their business counterparts." The student went on to list several other factors including summers and numerous time off, guaranteed jobs after tenure, limited accountability after tenure, and ability to earn extra income through writing and consulting, that Professor Sykes felt made being a professor a near no-show job.

Professor Sykes was flabbergasted and caught off guard by the students' remarks. She knew that she was putting in a sixty hour work week (not that she counted) and that she worked as hard, if not even harder, that her business complements. Yet how could she explain the inordinate pressure that faculty, especially non-tenured faculty, experienced on-the-job? How could she describe the numerous groups she was accountable to, though many not formally part of the university nor having a direct impact on her teaching and research performance?

People in higher education possess a sacred trust and duty and often must subjugate their own interests to the interests of the learner. That being said, our earlier definition of the academic community as a role set begs the question: "what does the expect from its academic community?" This is an important question because it requires the academic community, and the academic plan, to address the concerns of the professions representing these individuals. It also acknowledges a very important fact: people, especially faculty, have a much stronger allegiance to their profession than they do to their institution (Mosher, 1982). With the rise of the two-worker household, dramatically shifting regional economics, and the more temporary shifting nature of employment in higher education, it is not surprising to see greater employee mobility in the field of higher education particularly with administrators and staff members (Warren, 1982).

Going back to the question concerning academic expectations, we identify that the academic community is comprised of several internal stakeholders: faculty, academic staff, administrative staff, and trustees that represent the greater external community. These interest groups play differing roles in the institution and provide the services necessary to sustain the institution's overall learning environment as suggested in Figure 4.1 below.

---

[1] see Charles J. Sykes (1988) *Profscam.* New York: St. Martin's Press.

Figure 4.1
The Academic Community's Internal Stakeholders

University Stakeholders (internal) – Academic Planning

Faculty   Academic Staff   Administrative Staff
                           Trustees

Academic Programs   Administrative Services
                        Other Learner Services

Faculty and the Academic Community

Faculty members have always played an integral part in formulating, implementing and assessing the functions of the academic community. The American Association of University Professors (AAUP), a representative group, has defined the job of the faculty member as including three areas of focus besides teaching and research:

1. Student-Centered Work (i.e. coaching, counseling, advising, course development, student assessment, and alumni outreach, etc....)
2. Disciplinary/Professional-Centered Work (i.e. serving on college/professional committees, scholarly pursuits, and fundraising/grant writing for the college, etc....)
3. Community-Centered Work (i.e. providing professional advice, serving on boards of directors/trustees, informing the public, etc....) (AAUP, 7/25/02, http://www.aaup.org/Issues/workplace/facdo.htm).

Kezar (2000) has indicated that every aspect of the traditional faculty role is being reconceptualized. Workload, attacks on tenure, and changing job demands have been themes throughout the 1990s. The restructuring of traditional doctoral programs, the scholarship of teaching, and the rewarding of service show promise for assisting this time of transition. The rise in part-time and contract faculty, the growing antagonism represented in the growth of collective bargaining, and the lack of diversification of faculty, however, represent serious and looming problems.

As we described the multiple roles of the academic community in the last chapter (Figure 3.2), we suggested that what the academy wants and needs from its various faculties is to create a coherent community for the learner based upon the tenets similar to those described by the Carnegie Foundation for the Advancement of Teaching (CFAT, 1990). These tenets state that a college or university is an educationally purposeful, open, just, disciplined, caring, and a celebrative community which strives for excellence in the pursuit and assessment of said goals (Bogue and Saunders, 1992). The institution's expectations are that the academic community strives for these goals pursuant to the institution's specific purpose and mission.

We combined AAUP's functions of the faculty with CFAT's view of the academy with our own notion of the academic community as an overlapping role set, and created the following diagram to depict the faculty's roles in the learning community as suggested in Figure 4.2 below, as required by the academy.

Figure 4.2
The Multiple Roles of the Faculty

The Faculty Community as a Teaching Center
(Knowledge Dissemination)

Teaching, or more appropriately learning facilitation, is the core role of the faculty member although it is quite clear that there are varying degrees, by institutional mission, to which faculty will perform this function. Rowley, Lujan and Dolence (1998) reported that "faculty spend twice as much time teaching as doing research" (pg. 59) with teaching time ranging in percentages from humanities faculty (64 percent) to agriculture/health sciences (34 to 39 percent).

Ironically, there has been criticism that faculty need to get back to basics and focus on teaching. Goodchild (1986) described the Association of American Colleges' (AAC) recommendations to faculty as the need to restore the teaching orientation of the profession as its first obligation. The AAC's report further endorsed a revised faculty role emphasizing a greater teaching and formative orientation toward students' intellectual and character development and a revitalization of general education and of the liberal arts curriculum. Atkinson (2001) noted that higher education leaders are calling for more emphasis on teaching as a primary faculty role. Part Two of this book, entitled "How Should We Teach It?" will explore faculty instruction in detail.

The Faculty Community as a Research Center
(Knowledge Creation and Storage)

The second most common role for a faculty member is to add to the body of knowledge of his or her field through basic or applied research. This role has been broadened "to include scholarship associated with teaching, the integration of knowledge across disciplines, and the public service applications of knowledge" (Bogue and Saunders, 1992, pg. 254). According to Rowley, Lujan and Dolence (1998), faculty publish on average around one article every two years with research faculty publishing four articles per year.

In the information age, Rowley, Lujan and Dolence (1998) advocate that "ivory-towerism" (pg. 185), the tendency for faculty to concentrate within their own area of research and instruction, should and is giving way to a more market-oriented research faculty where faculty treat students as partners in academic research. McKee, Kiser and Lea (1999) claim that "universities are promoting the integration of their research with local and regional economic development (in order to) address today's complex, multidisciplinary problems" (pg. 155) with certain states in the United States establishing research grants to promote basic research, commercialization and transfer technology (Bogue and Saunders, 1992).

Controversy has surrounded the issue of the balance between teaching and research. Kerr (1975) noted that although many in higher education believe that good teaching and good research are synergistic, the reality is that most colleges and universities have far greater extrinsic rewards for research than for teaching. The academic community hopes for good teaching but rewards good research. Serow (2000) examined tensions between the research and teaching components of the faculty role in a research university, specifically less-active (LA) and more-active (MA) researchers. Particularly noteworthy was the presence of a strong allegiance to the historic teaching mission of public universities among both research types. Among the LAs, a cadre of politically adept senior faculty had achieved some success in preserving or expanding the place of undergraduate teaching in the reward systems of their departments and colleges.

The Faculty Community as a Mentor

Mentoring, historically an informal activity except at the doctoral level, is where faculty provide a student guidance and a clear understanding of both the content and process of learning and research in the faculty member's particular subject matter. Mentoring can occur within a classroom setting as part of the student-teacher relationship, or can occur outside the classroom through formal advisement, career counseling, and informal discussions. If mentoring is to be taken as a critical component of a faculty member's job, academic planning must promote faculty advising as part of faculty development (Kramer, 1985). Advising roles or tasks can be analyzed by faculty and administrators for their contribution to personal and professional development as well as to institutional need.

The Faculty Community as Providing Services to the Profession

Besides the direct contribution to the through teaching and research, faculty are expected to play a role in the development of their profession. This is done through such activities as mentoring of junior faculty (Mary Deane Sorcinelli (2002) "Principles of Good Practice: Supporting Early-Career Faculty", *American Association of Higher Education*, http://www.aahe.org/FFRR/ principles_brochure2.htm), participating in the governance of professional organizations, attending regional and national conferences, conducting workshops and seminars dealing with professional development, serving as reviewers, chairs and discussants at academic conferences, and serving as an editor and/or reviewer for academic journals.

The Faculty Community as Providing Services to the University Community

Colleges and universities expect their faculty members to serve the academic community through participation in governance, junior faculty mentoring, advising student clubs and fraternities and attending college events. These services are needed at the university, school and/or department level.

Shared governance, one of the cornerstones of higher education, has of late come under attack with the increasing subordination of traditional collegial governance arrangements to intrusive management procedures. Nielson and Polishook (1986) noted that the faculty role in college governance is eroding, and that this transformation in university affairs is enlarging the distance between managers and professors. Faculty believe that the college and university organization is rapidly evolving toward a hierarchical pyramid of control, centralized planning, top-down decision making, and a reward system based on bringing in outside money (Browne,1991). The long-term interests of higher education call for a return of faculty to their traditional role at the center of academic decisions. However, Collins (1996) observed that standards and policies promulgated by both the Middle States Association and the American Association of University Professors had strengthened the faculty role in the governance process between 1960 thru 1990.

The Faculty Community as Providing Services to the Community-at-Large

Community service is predicated upon one of the basic tenets of faculty rights, the notion of academic freedom. "It is recognized that in a world of rapid change and recurrent crises, a University best serves its community as an open intellectual forum where varying shades of opinion may be freely expressed and fairly debated" (Southampton College Federation of Teachers, 2000, pg.5). Associated with these rights is the responsibility to become active in the community and to share opinions and expertise with a wider audience. Whether that activity is community-based, politically-based, government-based, economic-based or religiously-based, the campus expects faculty to integrate their professional lives with the locality they inhabit.

Two types of community service, community activism and consulting, have caused some controversy and concern for colleges and universities. Boyer and Lewis (1986) indicated that although consulting has long been recognized as legitimate in most colleges, concern has arisen about the appropriateness of double-dipping, and particularly whether consulting and other supplemental income activities result in shirking other university responsibilities. The debate centers on six basic issues: who consults, whether consulting is increasing, whether faculty are shirking university responsibilities, whether faculty are exploiting consulting opportunities, whether they are motivated to consult primarily by economic reasons, and whether most institutional policies and procedures are adequate for governing such activity.

Community activism, what Ralph Nader called "a new kind of citizenship" (Nader and Ross, 1971, pg. 5), is characterized as "working on institutions to improve and reshape them or replace them with improved ways of achieving just missions" (pg. 7). In this role the faculty member gives voice (Hirschman, 1970) to his or her opinions and actively engages in behaviors that attempt to transform voice into action and social impact. Academic freedom does include "freedom from institutional censorship or discipline when writing and speaking as a citizen" (Southampton College Federation of Teachers, 2000, pg.5) but only to the extent that the faculty member "does not represent him/herself as an institutional spokesperson" (pg. 5).

The Faculty Community as an Assessment Center

The newest role to emerge for faculty deals with the issue of measuring performance and external accountability beyond the profession. Assessment refers to the documentation of change in students' growth – changes in knowledge, attitudes, skills, and values (Bogue and Saunders, 1992) but includes examining the broader dimensions of the teaching-learning process (Lewis and Smith, 1994). This broadening of the locus of analysis requires a multidimensional strategy for assessment which examines external influences, the institutional approach and context, and the uses and impacts of assessment (Peterson and Vaughan, 2001).

Kezar (1999) indicated that assessment is a prevalent issue, although a gap is apparent between administrator and faculty views of and beliefs about assessment. "Some faculty philosophically disagree or are unaware of their academic division's outcomes assessment plans" (Southampton College, 2002, pg.s S33-S34). Schilling and Schilling (1998) reported that certain conditions are necessary if faculty members are to view assessment as an integral part of its role. These include embedding assessment in a fiscal and policy context that supports innovation; basing assessment on evidence and forms of judgment that disciplinary specialists find credible; and identifying assessment as a stimulus to reflective practice.

Faculty Roles – a Summary

Each faculty member, within the confines of the institution's mission, creates his or her own role mix. Certain academic institutions may require far greater research, others service, while others may require student interaction and mentoring. The faculty must balance the needs of the institution and the needs of the learner with their own needs in order to maximize both effectiveness and motivation.

Trustees, Administrators and Staff and the Academic Community

The college campus is different from other organizations in that trustees, managers, supervisors, and staff are part of a learning community. If the primary outcomes as a campus are that of learning, the creation, dissemination, and storage of knowledge, and creating a learning environment, then everything everyone does has some relationship to learning or the support of learning, whether his or her position deals with the learner or faculty needs. (See Figures 3.3 and 3.5 in the previous chapter.) Furthermore, everyone's responsibility includes making the learning process better on a continuous basis. Learning may occur in a variety of locations and within a variety of circumstances, such as the classroom, the library, or the laboratory, study groups, and other forums. Beyond this, however, learning is impacted by everything else that goes on across the campus.

Trustees, administrators and staff, in order to be successful in an academic environment, must embrace the value system of the – a culture that values learning, the search for truth, and human dignity.

"Words and phrases such as *personal growth, intellectual development, the scholarly community, humanism, improving society, and liberal education*" (Birnbaum, 2000, pg. 204), surely values that are inherent to the academy, are absent from much of the management techniques employed in business. "There can never be a management system that supports in equal measure all the goals to which higher education is committed" (pg. 228). The culture of business rationality, the bottom line, clashes with university tradition and values such as shared governance and it would be undesirable, as well as impossible, to change the culture of higher education to fit (Miles and Snow, 1984) these business models.

For Birnbaum, academic administrators "make sense of institutional knowledge through experience and the knowledge they have developed over time" (pg. 200) through decentralized authority, producing quality products, providing responsive service, formulating strategies that are based upon distinctive capabilities, giving equitable rewards for performance, and being socially responsible. In essence the goal of managing an academic environment is effective human collaboration; creating social, technical and managerial systems that support and nurture the needs of the learner (Lewis and Smith, 1994) through the roles of the academic community and the faculty.

Society and the Academic Community

Prior discussions of the role of the academic community and the role of the faculty member have touched upon the three primary roles that the academic community serves in terms of its social responsibility: *the community as the ivory tower, the community as a partner, and the community as a leader.*

Bok (1982) described the long-established role of academia, the ivory tower, as including traditional values of academic freedom, institutional autonomy, and political neutrality. This time-honored role segregated the academic community from the community at large and allowed higher education institutions to pursue their primary mission of teaching and research without outside influences. Lynton and Elman (1987) observed that the prevalent emphasis on the quest for new ideas and knowledge is too narrow, that existing knowledge must be interpreted and applied in the real world, and that universities must focus on preparing individuals to apply knowledge both on the job and as private citizens.

Institutions were now being asked to apply their knowledge and skills to deal with such social issues as racial inequality, the decline of ethical standards, the need for technological innovation, the risks of scientific research, and the desire for economic development. Furthermore, the university was being asked to take the reigns of social leadership by attacking social injustice through such nonacademic means such as voting stock, boycotting companies, and taking formal stands on controversial issues (Bok, 1982).

Bonnen (1968) indicated that the organization and structure of the university has prevented a coordinated assault on social problems. The university is beset with conflicting pressures from both within and without. If it is to attempt to alter social institutions and impact society for the better, the faculty must become more conscious and respectful of the diversity of norms underlying behavior within the university. The reward system must be changed. The nature and processes of the university should be communicated to faculty and students. Some university outreach activities should be instituted. A major problem is the fragmentation resulting from higher education's organization into departments (Harkavy and Puckett, 1992).

Fitzpatrick (1988) suggested that colleges and universities can structure the learning environment to encourage the analysis and action needed to build a healthy society through academic programming. Universities were being asked to examine the role that students could play in public and community service through service learning (Hollander and Saltmarsh, 2000). Stephens et. al.'s (2000) study found a strong movement toward reinvigorating higher education's civic and democratic mission, and noted that colleges and universities are increasingly developing community-university partnerships around schooling, discourse about public issues, and youth programs.

In terms of societal needs, partnership and collaboration seem to be emerging roles for higher education. Votruba (1996) stated that the university had a social covenant which required rethinking their missions, rebalancing the faculty and unit-level incentive and reward system, allocating resources and holding academic units accountable, strengthening their capacity to organize knowledge, preparing faculty to apply their scholarship, and committing themselves to full and active partnerships with society. Industry-supported academic research, for instance, is economically and socially desirable and consistent with both the commercial mission of business and the research mission of higher education. This increased coupling is advocated because there is fine science and technique created in academia which is not effectively coupled to the nation's commercial innovation system (David, 1982). Brewster (1968) discussed the partnership between Yale University and the City of New Haven to develop solutions to the pressing social problems in the areas of neighborhood development, health, social work, tutoring, legal assistance, and employment.

This partnership, however, is not without potential drawbacks. Sacken (1992) in response to criticism that university faculty should become more socially responsible, examined the ramifications of pushing faculty to pursue extramural funding and controversy over "political correctness" in dealing with social problems, yet noted the potential negative impact on the primary teaching function of the university and of each professor.

Balancing the Needs of the Learner, the Academy, and Society: The Mission and Strategic Planning

Higher educational institutions are under tremendous pressure to provide numerous services demanded by the learner, the academy, and society. Furthermore, higher education institutions must deal with other external forces in their domain such as changes in the economy, competition, regulators, new technology, donors, and alumni as we suggest in Figure 4.3 below.

Figure 4.3
The Academic Community's External Stakeholders

University Stakeholders (external) – Strategic Planning					
Competitors	Regulators	Economy	Technology	Society	Donors/Alumni
Mission	Goals	Competitive Position		Distintive Competencies	

As an industry, the demands for excellence in teaching, advising and research, social advocacy, skills training and development, and employment counseling, just to name a few, are in general being met, but not every institution can individually meet all of these needs. The purpose of identifying and stating the mission of the institution is to clearly state which needs of the learner, the academy, and of society the institution will address and, in general, how the institution will address them. More specifically, the mission should address the institution's philosophy of learning (university-driven, consumer-driven, or collaborative-driven) and its specific mechanisms for implementing its learning values. This forms the foundation for which the learning community is built upon.

Rowley and Sherman (2001) suggested that various forms of colleges and universities have emerged based upon these differing learning philosophies: the classics (research, comprehensive, small, community, and specialty), and the new breeds (co-op, composite, perpetual, virtual, virtual indexes, self-directed teams, competency-based, corporate, company, alternative, and emerging). Each type of institution has a differing mix of resources, learner-orientation, and has dissimilar risks associated with its mission.

For example, community colleges are very consumer-oriented. They provide a low-cost education centered in skills and careers and offer classes in the day and in the evening to accommodate both traditional and adult learners. Being consumer-driven, however, has risks. The community college must offer academic courses and programs that learners want and must be prepared to alter their classes and curriculum to meet shifting demands. These shifting demands may result in under-subscribed classes and programs, causing either course or possibly program cancellations. The risk associated with consumer preferences, however, is offset by the fact that community colleges receive only a portion of their funding from consumers since they are economically supported by their local community. This provides an economic buffer to community colleges and provides them the resources necessary to survive shifting consumer preferences.

Small colleges and universities are also consumer-driven, but not in the same way as community colleges. Small colleges have smaller class sizes, fewer classes, and a more academic-driven faculty than community colleges. They have a much greater sense of community with the focus of engaging students in the academic process. Smaller colleges are less consumer-driven than community colleges since faculty have research and professional obligations that may not directly address the needs of their learners. However, this risk is offset by the ability of smaller colleges to react to market demands quickly. They have far less bureaucracy than community colleges and can change their academic programs to meet consumer needs. Smaller colleges' real risks are associated with small class sizes, limited programs, and unless they are public institutions, tuition dependency. Small colleges do not have the luxury of canceling many of their lower-enrolled classes since this will adversely impact students who may opt to leave the institution. This means that smaller colleges must develop core programs in their institutions that will guarantee continuous yearly enrollment and minimize the need to cancel key classes.

Elaborating on the Mission: Strategic Planning

If differing types of colleges and universities have differing missions and roles associated with those missions, then one of the important functions of strategic planning is to minimize those roles by defining and then addressing the needs of the learner and of society in the context of the college's mission. Rowley and Sherman (2001) noted that the institution's mission defines its market position and its role in the marketplace, and that this role can be defined through the college's competitive advantage and its strategic approach to the market.

A college's competitive advantage is derived from its distinctive skills and competencies; that is, the university's centers of excellence produce a value for the learner superior to other institutions. For instance, community colleges' competitive advantage is usually low-cost. They charge less than other institutions, even public four year colleges, and provide an adequate education. Small colleges, on the other hand, compete by differentiation. They offer smaller class sizes and personalized instruction, a value that certain learners are willing to pay more for. All institutions also have to determine the breadth of their programs and services relative to their resources. This may also lead to a competitive advantage in that learners may perceive value in greater choices and/or specialized programs.

Strategic approach refers to the relative activity or aggressiveness of the institution in the marketplace. For instance, proactive educational institutions tend to be first movers and pioneers. They constantly introduce new academic programs and services in anticipation of the needs of the marketplace. Defenders, on the other hand, ignore market changes and focus on increasing the quality of their current programs and services. They invest their funds to enhance their centers of excellence, not to create new ones. Analysts wait for proactive institutions to create successful markets and services and then enter with higher quality or lower price; a follower strategy. Reactors are institutions without a strategic approach; their strategies are in response to changes in the marketplace and are detached from their institutions' mission.

The purpose of the strategic plan is to enact the mission of the institution, in conjunction with the institution's external environment, through the development of both a competitive advantage and a strategic approach to the market. The plan aligns the mission of the institution with the needs of the learner, the academy and society.

Academic Planning: Implementing the Strategic Plan and Academic Mission

As we described earlier, strategic planning defines the college's position in the marketplace relative to its mission. In order to carry out the mission and enact the strategic plan, the institution must develop both a broad-based plan and supporting plans that operationalize the mission. Academic planning is the broad-based plan that addresses the multiple roles of the academic community (learning center, spiritual center, career center, fitness center, entertainment center, and living center) and the relative mix of those roles in the context of the mission and strategy of the institution. For example, community colleges will have strong career and learning centers given their consumer-driven orientation but may have minimal living and fitness centers given the nonresidential nature of their learners. This may differ dramatically from comprehensive universities who, given their breadth of coverage, will have to invest in all of their centers in order to meet the needs of their diverse learner population.

The academic plan must also be implemented and the supporting or functional plans that comprise the academic plan can be broken down into four types: academic program plans, faculty development plans, administrative support plans, and learner (student) service plans as we suggest in Figure 4.4 below.

Figure 4.4
Hierarchy of Planning in Higher Education

Strategic Plan			
Academic Plan			
Academic Program Plan	Faculty Development Plan	Administrative Support Plan	Student Services Plan

The Academic Program Plan

The term academic program plans refer to the specific plans that are developed from a discipline perspective and address a particular course of study by the learner (Bogue and Saunders, 1992). These plans are curriculum-specific and tend to focus on degrees, majors, and minors, may include a university-shared core of courses, and tend to be owned and managed by a specific department and/or school. There are exceptions where programs are interdisciplinary in nature and shared between departments and/or schools. Academic programs also include the college-wide programs of a scholastic nature, such as honors programs, remedial programs, travel abroad and/or exchange programs, where the focus is on the development and implementation of a particular type of learning. We will address these aspects of academic planning in detail in Chapters Five and Six.

The breadth and depth of academic programs offered by the institution is certainly one of the easiest ways an institution of higher education can differentiate itself from competitors. For example, Southampton College of Long Island University, with only 1500 students, has developed a center of excellence in Marine Science which has a national clientele and has produced nearly thirty Fulbright Scholars, while, just thirty miles away, Dowling College offers a unique program in Aviation Management and Aeronautics. The State University of New York at Stonybrook is also within a sixty mile radius of both of these institutions yet, as a comprehensive research institution, offers a much broader array of academic programs than both institutions combined.

The Faculty Development Plan

Another major part of the overall plan is the faculty development plan. This part of the plan determines the mix of roles of the faculty member within the academic institution, especially teaching, research, advising, assessment, university, professional and community service. The plan balances the needs of the institution, the learner, society, and the needs of the faculty members. Based on the faculty members' skills, traits, style and abilities, the plan may include such developmental techniques as mentoring, coaching, workshops and seminars, interactive skill training, role playing, and instructional training (Blanchard and Thacker, 1999). Most plans must go through a series of approval processes, starting with the department, and, in certain states, may include approval from a state department of education.

Faculty development, and the specific focus of that development, can also lead to the creation of distinctive skills and a competitive advantage. The University of Phoenix, renowned for its on-line course instruction, has continuous online instructional training for faculty members including the Faculty Writing Workshop; Critical Thinking Across the Curriculum; Grading, Evaluation, and Feedback; and Learning Teams. Combined with peer reviews and end-of-course student evaluations, faculty members hone their skills as on-line facilitators (Trippe, 2001).

The Administrative Support Plan

The term, administrative support services, refers to those services that are outside the purview of the academic schools and are not directly related to student services. These services would include such functions as buildings and ground maintenance, fundraising and grant administration, public relations, financial management, mail delivery and personnel, and are often managed in a business-like manner. As support services, they exist to assist both the faculty and the learners in creating a comfortable and efficient learning community.

The strengths of these operations, although they impact hygiene factors, cannot be understated. Many universities tout their beautiful settings and their immaculate facilities and are constantly erecting new buildings and/or refurbishing older ones. Support services can add to the competitive advantage of the university by either adding perceived value to the learner's education like pleasant learning conditions, fast and easy access to the internet or reducing tuition costs through efficient operations.

Student Services Plan

Student services cover all of the student-related operations that do not deal with the delivery of academic content and play an integral role in creating and nurturing the learner's educational experience. These services traditionally include such functions as admissions, financial aid, the book store, registrar, advising and student housing. They address such students' needs as day-to-day living, entertainment, housing, physical fitness, and psychological and spiritual counseling.

Student services can be delivered in distinctive ways that may complement the institution's academic plan and overall strategy. The student union at George Mason University, for example, integrates traditional functions such as food services, meeting rooms, offices, study areas, bookstore with recreational activities and academic uses. Administrators hope the facility will bring faculty, staff, and students together and build a sense of campus community (Geraghty, 1996).

Planning to Plan: The First and Last Requirement of Academic Planning

We cannot end this chapter without a brief comment on the need of the academic institution to commit to the academic planning process. Rowley and Sherman (2001) observed that, in many cases, planning fails because the key stakeholders involved in formulating and implementing the plan were not prepared for and committed to the need for planning and the possible changes resulting from that planning. "What we mean by *being prepared* is that employees need to come to understand the changes desired, possess the resources and skills necessary to make the changes, and feel that the changes will benefit all involved, including themselves" (pg. 240).

The institution needs to create a culture that supports academic planning and change, empowers employees, and provides them with the necessary tools to enact the academic plan. As Rowley and Sherman (2001) noted, higher education does not have to look far in order to find a culture that nurtures planning. By adopting lifelong learning as not only a doctrine for their students but as a doctrine for their own operation (creating a learning community), academic planning will become a natural and expected part of the institutional learning process.

Knowledge, Learning, and Academic Disciplines

The faculty members of the English Department of ABC University were once again about to be subjected to what the senior faculty called their "monthly torture" the monthly departmental meeting. The usual topics were always bandied about the room; the incompetence of the administration, the poor quality and ability of their new students, the inadequacy of their physical facilities; in essence, the demise of academia as they once knew and loved it. These sessions tended to have no real purpose or goal and the faculty members were cognizant enough to know that things had not changed on the campus in decades. Things would not change, for the next few decades as well. Isn't that what academic tradition is all about?

Yet this fine day would be different from all of those other days, and they knew this meeting was dissimilar from the rest. The chair of the department had been charged by the university's outcome assessment committee to evaluate the departments' academic programs, its faculty and administrative practices. Based on a history of faculty resistance to change, it was an onerous task that she knew would not go over well. The committee had specifically provided her with a series of questions they wanted answered, questions she knew her faculty members would struggle with since they had never been asked to think this way before. What do learners need and want to learn to satisfy society? What is quality education and academic excellence in your discipline, and will the discipline grow or wane? What would require her faculty to give outcomes assessment serious time and thought? But how could she capture her faculty members' attention and interest when they so often got caught up in the mire of college politics, and hid behind the throne of tradition?

As we have suggested throughout, the academic planning process needs to be less provider-driven and more focused on the needs of the learner and of society. A learner-focused learning environment is one in which the needs and wants of a wide variety of constituencies becomes apparent. For colleges and universities, creating a learner-centered environment can be a challenge if the tradition of the campus is not particularly supporting of taking learner needs and wants into account as the faculty develops the academic program. This can be seen as a challenge not only to tradition, but to academic freedom and faculty governance as well.

What is required is a change of perspective for faculty members in developing courses and course materials that are more learner-focused than traditional teaching (particularly in using the lecture method of teaching). It is also important that the academic process create an overall learner-centered environment for the college or university as it creates the academic plan for the institution.

This chapter examines a wide variety of issues that faculty members and academic planners can use to reorient thinking toward a learner-centered environment. We construct the balance of this chapter in a series of questions and then engage in a discussion as to how academics might address these issues.

What Do Learners Need and Want to Learn to Satisfy Themselves and Society?

In the United States, much of Europe and parts of Asia and Australia society is moving through the secondary stages of the Information Age. Computer usage has become so common that, in the 1980s and 1990s, it became a standard for how we gather information, make decisions, and generally conduct business. As we have moved into the secondary stage, we have come to expect continual advances in technology that improve the way we do things in almost every part of our lives. We have also gotten more comfortable with the revolutionary things technology can do. We not only accept new technological changes easily, we tend to expect that the changes will continue to emerge and even become excited about what might be just around the corner.

Technology pervades our lives in business, at home, and at leisure. There is very little left in our lives that is not impacted in some way by the inventions of the Information Age. So what is the role of academia in all this?

Traditionally, the academy has been one of the most significant venues for the development, analysis, and dissemination of knowledge. Nearly all of our current knowledge base comes out of the academy, especially that part which examines causes and effects. Research agenda, curriculum development, and teaching activities have all traditionally been geared for understanding societal realities and providing society with explanations and potential interventions that speak to those issues that concern society the most. It is this tradition that compels the academy to be fully immersed in the development of the Information Age.

Interestingly enough, the Academy no longer has an exclusive franchise on knowledge development or dissemination in the Information Age (Rowley and Sherman, 2001; Rowley, Lujan, and Dolence, 1998). Research and development activities at IBM, Hewlett Packard, and Microsoft have created many of the components and methods that fuel technological growth today. This is not to suggest that colleges and universities have not contributed to this development; they clearly have. Yet, it is interesting to note that the franchise is now being shared instead of dominated by the academy. So in a real way, the academy has had to examine the world created by others and then plug in its own resource base to learn how to use its traditional strengths of research, analysis, and dissemination to support the emergent knowledge base of the Information Age. Evidence strongly suggests that it is doing so.

Rowley, Lujan, and Dolence (1998) suggested that the Information Age requires a significant increase in the total number of Information Age college-educated workers. While no one knows exactly what the demand is in terms of a specific target number or percentage, it is evident that demand will easily top 20% (a doubling of Industrial Age needs) and perhaps go significantly higher. This, then, is hard evidence that society needs the availability of college education more now than ever.

Education for What?

The demand for a more widely educated population in the Information Age comes with new priorities. Computer literacy is already a given, but computer-savvy, and perhaps more importantly software-savvy, is becoming a more important skill. It is really the software that has helped open up personal computing, business computing, and computing over the Internet to a whole new range of opportunities and possibilities.

We do not imply here that all of this development is just business related. If that were so, we could narrow the discussion of academic development to the business school and not worry about the balance of the campus. As we stated earlier, the Information Revolution is part of all of our lives and a part of nearly every aspect of our existence. Computers and software are issues in medicine, science, architecture, construction, the law, transportation, communication, and a plethora of other societal sectors. Just looking at the websites for churches and synagogues is a good reminder that even the religious portion of our lives is somehow connected to technology, and much of it is online.

The academy needs to more adequately address the significant paradigm shift that society is experiencing. Learners in today's college or university seek knowledge that will adequately prepare them not only to live in the Information Age, but to thrive there. Using the monumental strengths of academic research in all its forms, along with a dynamic learning environment that takes theory into practice, all vital knowledge components should be reflected in the institution's academic and strategic plans.

When Do Instructors Know if They Have Been Successful?

On the surface, this might seem like an odd question. It is seldom asked, and even when it is often answered by satisfaction surveys. Yet it is incorrect to believe the results of satisfaction surveys from either students or employers, and assume that material has effectively been transferred from the instructor to the student. It is also naïve to think of the learning process as a one-way event (professors teach students, students learn, end of story). There need to be other measures – measures that not only require that learners are able to demonstrate that they are mastering the materials the curriculum has identified as important, and instructors need some other levels of assurance that their methods of knowledge transfer are effective.

The traditional measures of claiming success, test scores, grade point averages, and graduation rates all may suggest success, but only in superficial terms. If one relies on multiple choice exams, for example, or even worse, true and false exams, the reliability of such testing methods are pretty small. It is well known that many students figure out the logic behind these types of exams and the actual taking of the exams is much more an exercise in playing the game than in demonstrating mastery of the material. Unfortunately, these types of exams are plentiful and many publishers include test banks with multiple choice and true and false questions in both paper and electronic form, making it easier and easier for instructors to use these methods. Considering the general student preference for these testing methods, and the issue of the course/instructor evaluation at the end of the course which is an especially big issue to those looking to achieve tenure, promotion, or making themselves attractive to other potential campuses as future employers, it is highly likely that effective knowledge measurement has not occurred.

Most doctoral candidates know that one of the final hurdles of completing their degree is a series of both written and oral exams. Most of these exams are quite rigorous, and being able to pass them successfully is a momentous event. Yet the message about learning is quite clear – under intense examination by experts, the doctoral candidate has proven an expert mastery of the material and is now in a position to teach or research this material when assuming a career in the academy.

We are not suggesting that all students in all classes be given 2 days of written and 1 day of oral examinations in each course they take. This is unacceptable in terms of both time and resources. Nonetheless, it seems that in identifying two opposite ends of the evaluation issue, some sort of mid-point might be more effective. Other methods of evaluating the learning process are more reliable. These include portfolio generation and analysis, individual project completion and presentation, case analyses, essays, written papers, laboratory experiment outcomes, and field application and testing.

For an individual college or university to suggest that its learners have achieved the level of education reflected in grades and certification, it should adopt a campus-wide policy that provides clear guidelines at to what sort of evaluation methods are appropriate and acceptable. Individual colleges, schools, and finally departments can then choose those methods that are most appropriate for them and then be in a position to more effectively defend the accuracy of their grading.

In any event, we firmly believe that many American colleges and universities are not doing their jobs effectively. If they cannot demonstrate effective knowledge transfer evaluation measures, these criticisms could become catastrophic.

What is Quality Education? What is Academic Excellence?

Pascarella and Terenzini (1991) found that high quality exists in a college "with a distinct advantage in terms of the academic ability, educational aspirations, level and clarity of career ambition, and family financial resources of the students they recruit and enroll (pg. 374). Sherr and Lozier (1991) further suggest that while most every college or university would want the services they provide to be of the highest quality, few would agree upon just what exactly that means. We think that Pfeffer (1977) may have gotten closer to the issue of high quality in higher education in his definition of organizational effectiveness. He stated that an organization is effective when it accurately understands its resource base, correctly perceives demands made upon it and then responds appropriately.

This external view of the issue of quality makes a great amount of sense. As we recognize that colleges and universities continue to come under the scrutiny of their external constituents (particularly governments and funding sources), being able to define quality in terms of meeting constituent demands helps. What is troubling about the Pascarella and Terenzini quote above is that not all campuses are able to attract the types of students the two authors describe, and perhaps in the Information Age, we can't be so parochial anyway. Society in general has a need for a more highly educated work force, and not just those whose parents can afford it. Educating learners of a wider variety of ages, a wider range of ethnic classifications, and a greater spectrum of social and religious groups should not be seen as a hindrance in any campus being able to provide high quality education. In fact, this growth of diversity should increase the quality level. With diversity comes a greater expanse of knowledge and the ability in an academic setting to understand phenomena even deeper because of the plethora of differing views that emanate from diversity.

Excellence in an academic setting implies a state of affairs that results from activities that match the needs and demands of society. Excellence is a process of continual improvement in which the campus tests its knowledge products against emerging realities of society and its own ability to deliver such products. Now that the Baldridge Award is something that colleges and universities may apply for, the issue of excellence and high quality becomes a much more public and much more introspective set of experiences. Campuses are challenged not only to perform and report excellence, but have in place on-going procedures that continually seek to improve the campus and its knowledge products.

We recognize that cheating exists. Most any evaluation method an individual instructor or campus might put into place some highly motivated and intelligent student might be able to find a way to thwart. As we face more and more on-line course delivery for cutting down on cheating continues to be a serious issue. Other than vigilance, we can offer no magic cure for cheating, but we also recognize that the Information Age and technology are addressing this problem and there are tools being developed that should cut down on cheating, particularly plagiarism. However, seeking to create an excellent learning environment that truly captures the curiosity and interest of learners is the best weapon against cheating. When learners understand that they are learning for their own good, cheating no longer is a serious option.

Academic planning is an excellent mechanism allowing academic leaders and faculty members begin to explore what high quality and excellence means. There should be no question that attaining and supporting high quality and excellence are noble goals. It may well be in the near future that being able to demonstrate these aspects of campus life will be tied directly to resources provided by others. As a vehicle for translating goals into practice, the academic plan can assure that all campus offerings meet quality and excellence standards as defined by themselves and their constituency base. This clearly supports the suggestion in Chapter One that college and university academic planning needs to test the current curricular offerings and be willing to alter those offerings to better be able to meet the needs and demands of society. This could well create a new knowledge base as continual improvement demonstrates the need for change.

Where Will this Knowledge Base Come From?

As we suggested earlier, the academy no longer has an exclusive franchise for knowledge creation, development, and dissemination. While the academy has hardly become irrelevant, its role has changed in that it now must create partnerships with other knowledge sources and then be able to translate what we are coming to know to today's learner.

What are the Research Institutions Doing to Help the Disciplines?

The status of research institutions has been a major draw for academics, learners, and other groups in society alike. These special places have the distinction of providing venues for the creation, analysis, and dissemination of new knowledge. This is a natural place to at least begin the process of enhancing disciplines to meet society's needs and demands.

In order to effectively match research and discipline growth, the traditional role of academic research must continue to grow and flourish. Laboratory research, field research, and applied research are all vital elements in the knowledge creation process the academy has mastered over the centuries. The free exercise of these activities is much of the heart and soul of the principles of academic freedom, and every college and university needs to vigorously support and defend these activities. As this translates into practical knowledge within an academic discipline, it can then be disseminated and provide a more up-to-date knowledge base for educating discipline members or further research.

Where Else Does Knowledge Come From?

In colleges and universities, however, there is another source of knowledge creation that not many campuses take advantage of: their learners. While the traditional student continues to exist (young, immature, leaving home for the first time, anxious to enjoy the amenities of a traditional college campus, and wanting to be spoon-fed their education), the ranks of the college student are changing. Dolence and Norris (1995) describe these new students as "learners," individuals who come to a college or university to continue a learning process which many understand is a life-long process. This group includes those who entered the work force right after high school, but enter college because they know they need the products of higher education; those who began college, dropped out, and discovered that they really should have stayed and those who see the campus as a place where they can continue their education after having already received a college degree. It is this new group of learners that presents another avenue for knowledge discovery. These are people who have a significant idea of what they don't know and what they need to learn. As such, they hold the promise of becoming research partners during their time in the college classrooms and laboratories. What these people already know can be added to what researchers are seeking to know. The result can be vastly improved academic research.

In terms of partnering with non-academic researchers, two things must happen. One, campus researchers have to understand where and why this non-academic research agenda is developing and must be willing to include this research in their more pristine campus labs. Two, they must extend a hand of friendship to the non-academic sector and help provide a climate for mutual respect. By creating these linkages, the knowledge process will become much more flexible and uninhibited.

This is also knowledge that can, and should, be translated into the classroom. Academic planners need to have a view of the world and of disciplines that transcends journal-published theory and research, and encompass non-academic knowledge base as part of the overall learning products they provide.

What Disciplines Will Grow, Which Will Wane? How do We Know This?

It is apparent that disciplines related to the future will be disciplines that will experience growth, perhaps even major growth. In terms of demand and content, these disciplines will need the support of the academic plan and the campus resource base to grow in a timely manner.

Disciplines in all technology-related fields will certainly grow. Since it is reasonable to assume that current technology will spawn future technology, the related disciplines such as computer science, management information systems (also known as computer information systems), mathematics, and physics should experience increased demand and discipline growth. Other disciplines in the general area of business, engineering, medicine, science, and education will continue to grow as their continuation of support for society and the new age will continue to be in high demand. Language disciplines (especially English), sociology, economics, psychology, and communications will also see growth, but perhaps not as dramatic as the other areas.

This is where the discussion gets sticky. What about the rest of the disciplines found on typical college and university campuses? What happens to the arts, music, literature, history, philosophy, and the many other disciplines that bring understanding and beauty to our society? Do these go away? To answer these questions most directly, one has to be hard-nosed in one respect and encouraging in another respect.

In the more callous approach, the market will tend to dictate the fates of disciplines that are popular and not popular. Simply, if learners fail to enroll in courses, they begin to shrink. If demand begins to approach critical lower limits, departments can be combined to survive a bit longer (with a lower level of resources) and might even be closed. Demand is an important consideration, and as the academic plan moves forward it must do so with a conscious connection to market demand.

But there is also a more encouraging side of the issue for non Information-Age-disciplines. That is the notion of the liberal arts education, and the clear need for colleges and universities to provide a broader educational experience to its learners than that found in the academic major programs. One of the authors of this book likes to tell his business students at least twice a semester that he believes they will have been short-changed in their degree program if they leave the University without a healthy respect for poetry, classical and modern art, music from all the ages, drama, ballet, opera, and especially Shakespeare. The point is that one of the major societal purposes colleges and universities play is to provide a well-rounded education for its learners. This means that each campus needs to assure that it provides education beyond the majors, that learners are exposed to these opportunities, and that they take advantage of them. For the academic planner, the challenge here is to make sure that departments and faculty members find ways of connecting these liberal arts courses to the knowledge the learners are seeking from their major fields of study. This is not always done, and when learners take courses because they are required instead of because they benefit their overall education, high quality and excellence are not occurring.

Does Knowledge Ever Go Away?

Probably not, but knowledge does tends to ebb and flow based on demand. If one looks at the stacks of books in our libraries it is apparent that all the knowledge that has been contained there is still around, just store-housed. One real problem with knowledge is that there is now so much of it that it is often hard to keep it organized and usable. The digitizing of the world's basic library resources should help to address this problem, but then perhaps much found in older books in the darker sections of the library stacks isn't helpful anymore. With the explosion of knowledge in the new age, and the promise that

that explosion will continue and intensify in the future, the organizing of knowledge is becoming a major concern.

Certainly, over time, the old knowledge may well have usefulness, so it would be a clear mistake to do house cleaning in our libraries to toss out the old to allow in the new. The issue is how do we manage? This is an additional concern to academic planners as they try to get a handle on the state of knowledge in the college or university's discipline bases, and then begin to make resources available to support those areas that need support and begin to withdraw resources from those areas that are no longer as crucial to the overall societal demand for education.

In this regard, while knowledge may not go away, certain disciplines have. It is almost impossible to find home economics on any American 4-year college or university campus. The demand for military science waned to the point that many campuses have abandoned it. Partially as a market function, but also as a function of determining that certain disciplines no longer merited further research or resource allocation, the body of disciplines is constantly changing.

Are the Disciplines Basically Evolutionary or Revolutionary?

The nature of some disciplines is to be evolutionary, building on the knowledge base that comes from the past with more recent and current research to keep the heart and soul of the discipline vital and relevant. The study of languages, as an example, would begin with a basic understanding of what we already know about the language (words, syntax, meaning, phraseology, and tone). It would then be up-dated through the study of modern usage, impact of television and movies (particularly American television and movies), music, societal and religious influences, and the internationalization of languages.

Other disciplines tend to be revolutionary in nature. Certainly computer science is a new and dramatically different discipline that has only become academically formalized in the last half of the 20th Century. Science has always been revolutionary and continuously reinvents itself as breakthrough after breakthrough occurs.

So, why is any of this important? Perhaps the greatest impact of the nature of disciplines in this context is that the revolutionary disciplines are far less predictable than the evolutionary disciplines. This creates a problem for the academic planner. It is possible that disciplines which have appeared suddenly will lose their importance just as suddenly. For example, in the 1980's topics such as "Theory Z" and "In Search of Excellence" were fads in management, but are hardly mentioned in the contemporary literature. How many resources should be siphoned off the campus budget to support a new discipline if the future of that discipline is uncertain? Couple this with the need to stay current, meet society's demand for new knowledge, and the desire to improve continuously and it is easy to see why this topic can create problems for the academic planning function.

Do We Create the Disciplines or do the Disciplines Create Themselves?

What we are suggesting in the modern world of higher education is that disciplines can have a life cycle. They can come and they can go. But who decides when a discipline exists, or is there some other activity that makes disciplines evident? In other words, is there any control that would provide a structure for the timely creation of a new discipline?

Historically, the academy created disciplines to address societal needs. Sigmund Freud was instrumental in the formation of the discipline of psychology, for example, because he and others saw behavioral problems from a different perspective. They discovered the psychological world as a set of new explanations for why people behave as they do, and this growing body of knowledge created a discipline that continues to grow and thrive today.

As one looks at trends in the contemporary world, however, it is clear that disciplines are creating themselves and then being adopted into the academy. The Microsoft revolution, the Internet, long-range jet passenger planes, fiber optics, software development, and mass communication have all been incorporated into the fabric of academia. In the business school, we are examining the importance of creating "e-business" as a set of courses, or perhaps as a new department within the business school in response to the huge impact business on-line has had on business in general.

The future will most likely reflect this type of discipline growth. For academic planners, again, the suddenness, the speed of change in emerging discipline bases, and the resulting demand for new resources is key to determining the best mix of disciplines a campus should offer.

What New Disciplines Should a College or University Plan For? How Do They Know This?

The academic disciplines that make up the academic offering of a college or university make the practical decision as to which portion of the knowledge base should be presented to learners. They then employ professors and instructors who are regarded as experts in their fields. They determine the relevant subjects in the field and how best to bring these to learners. Faculty members in today's institutions of higher education make decisions about the knowledge base and how it will be shared with learners. These issues have a dramatic impact on the overall quality and excellence of the education found on one campus or another.

To maintain high quality and excellence, each campus needs to develop a clear understanding of what its constituents demand of it. Service areas (that community or set of communities that have significant ties with a given college or university) differ from one setting to the next. Understanding what a specific service area needs and wants is the responsibility of the college or university. With this understanding, it can then make an informed academic decision about what it should offer. Since nearly no campus has all the resources it wants, each campus can only offer a portion of the discipline-based programs the service area may need. There is no way to escape this delimiting reality. However, with the understanding that no campus can do everything, it can do some things that meet service area needs well. Then, the challenge is to provide those areas of study and service in an environment that supports excellence and continual improvement. The result will be a set of disciplines, old and new, that meet service area needs. In the present age of evolving technology, certainly being ahead of competing institutions in being able to offer new programs that address the rapidly changing realities of life will suggest new courses of direction that will define the overall academic core of the college or university.

To determine what discipline mix is most appropriate, the college or university must engage in marketing research activities that will clearly identify the needs and wants of the citizens, businesses, governments, and community organizations the institution serves. Another important factor is to understand the desires of major funding sources, such as state governments, donors, alumni, as well as employers and other consumers of the intellectual properties of the

college or university. This is time-consuming and it can be costly.
Regardless, it is extremely important to do. These are the mechanisms
that will inform the campus as to what its role should be while keeping
the campus a strategic asset to the service area.

How Does Credit Hour Production Fit into a Model?

In later chapters, we go into depth about the learning process
and examines how best to transfer knowledge from instructor to
learner. However, the issue of credit hour production is an additional
consideration in looking at the current structure of disciplines in
today's institutions of higher education. Credit hour production is
another one of those elements of academic life that is often overlooked
and taken for granted as another surrogate measure of knowledge
transfer. The assumption is that a course should provide a certain
volume of knowledge and this volume is described in the paradigm of
credit hour production. For example, in a semester system, a three-
hour credit course contains approximately 45 to 48 contact hours. The
term "contact" is important here, because there is an assumption that
students engage in a learning process with an instructor for at least 45
to 48 hours over the course of the semester <u>and</u> that this is the precise
time needed to effectively transfer knowledge.

Discipline-related courses are all measured in credit hour
production, and often are reflected in master syllabus documents that
describe how each of the 45 to 48 hours are used in the course,
providing at least some measure of portfolio review in terms of
understanding the quality level of the course offering. Campus budget
officers look at credit hour production in a different way and can assign
weights on certain courses where the production is high and tuition
revenues are maximized, and those where production is low and there
is a drain on the resource base.

Credit hour production is not just a campus yard stick. Many
funding sources look at credit hour production, as well, as a measure of
how well the college or university is using their resources to provide
education.

Essentially, credit hour production is an economic measure,
not an academic measure. With the exception of potential portfolio
analysis of the content of the course, the basic purpose of measuring
credit hour production is to determine economic impacts. Based on
these analyses, certain courses could be expanded while other courses

could lose their funding. These decisions can have a major impact on the academic plan.

Should Cost Be the Deciding Factor in Developing a Strategic Academic Plan?

One can ask any graduate school this question and be given a very definitive "No!" Graduate classes cost more – they have smaller class sizes and higher-priced faculty, often full tenured professors, making the costs of graduate classes necessarily higher than undergraduate classes which are typically larger in size and taught by lower-level professors or instructors. Doctoral education can be horrendously expensive when one considers that classes might consist of as few as two or three students and a full-tenured professor.

Reengineering graduate classes to reduce costs would probably be a fatal mistake. Reducing the quality of graduate education could result in reducing the overall quality of the campus and research capabilities. So, campuses with graduate programs have to buy into the fact that they are more expensive, but clearly worth it. If their analyses do not end on this note, then they should consider reducing their commitments to graduate education.

But this is not just an issue of graduate education. There are many classes in the undergraduate curriculum which will also produce lower levels of credit hour production and should not be considered candidates for reengineering because of it. Typically, senior level classes within a major will have smaller classes, in which learners interact more vigorously than they would in earlier classes. This promotes more effective learning, and is an appropriate part of preparation in the major prior to graduation. On the other hand, because of the less lofty goals for such courses, one can better justify survey courses in the earlier years that are larger in structure and taught by less qualified instructors or professors.

It is only where one finds courses with low credit hour production that are the result of a fading discipline base or waning market demand that the economic model does apply. Here the academic planning function must look seriously at the causes of poor production and make the decision to reduce resource allocation in these areas and re-channel them to those areas where they can be more effective.

Where Will the Resources to Support These Discipline Decisions Come From?

Capital will continue to come from all the traditional sources of resource allocation, but it will be difficult to have this base expand based on an institution trying to make a case for expansion into a new discipline or set of disciplines. Most state funding agencies are more likely to tell the institution that it needs to reorder its priorities and cut back in some areas if it wishes to expand in others. Other funding sources (those that private colleges depend upon) are likely to take the same approach. This leaves the modern campus with little choice other than to find new sources of funding. This can be done through grant activity, appeals to alumni, and appeals to the community and businesses, but none of these are particularly long-term solutions or sources that come without strings attached. Partnering is a potential source of longer-term support, especially if the educational facility and the partner can work together in educating learners who will become employees of the partner. At bare minimum, strong college and university foundations are essential for helping determine other resource bases and securing them to support new disciplines and programs.

Attaining a high quality faculty is another resource issue that creates problems for colleges and universities, especially in emerging disciplines. The market mechanism exists. Potential faculty members in emerging and popular disciplines will be very much in demand and can command higher salaries. For many traditional faculty members, this is often a bitter pill and it is understandable. However, it is not supportable, and clearly, no institution can afford to give into complaints of existing faculty members and not hire new faculty in new discipline areas to prevent an escalation of campus politics or bad feelings. If the new discipline fits the needs of the service area and if the strategic plan of the college or university calls for the institution to move in that direction, hard resource choices must be made to assure the longer term relevance and survival of the campus. To fund these new faculty members, the administration can use the traditional sources of campus funding, and perhaps will win support from these quarters. However, it may also be the case that the campus will have to use many of the sources suggested above, including the endowment of new faculty chairs to create the resource base that will support the faculty base of a new discipline.

None of this is easy. With resources already tight on nearly every campus, adding new disciplines, faculties, and the support those new faculty members need presents a challenge to the academic planning process, the central administration, and the strategic plan of the college or university. Yet, none of this should prevent the academic plan from doing the right thing. Academic planners need to put the welfare of the institution ahead of campus politics and seek to not only find the discipline mix that makes the most amount of sense, but also the funding bases that they need as well.

What are the Relevant Time Frames to Adequately Accommodate the Needs for Change?

We suggest that the section title we use here is correctly presented as a plural rather than singular. Changes have different intensities, different logistics, and different time requirements. Add to this the rapidity with which societal changes are occurring and one starts to see that the strategic planning process and the academic planning process are in fact continual activities rather than one-time events.

For example, if a campus decides that it is in its best interest (as well as in the best interest of its service area) to create a school of medicine, the decision should come as a result of an exhaustive study for services needed by the service area and the availability of those services Costs of a school of medicine are astronomical, and the need to generate research grants is a paramount consideration Assuming that all of these conditions are met and the decision is made to go ahead, implementation may well take years. For a school of medicine, this slow approach is prudent and practical. Further, medicine is not a new discipline, and the evolution of its disciplines is slower paced than one might find in more purely technology-related disciplines.

On the other hand, if a campus decides to create an e-business program which leads to an e-business major and degree, it doesn't have as much time to consider, plan, and establish it. Imagine constructing a building for this new major: the building would most likely represent the state-of-the-art in terms of learning technologies, but if the college or university takes too much time in coming to a decision about the accoutrements of the building it could find that once built it was obsolete. The deep analysis that must go along with this particular decision is not excused from rigor, but it is also confined to a quick

What the Academic Program Plan Should Look Like

Six months had passed since the president had delivered the dictate that each and every department of the university was to submit a proposal for new program development to the university academic vice president for analysis and approval. The faculties had managed to get over their initial shock and, as one might expect, reacted quite negatively to being told, not asked, to create new academic programs. Finally, their anger was vented, their chests appropriately pounded, and many members of the faculty realized that a wonderful opportunity had presented itself, a chance to add to their series of course and program offerings. New offerings meant new resources, i.e. new faculty members, graduate assistants, equipment, office and classroom space, and those departments and schools who were first to the trough would obtain the lion's share of the wealth.

For many years the School of Humanities had taken a back seat to their more proactive, entrepreneurial cousins in social sciences, business administration, and natural sciences. Humanities had a small percentage of students majoring in their disciplines (i.e. English, philosophy, foreign languages, etc...) and had been relegated to the role of a service school; providing mainly writing, public speaking, basic philosophy and language courses that were required for other majors or the liberal arts core curriculum.

The Dean of the School of Humanities, a very prominent essayist, had been recently hired for the position because of her notoriety and public presence and had an excellent academic education in undergraduate, graduate, and postgraduate Ivy League schools. Her presence on campus and in the School of Humanities was considered a coup by the president and the university trustees. The faculty members of the school were less impressed and enamored with the decision, nonetheless, cooperated with the dean during those rare times that collaboration was necessary.

The Dean wanted to elevate the school in reputation within the university and the outside world, and she knew that with the right academic programs and curricula, this task could be accomplished. Here was an opportunity for more easily achieving this goal, but how could they take advantage of it? The dean knew little about academic program planning. Did every department in the School need an academic program plan or was there a school-wide plan that encompassed the departments? How did the school's academic program plan fit into the university's academic plan? How permanent is the plan? What form should the academic program plan take? Is it a good idea for there to be a series of plans or a single plan? The dean knew that she needed a quick education on the topic before she discussed her plans with the faculty.

The Academic Program Plan: An Overview

As we discussed in Chapter Five, academic program plans are discipline-specific, explicit plans that address a particular course of study by the learner. These plans revolve around specified curricula, usually include a university core experience of classes, and tend to be administered by a specific department. There are also programs which are interdisciplinary in nature and shared between departments, schools, and college-wide academic programs.

The result of implementing a university academic program plan is the academic program mix (Shirley, 1988); a portfolio of courses and program offerings available from the institution including the prioritization of those programs and the relative expectation of new program development over time. Kotler and Fox (1995) broadened this concept to include affiliated services. Internal factors such as faculty capabilities, the mission of the institution, library resources, facilities, and cost, and external factors such as student demand, employer needs, competing programs, community impact and local resources need to be considered in making academic program mix decisions (Shirley, 1998).

Heydinger (1980a) indicated that the environmental conditions facing postsecondary education during the 1980s called for institutional program planning styles that are comprehensive, systematic, public, regular, and expansive. Heydinger (1980b) also noted that each institution has an existing planning style, and new approaches to academic program planning must take into account institutionalized planning practices. Hayes and Newsom-Hales (1978), on the other hand, discussed a practical approach to academic program planning and evaluation based on student needs and social utility. Their proposed approach focused on fundamental characteristics of the academic program planning and evaluation process which were desirable and which insured that educational designers did not lose sight of the more humanistic elements of the educational process.

Academic Program Planning: Program Management (Consumer-focused)

In suggesting that academic programs are essentially products or commodities, Kotler and Fox (1995) recognized that academic program plans delineated institutional product lines, a group of closely related academic programs, and specific products or programs. Programs can be branded – given a name, term, or design that differentiates it from competitor products. As such, programs are also subject to typical product life-cycle patterns (introduction, growth, maturation, and decline) which can also be cyclical, wax and wane over time, or even be fads. Program planning and development are necessary to forecast program declines and to introduce new programs that meet new market demands.

Program growth, under this traditional marketing approach, is just a matter of repositioning academic programs as we suggest in Figure 6.1 below.

Market Penetration. Market penetration occurs when any college or university strategies the institution's market share of students through increased program usage, frequency of use, quantity of use and new program applications (Walker, Boyd and Larreche, 1999). Colleges or universities offer the same programs to the same target market, but in increased volume by adjusting its marketing plan (price, program, promotion, and distribution) to match the needs of potential students.

For example, a college that offers a major in business administration may increase program enrollments by improving program quality (such as obtaining accreditation by a collegiate business accrediting body), discounting tuition (such as having a policy that second family members attending the institution will pay one-half tuition), or by offering the program through distance learning (new distribution channel). As each of these marketing tactics addresses the same target population with the same program by merely modifying some of the tangible and/or intangible benefits of the program, the risk associated with this program planning strategy is quite low.

Program Expansion. If the current customer base has strong brand loyalty but no longer needs the current programs offered by the institution (for example, potential students already have the highest level degree offered by the institution), then creating new programs that are related to the existing academic programs is a low risk method for garnering higher enrollments. These program expansions can take the form of higher or lower degrees (moving from certificate programs to associates, to bachelors, to masters, to doctoral programs or visa versa), alternative degree programs (such as a B.A. as well as a B.S. in Business Administration), as well as related new degree programs where the institution has the faculty expertise, library holdings, and facilities to expand easily. For example, Southampton College has a program in psychology/biology that it developed from the expertise in Marine Science Department and developed it to address the needs of certain students for a less physical science-intensive program.

Figure 6.1
Program Growth Vector Model[1]

	Present Programs	New Programs
Present Markets	Market Penetration	Program Penetration
New Markets	Market Expansion	Diversification

Market Expansion. Market expansion occurs when a college or university looks for new markets for their current mix of academic programs. There is some risk associated with this strategy since the institution is dealing with new psychological and sociological demographics and new consumer preferences. A college or university can expand geographically, enlarging its scope of operation, or the institution can employ alternative, asynchronous instructional delivery methods.

For example, Long Island University is comprised of three major campuses, three satellite campuses and operates, through its Friends World program, eight international regional centers while the University of Phoenix employs on-line education coupled with over

---

[1] Adapted from David A. Aaker (1984) "How to Select a Business Strategy" in Glenn Carroll and David Vogel (eds.) (1984) *Strategy and Organization: A West Coast Perspective*. Boston, Mass.: Pitman.

100 locations nationwide. Many universities expand their geographic boundaries through exchange programs and joint degree programs, for example Moscow University Touro offers both Russian and American undergraduate degrees and is affiliated with Touro College of New York. (http://www.touro.ru/main.php?trg=2)

Diversification. The riskiest growth strategy is diversification, that is, create new programs for new markets, since it involves learning new operations as well as dealing with new consumer groups. If successfully implemented, however, diversification can reduce the overall risk of the institution by broadening the program mix – the broader the program mix, the less dependent the institution is on one specific program and the less susceptible the institution is to any one particular change in its marketplace. Diversification can be either concentric in nature adding programs that are similar in nature or related to the current programs of the institution, or conglomerate in nature, unrelated to the current program offerings.

One related diversification strategy, vertical integration, refers to providing products and services to students that would normally be provided by the college's suppliers (backward integration) or providing products and services that students might normally purchase after their college experience (forward integration). For example, some colleges require that students in certain academic programs purchase essential equipment for those programs (engineering schools may require students to purchase a wireless laptop computer). The college may make this purchase easier by integrating the purchase into their operation (the college sells the computers) and/or bundling the purchase with the price of tuition (the equipment is included as part of the tuition).

In horizontal integration, the college expands through mergers and acquisitions. Union Institute and University, a well known university without walls, purchased Vermont College to provide personalized, classroom education as a form of unrelated diversification; St. John's University in Queens, New York bought La Salle Academy (a military school) in Oakdale, Long Island in order to expand their geographic region and to offer a rural setting for their students; related diversification (Pride and Ferrell, 2003).

Diversification can also occur through organizational relationship, joint ventures, or networks (Walker, Boyd and Larreche, 1999). Western Governor's University (WGU) is a virtual university comprised of offerings from forty colleges and universities from twenty-two states. WGU has also signed an agreement with Open

University (OU) of the United Kingdom to bring OU's on-line programs into the US market (Rowley and Sherman, 2001). Many colleges and universities have articulation agreements with two year community colleges or with neighboring institutions that offer differing degree programs. These agreements may include early admissions to an advanced degree program or guaranteed acceptance of transfer credits.

Portfolio Approach to Academic Programs

Figure 6.2
Boston Consulting Group's Growth-Share Matrix

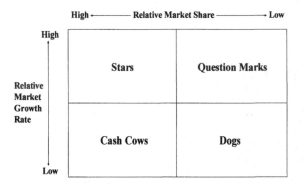

A logical extension of the notion of academic programs as products is to then treat the academic mix of programs as constituting a portfolio; a set of program holdings that can be evaluated in general terms and evaluated against one another. The notion of the portfolio also suggests that, like personal investment portfolios, under-performing programs can be deleted from the program mix while well-performing programs would be favored with continued college investments. The most basic portfolio model employed by the business sector is the Boston Consulting Group's (BCG) growth-share matrix as represented in Figure 6.2 above (Hunger and Wheelan, 2000).

This 2 by 2 matrix is a rather simple method for segmenting and evaluating college programs. The vertical axis indicates higher education's growth rate[2] (could be measured for the industry as a whole or for the institution's particular market segment) while the horizontal axis shows the program's market share relative to either its largest competitor or the industry's market segments average. Each circle represents a particular academic program with the size of the circle indicating the relative size of the program and with the placement of the circle within a quadrant being based upon the program's market share and growth rate.

Question Marks. Also known as problem-children, question mark programs are those found in fast-growth markets with relatively small market share. They tend to require capital for expansion so as to keep up with industry leaders or they will lose their small market share and decline once the market matures and the growth rate slows down. The risk is that further investments in these programs will not be enough to catch up with industry leaders and that the program will quickly deteriorate without recouping the college's sunk costs (Walker, Boyd and Larreche, 1999).

An excellent example of a potential question mark is virtual universities and internet education. There are many colleges and universities who did not enter this market early, or allowed other institutions to obtain a large portion of this market. These late comers do have some internet instruction, but it is haphazard at best, unorganized, and managed by the professor who is teaching his or her course. The question for these colleges and universities now, especially those with access to minimal resources, is whether it is worth the time and effort to introduce a substantive, organized internet program knowing that they may not be able to acquire substantial market share. Secondly, these institutions need to question the role of internet instruction relative to their mission. Are they jumping on the internet bandwagon as a me too, knee jerk reaction to market trends or have they thoroughly examined the ramifications and costs of a viable internet program and how this educational delivery system meets their learners' needs?

Stars. Academic programs that are stars are market leaders in a high-growth educational sector. In order to maintain their industry leadership, however, further investments in these programs must

---

[2] One can calculate growth rate in several ways, change in: enrollment, credit hours, number of classes, number of faculty/staff, annual revenues, and annual operating budget, etc....

[4] Condensed and modified to fit academic program planning.

continue to offset potential new entrants (who are attracted to the high growth nature of the field) and innovative competitors.

Southampton College has unfortunately learned this lesson the hard way. Their premier program, Marine Sciences, was at one point the market leader in the field with over 500 students enrolled in the program (about 1/3 the total students attending the institution). As competitors entered this market, they brought with them modern facilities and state-of-the-art teaching technology. However, Southampton College took no action to resist the competition, allowed their infrastructure to age and become obsolete, which resulted in a twenty percent drop in program enrollment.

Cash Cows. These academic programs are the undiscovered pearls of the institution, they are market leaders in a slow growth market; a mature market which has become quite stable and predictable. Investment in these programs tends to be less intensive than in stars or question marks since there is less potential and existing competition and less need to invest in new infrastructure and marketing. More importantly, cash cow programs are those programs that the college milks for growth capital to fund its stars and question marks. In most universities around the country their business programs have served as their cash cows since enrollments in these programs have been quite stable with lower infrastructure requirements than other fields.

Dogs. Academic programs with low-market share and low-growth rates are called dogs because they tend to generate little revenue for the institution and have little prospect of doing so in the future. Academic programs in this category tend to be harvested; that is, the institution puts minimal investments into the program until the program is either phased out or refunded given a change in the growth rate of the field. Many academic programs in this category are taught out; the institution closes admissions to the program and allows the existing students in the program to complete their education within a certain time frame.

Academic Program Development. Based on the four quadrants of the BCG model, one might expect that most new academic programs within an institution will originally start out as question marks, that new programs will be introduced only in high growth academic areas. Assuming these programs receive the proper funding they will grow into stars by gaining market share as demonstrated through increased enrollment. As more colleges and universities introduce similar programs, the demand for these programs will wane, causing a slowing of the growth in the market. High market share programs will become cash cows if they survive the competitive shakeout; lower market share programs will become dogs and should be deleted from the program portfolio.

A Cautionary Note. Institutions can use the BCG model, or other portfolio models such as the General Electric Industry Attractiveness-Business Position Matrix or Hofer-Schendel Product/Market Segment Evolution Matrix (Hofer et al., 1984) to analyze their academic program holdings but certainly these techniques are not fool proof. Walker, Boyd and Larreche (1999) indicated that the BCG model in particular has several limitations:

1. *Market growth is only one measure of academic market attractiveness.* There may be other reasons that an institution might want to start an academic program in a certain area. For example, a new program might require minimal investments in faculty and infrastructure to yield high margins between cost and tuition, or the program is a logical extension of existing programs. The institution has to define what features of an academic market make it attractive to enter, within the context of the institution's mission, and use those factors in determining market attractiveness.

2. *Market share, enrollment, is only one measure of competitive positioning.* The notion that an institution should benchmark its programs, is a valuable one, however, colleges and universities may feel that the size of their academic programs alone is inadequate in describing the strengths of their programs. Other factors such as quality of the faculty, reputation of the institution, unique program attributes, specialized program accreditation, access to resources, and student/alumni loyalty may be additional factors that help differentiate one institution's programs from another and make it more viable.

3. *The model provides only very general guidance on strategic choices and does not consider implementation issues.* Besides cash flow into or out of a program (invest or harvest), the model does not provide guidance as to other actions that an institution can take to make its question marks stars and its stars cash cows. The portfolio produces, at best, a build, hold or divest strategy which needs to be integrated with the institution's overall strategy and the institution's approach to the market whether it be proactive, defensive, analytical, or reactive.

4. *The model does not account for academic program synergy and relatedness.* Many academic programs have commonalities, that is they share program components, and are synergistic (their whole is greater than the sum of their parts). For example, many accounting and business degree programs share many of the same courses as part of their program core requirements. A decision to discontinue one program may have deleterious effects on the other since basic business courses may have to run with very low course enrollments in order to continue offering one program.

Birnbaum (2000) also noted that although "the notion that one should stick with winners and drop losers [is] intuitively appealing ... institutions are more likely to base their judgments on quality, centrality, mission and academic politics [rather] than on a purely financial bottom line" (pg.6). Given these caveats, institutions could employ portfolio techniques to understand their program mix from a profit-performance perspective yet include additional factors in their analyses in order to determine the broader utility of their programs. Colleges may choose to include loss leaders (programs that actually have negative cash flow – dogs) in their program mix because they are fundamental to the institution's mission or have non-financial, intangible benefits such as adding to the university's reputation.

The SWOT Approach to Academic Program Analysis

An alternative method to analyzing a college's programs or program mix is to perform an organization audit or SWOT analysis. SWOT refers to the strengths, weaknesses, opportunities, and threats that are associated with a particular program or program mix. This business technique but has recently been transferred to academia (Kotler and Fox, 1995; Cordeiro and Vaidya, 2002). Dolence, Rowley and Lujan (1997) recommended that the analysis process be comprised of the following steps: [4]

1. Develop key performance indicators (KPIs).
2. Perform an external and internal environmental assessment.
3. Using indicators and assessments, evaluate institution's SWOT analysis.
4. Brainstorm on results by evaluating potential impact of SWOT on institution.
5. Formalize program strategies, goals and objectives.
6. Implement changes based upon academic program plans.
7. Outcomes assessment of program implementation (pg. 2).

KPIs

Dolence, Rowley and Lujan (1997) define a KPI as "A measure of an essential outcome of a particular organizational performance activity, or an important indicator of a precise health condition of the organization" (pg. 17). In terms of academic programs, KPIs might include full-time equivalent (FTE) program enrollment, program entrance and graduation requirements, and percentage of Ph.D.'s teaching in the program. These are synonymous with many of the quantitative and qualitative measures employed in college and program outcomes assessment and total quality management programs (Fields, 1993). KPIs need to be prioritized for both the overall academic program as well as individual programs and can be further segmented by academic school, department and course. Meaningful KPIs must include the following characteristics:

1. Quantifiable and Measurable: Can we define this KPI so that we can collect comparative data between programs within and without the institution?

2. Importance: What is the value in collecting this data? Does this data help us analyze how the overall academic program and specific programs support our overall institutional mission and academic strategy?

3. Level of Analysis: Which level or levels of analysis (institution, program, course) does this KPI cover? (Dolence, Rowley and Lujan, 1997, pgs. 20-21).

Developing and utilizing KPIs is not as easy as it may seem. California State University, Los Angeles developed eight KPI areas (academic quality, enrollment management, financial aid and student support, institutional advancement, image and reputation, sponsored research, facilities, and revenues/expenditures) but found that their strategic planning committee, as well as their individual academic units, were bogged down in data collection and analysis. Much of the data "was not being used to guide planning ... the original objective of strategic planning – to establish broad direction and goals – had become lost" (Cordeiro and Vaidya, 2002, pg. 25) and they eventually dropped the use of KPIs for a more expansive, "higher level" (pg. 26) approach.

Based upon Cal State's experiences, it is evident that if KPIs are to be employed in program planning and evaluation, the use of KPIs must be tied into the university's mission, receive support and input

from the president and the campus community, and be integrated with
the budgetary process.

Analyzing the External and Internal Environments

All organizations, including colleges and universities, are
significantly influenced by many internal and external forces (Lewin,
1951).   Higher educational institutions have unique internal and
external stakeholders who bring with them their own particular
dynamics.

One can divide the institution's external environment into two
subsets: the task environment or the organization's operating domain,
and the remote or broader environment (Kotter, 1978). The college's
task environment includes industry forces such as suppliers,
competitors, regulators, and buyers; any external organization that
impacts the institution's value chain (Kotter, 1978; Porter, 1985). The
broader external environment includes political, economic, social and
technological trends.   Changes in the broader external environment
may impact both the organization's task environment as well as the
organization's internal operation.

Forces or changes in the external environment that have either
a negative or positive impact on the institution and its programs are
referred to as either threats or opportunities.   Whether the force or
change is a threat or an opportunity is determined by the college's
ability to take advantage of the force or change.   For example, the
growth of the internet (technological change – broader environment)
impacted the way in which learner's could purchase and receive
knowledge (buyer – task environment), which therein may have
impacted the college's instructional delivery system and billing. This
has certainly lead to opportunities for certain colleges who could adapt
their internal operations to accommodate these changes as well as lead
to new market entrants, and have become threats to those institutions
who could not or would not make the needed changes (Lawrence and
Lorsch, 1969).

The internal environment of any program or college program
mix is comprised of the shared values (the program vision or mission),
the skills of dean/faculty and supporting staff, staff and dean/faculty
motivation and interests, program structure, leadership style, and
program strategy of the dean/department or campus committee that is
responsible for the program or program mix as shown in Figure 6.3
below (Rowley and Sherman, 2001).

There are numerous ways in which to analyze the internal environment of an organization from a program planning perspective. Dolence, Rowley and Lujan (1997) indicated that an analysis of program performance (productivity, benchmarks, policies, and procedures), program design (structure, function, infrastructure, integration), and program strategies (mission, goals, objectives, strategies, and resources) should allow universities to determine their strengths (what they do well) versus their weaknesses (what they do poorly) as defined through their KPIs. They then would construct a matrix to correlate their KPIs with the internal factors in what they coin a cross-impact analysis.

An alternative approach cited by Porter (1985) would be to determine how the department's or committee's infrastructure, human resource management, technology development, and procurement added value to each step of the college program's value chain including inbound logistics, operations, outbound logistics, marketing and sales, and service. Those administrative operations that did not add value to the learning experience for the student would be considered a weakness while those that added value would be considered a strength.

Figure 6.3
External and Internal Environments

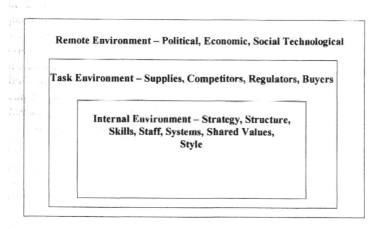

Finally, Dittrich (1988) recommended examining the physical, financial, human, and marketing assets of a college or program. This approach is similar to the functional approach cited by Pearce and Robinson (2000) which examines the marketing, finance, operations, and human resources of the institution or program. Both approaches emphasize the development of distinctive competencies and specialized resources that will lead to a program's competitive advantage (a strength).

     Conducting the SWOT Analysis. Using KPIs to describe the college's program mix and/or specific program attributes, Sherman (1991) recommended adopting a procedure that begins by developing a listing of the key institutional strengths and weaknesses (S/W) and key institutional opportunities and threats (O/T). Next, the analyst makes a judgment as to the relative balance of each combined measure on a +3 to –3 scale where strengths and opportunities are positive and weaknesses and threats are negative. In an alternative method, Dolence, Rowley and Lujan (1997) suggested that the analyst conduct what they called a cross-impact analysis between KPIs and each SWOT index and rate the influence of each KPI on a 6 (strong positive influence) to 1 (strong negative influence) scale, with 0 indicating no impact.

     Regardless of the specific method or scaling system, the purpose of converting qualitative judgment to quantitative data is to then graph the results of the analysis using the results of the internal assessment (S/W) as the 'X' axis ordinate and the results of the external assessment (O/T) as the 'Y' axis ordinate. The plotted results will fall into one of four quadrants, with each quadrant representing a set of specific actions that should be taken in terms of bettering the program or program mix as seen in Figure 6.4 below.

     The results are not unlike the results obtained from a portfolio analysis. The program or program mix (summary of the results of all of the programs) falls into one of four quadrants, and the college is provided with a set of program planning options to choose from. The college should either grow their programs or program mix, maintain its current operating level, shrink or harvest its operation, or divest itself fully or partially of some of its programs. Many of the specific options have already been described earlier under the topic of academic programs as products, particularly growth and maintenance strategies. Note that some of the specific options cross several quadrants -- concentric and conglomerate diversification, and divestiture.

Figure 6.4
SWOT Chart with Resultant Program and Program Mix Recommendations[5]

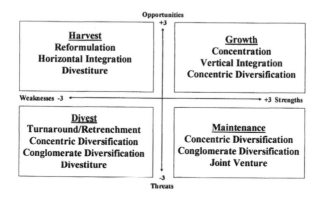

Reformulation/Turnaround/Retrenchment/Divest Options. These program options are quite similar and require that the university rethink the mission and objectives of the program mix or program in question. For example, programs with recent historical trends of decreasing enrollments should be examined to determine whether drops in enrollment are part of a larger industry trend or a function of the internal operation. Whether identified as a threat or a weakness, the institution needs to better position the program relative to competitors, alter the program to meet market demands in an internal focus, shrink the operation of the program to accommodate the shrinking market, or remove the program completely from their program offerings.

Unlike the portfolio techniques described earlier, the SWOT approach provides the institution some flexibility in that the institution defines what the key performance indicators are for its particular organization and uses those indicators to perform a self-assessment. The SWOT approach also offers the institution some elasticity in terms of options the institution may choose given the results of that analysis.

Another Cautionary Note and Final Comment. Birnbaum (2000) criticizes SWOT analysis and other strategic management techniques which have been imported into higher education by claiming that "strategic management [is] too new to have settled on a proven set of procedures" (pg.74) and warned that this "lack of proven

---

[5] Adopted from Sherman (1991) and Pearce and Robinson (2000).

procedures does not inhibit the continuing development by consultants of prescriptive products" (pg. 74). Ironically, Birnbaum continued his argument by citing Mintzberg's (1994) comment that strategic planning wasted a great deal of time, yet in Mintzberg's most recent strategic management text (Mintzberg et. al., 2003) he himself noted that although "there is no 'one best way' to create strategy ... quite different forms work well in particular contexts" (pg. ix).

Rowley and Sherman (2001) concur with Mintzberg that program planning must be tailor-made to the institution. They stated that, "The differences one finds from one campus to the next are gigantic, and attempting to use a cookie-cutter method of planning, let alone a method that is not sensitive to the unique circumstances and needs of colleges and universities, is bound to fail" (pg. xxi).

The Academic Program Planning Matrix. The academic program portfolio approach that arises from the prior analysis of the learning environment cited in chapters one and two treats the academic program plan as a compilation of the academic programs of the institution and whether these programs impact the academic centers that address learners' needs and impact the faculty's roles in addressing learner and institutional needs. Referring back to Figure 3.3 in Chapter Three and examining the roles of the academic community and the multiple roles of the faculty as we suggested in Figure 3.5, the academic program plan is defined through a three dimensional matrix.

In this matrix, the X-axis represents the variety of faculty roles; the Y-axis represents the mix of college centers; and the Z-axis represents the actual list of academic programs found on a campus. In constructing the matrix, one would first define how college centers and faculty roles impact each center. For example, a business undergraduate program would impact the learning and career center of an institution. Further, certain business programs may also have elements that are entertaining (such as a business club or guest speakers), impact living accommodations (such as a business fraternity house), or even have a fitness element (such as an executive exercise program). Similarly, business faculty members would teach in the program and would assess learning. However, this program may or may not necessarily emphasize research, mentoring, or community, university and professional service. Once each program within the institution has been described in this manner, the analysis will be amalgamated on the matrix to provide an overview of the existing academic program plan as we demonstrate in Figure 6.5 below.

The benefit the institution can derive from plotting programs on this matrix is that the composite matrix serves as an assessment instrument that will depict the relative demand for specific center's support as well as faculty services. These demands can be compared to actual services provided as well as the mission of the institution to determine the relative fit between the academic program plan, the academic plan, and the strategic plan of the institution. Second, future programs can be gauged against the current program mix to determine whether they reinforce current areas in the program plan or whether they cover centers and faculty roles that have limited or no coverage.

Figure 6.5
The Academic Program Planning Matrix

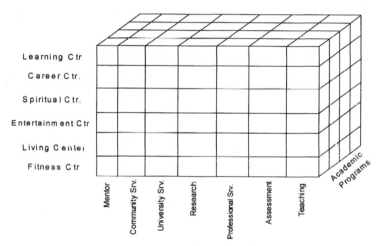

Academic Planning: Learner Collaboration (Community-focused)

In earlier chapters in this book, we emphasized the need to include the learner in the formulation and development of the learning community. Program planning, as a subset of the institution's strategic and academic plans, must also address the role of the learner in the program planning process. Earlier methods of program planning either tended to treat the learner and the learning environment as a given, only to be modified through program review, or were based on the institution's most logical response to the internal and external forces such as market demands and institutional mission. In neither case is the learner central to the program planning process nor, more importantly, the learner's needs are at best only indirectly addressed.

Revisiting the Learning Community

Rogers (1969), who coined the phrase "client-centered counseling", transferred these concepts to an educational setting, one in which the instructor becomes a counselor-educator and the student becomes fundamental to the learning community. Rogers identified a number of traits of student-centered teaching including the following:

1. Teachers cannot actually teach others, they can only assist in the learning process.
2. A learner will only learn what he or she believes is important to his or her own existence and growth.
3. Learners will reject or distort knowledge that challenges their self view. Learning must fall within their zone of acceptance (Barnard, 1938).
4. Learners can only receive new and potentially threatening knowledge if their attitudes become more relaxed. They will be more receptive to disparate information if they perceive that they are in a safe learning environment (see Schein [1987] on the concept and techniques of unfreezing).

Translating Rogers' work into a more practical approach, Boy and Pine (1982) developed the following principles:

1. Learning is a process of changing behaviors in positive directions.
2. Learning is an experience that occurs inside the learner and is activated by the learner.
3. Learning is discovery of the personal meaning and relevance of ideas.
4. Learning is a consequence of experience.
5. Learning is cooperative and collaborative processes.
6. Learning is an evolutionary process.
7. The richest source of learning is the learner himself or herself.
8. The process of learning is affective as well as cognitive.
9. Learning is enjoyable
10. The learner is a free and responsible agent.
11. Learning is an experience that expresses values.
12. The process of problem-solving and learning are highly unique and individual.
13. Teaching is learning (pg.s 239-240).

Boy and Pine (1982) further described the learning community as an environment that facilitates learning to include an atmosphere where students: feel respected and accepted, are allowed to make mistakes, discover the personal meaning of knowledge, and evaluate their own progress in the context of their individual situations. Academic program planning within this context must assist in *creating an academic community that develops the whole person*, "not simply someone who is informed from the neck up but someone who exists in a significant relationship to others and to himself" (Rogers, 1969, pg. 201).

If academic program planning is to speak to the needs of the learning community then it first and foremost must include learners in the formulation and implementation of that plan as well as directly deal with the needs of the learners. Learners must be active participants in the program planning process as well as the focus of the content of the planning in the context of the institution's mission.

The Collaborative Community: Some Attempts

Today's colleges and universities have already adopted some collaborative approaches to program planning and development in response to the differing life styles of their learners. Students are now allowed to demonstrate learning outside the traditional classroom setting and receive college credit for prior learning through challenge and waiver examinations, internships, cooperative education, life experience credit, and independent study. High school students may now obtain college credit through advanced placement examinations and/or through college sanctioned courses offered through the high school. College courses are being delivered off-campus, during the evenings and weekends, using differing semester formats, through multimedia, and the Internet. Academic advisors and counselors work with students in helping them select courses, degree programs, career paths, as well as deal with nonacademic issues such as personal and health issues. All in all, colleges and universities in the 21st century have become far more sensitive to their learners' needs and have taken great strides to personalize the college experience for their learners.

All of these accommodations to learners and more, however, do not place the learner at the center of the educational experience nor do they ask the learner for input into the development of his or her course of study – the academic program. Students must still follow a set curriculum, obtain a certain number of credits in certain designated course topics (liberal arts core, major/concentration, specialization, and minor), and attain a specific number of credits and the appropriate grades in order to obtain a degree. In essence, there is a fairly strict standardization of the learning process as well as to the performance of the learner in that process.

Whether this standardization has been created for efficiency sake or imposed by state and regional accrediting bodies, the one method fits all approach to college education, even with the newly offered variations described above, still might require that the learner modify his or her needs and/or demands to fit the institution's academic programs. Since not all learners can adapt to these unvarying program structures, several colleges and universities have arisen in the past few decades that are nontraditional in nature (Bear, 1997). In the next section we will describe two reputable, innovative programs and describe a methodology for collaborative academic planning.

Towards the Creation a Collaborative Community

Collaboration with the learner needs to occur at the macro level, that is, on the content and methods of learning, the academic program plan. Several colleges and universities, most notably Empire State College in New York and Union Institute and University in Ohio, have embraced some form of the collaborative community model as the format for their academic programs.

Empire State College. Through a combination of prior coursework, contract learning, credit for experience, standardized tests, and other methods of evaluating prior learning, the Empire State College (ESC) allows adults to complete undergraduate and graduate degree requirements – collaboration occurs at the course level with adult learners working closely with faculty mentors/advisors. Students can complete a degree tied closely to individual, career, and educational goals (Hawkes and Pisaneschi, 1992). This non-residential institution serves students throughout the state, with faculty in over 40 regional learning locations (Hall and Bonnabeau, 1993).

Contract learning seems a particularly well-suited format for the older, working, married adult who may have attended several colleges some years ago. Students differ at entry and throughout the degree program at ESC and in their ability to handle independent study. The learning contract is the cornerstone of the learning experience and has substantial educational benefits apart from the subject matter the contract addresses. As the term implies, there is a solid commitment to a plan of study developed by a student and a faculty member after whatever deliberation both deem necessary. The learning contract specifies the learning activities to be undertaken, the duration of the study, the criteria by which the work is to be evaluated, and the amount of credit to be assigned. The learning contract addresses itself to various dimensions of learning: the long range plan(s) of the student, specific purposes or topics, the learning activities to be undertaken and the means and criteria of evaluation. The student clearly states his or her long-range plans, aspirations, or goals. These interests provide a conceptual framework around which a sound degree program is developed. Thus, each contract relates to the degree program and is an avenue leading toward the attainment of a degree (Avakian, 1994).

The role of mentor becomes crucial if the college is to foster self-learning. An experienced, resourceful, and mature group of faculty committed to the ideal of independent learning is needed to effectively work with students having different styles of learning (Lehmann, 1975). This program requires nontraditional concepts of faculty, since their role as mentor in a contractual learning situation is more diverse than that of a traditional faculty member. The ESC mentor role involves several activities: advisement, intellectual development, evaluation, and personal career development (Bradley, 1975).

Union Institute and University. Union expands the concept of the learning contract to encompass the entire learning experience for the doctoral student. The learning contract becomes the learning agreement (LA) for the entire degree program. The LA may take many forms but must include the following components: proficiency in the fields of study, an internship, personal development, a project demonstrating excellence (PDE), and sponsored learning sessions.

The learner develops the learning agreement with their doctoral committee. "Doctoral learning may include plans to attend classes of various sorts, seminars, laboratory sessions ... --whatever helps learning, wherever it can be found, however a learner finds that he/she learns best, so long as it is approved by the Doctoral Committee" (The Union Institute, 1999, pg. 7). Learning objectives are then developed for each major component along with outcome assessment instruments, including assigned evaluators. Assessment instruments can be as traditional as papers and other forms of written documentation but can be as creative as video tapes, presentations, computer programs, and works of art.

The learner is the chair of the doctoral committee which is comprised of a core faculty member and second core reader from

Union, two adjunct professors, and two peer learners. "Committee decisions are made by consensus, which means that all members agree on all points of the program" (pg. 10) with the full committee meeting twice; once to certify the learning agreement, the second a pre-graduation meeting to evaluate the learner's performance as per the learning agreement.

Based on the decentralized structure of Union's academic program, the role of the committee is vital to the learning process. The learner selects his/or her own committee members, starting with the first core. The core faculty member is the "keeper of the process" (pg. 12) and ensures that the learner/chair understands all of the procedures. The core also approves all of the other committee member selections. The second core is the outside reader and critically analyzes the work of the committee and the learner, more specifically, the second core reports on the strengths and limitations of both the learning agreement and the work submitted for graduation. Adjuncts are chosen for their expertise and scholarly background and ensure a high level of learner scholarship. Peer members support and encourage the learner and also assess the learner's work.

After the learning agreement is approved by the committee, the learner then works on the major components of his or her academic program. Once the program is completed, and all of the components of the program have been evaluated, the learner writes both a program summary and a draft transcript. These products are then evaluated by the committee, including the second core, and discussed at the pre-graduation meeting. Learners usually have additional work to complete after the pre-graduation meeting in order to complete the program.

Comments and Concerns. Both the ESC and Union academic programs have elements of collaborative learning utilizing a decentralized system to facilitate learner collaboration. More specifically, both ESC and Union empower their faculty and learners and provide an organizational climate and culture that supports learner initiatives. However, these types of programs are certainly not without pitfalls. Rose (1987) indicated that contract-based institution faced numerous problems in implementing their programs – programs were often highly conventional and similar to traditional ones and programs were highly specialized with little breadth. Interrelated reasons for these seemingly antithetical situations were that many adults attended college simply for the credentials and did not perceive themselves as voluntary learners. Other students wanted to dictate what they were to learn or were ill-prepared academically or not well-directed. Faculty issues and the general process orientation of the individualized approach compounded these problems. Adults who sought flexibility of access rather than content reshaped the original purposes of these academic programs. The result of assuming too much about the learner's ability to work was academic programs that did not empower students but left them feeling shortchanged or manipulated.

Second, cost analyses of these decentralized academic programs are quite difficult to undertake. Debus (1975) commented that it is essential that cost information be on an individual student basis. Therefore, the basic unit of analysis chosen is the individual student contract. The costing model developed assigns to each student contract its share of all costs -- both direct and indirect. Most elements of cost are gathered in cost centers by the common definitions.

Frequency Asked Questions (FAQ) About Program Planning

Although we have covered the background and some basics of program planning, and will cover the program planning procedure in detail in the next chapter, we are sure that there are some practical considerations that many administrators and academic supervisors have either not considered or may not have the answers to. In this portion of the chapter we would then like to pose and answer several questions related to the program planning process that we ourselves have seen.

Does Every Department Need to do Academic Program Planning? The most obvious answer would seem to be *yes* since the college's program mix needs to be analyzed on a per program basis (is this particular program viable?) as well as holistically. However, those departments that offer secondary programs (those programs less vital to the institution's mission) may have less planning demands placed on them than those departments which are central to the institution.

How is a Campus-Wide Plan Assembled? Campus-wide plans can be assembled through a bottom-up process (individual departments construct their own plans independently which are then combined at the school level, school level plans are integrated to form the academic program plan at the university level), a top-down process (the university level plan is developed as an integrated whole and then broken down at the school or college level, and then the department level), or a top-down/bottom-up process (a campus wide initiative for planning starts at the top but includes initiatives at the school or college level, and then the department level which are fed back to the university level to form the program plan).

How Permanent is the Plan? Usually academic program plans are created for three to five years and usually based upon the program review cycle of the institution. No plan should be written in stone, however, and the planning process should be flexible enough to allow for program changes given shifting conditions.

What Form Should the Academic Program Plan Take? It would seem fairly evident that the program plan should take a written form where the academic program is delineated for the entire university, then the specific schools or colleges, and then the specific departments within those schools. Some institutions may be tempted to put their academic plan on the internet which is fine as long as access is limited to those individuals who have the authority to read the plan. Since the plan comprises part of the competitive strategy of the institution one would not want competitors reading the plan.

Is it a Good Idea for There to be a Series of Plans or a Single Plan? Usually a single long-term plan, such as an academic program plan, is comprised of both shorter term plans that serve as milestones for the long-term plan, and implementation plans that break down the program plan into its functional and departmental plans. Contingency plans or what-if plans are also an outcome of the program planning process and are based upon the need to account for differing situations arising that are counter to the planning assumptions about the market and the institution inherent in the academic program plan. A series of plans may be necessary as planning is a continuous process.

Who *Should* Have Access to the Academic Program Plan? Who Should be Allowed to "Debate" the Academic Plan (or Plans)? In an environment of openness and sharing information, it is clear that any key stakeholder group which is impacted by the academic plan should have the ability to peruse the plan and make comments about it. More specifically, faculty, staff and learners should be part of the planning process and therein have access to the finished product.

Is it a good idea to have the Governing Board approve the academic program plan? Although not involved in the day-to-day activities of the university, we believe that an academic program plan cannot succeed in the long run without the approval and active support of the governing board. As Rowley and Sherman (2001) noted "there is no question as to where final authority resides, even in issues related to shared governance ... boards make final decisions on academic issues" (pg. 156). The board must become part of the academic planning process so as to obtain their approval for both the process of creating an academic program plan as well as the content of the plan.

How to do Academic Program Planning

They were all seated around a large table, in a cool dank room. The shades were drawn and there was very little natural light, just tinges infiltrating the corners of the room. The chairs of the School of Humanities were wondering just what they were there for. They sat pensively, as if a scimitar was hanging over each and everyone's head and they were just waiting for the hand of fate to come crashing down and chop off their heads.

Finally, the chair of the English Department broke the interminable silence by clearing her throat and exclaiming "Well, I haven't got all day. Does anyone know what this bloody meeting is about besides what the memo from the dean stated – academic program planning? You all know that I think that meetings are a waste of precious time and effort. And what's so special about academic program planning? First of all, planning is an oxymoron at this or any other academic institution. Who ever heard of a university that really knew how to plan, could plan, or wanted to? Secondly, we already have program planning through the program review process. Every five years we internally evaluate our programs and send them to a college-wide evaluation committee for comment and approval. What more do we need to do? If this is another hair-brained scheme of administration to cover their asses with the Trustees over shrinking enrollments, I swear they are going to pay dearly!"

The comments by the Chair of the English Department were greeted with a roar of voices. A tumultuous discussion erupted from the other academic chairs. As these discussions decayed into snide comments and the usual attacks on administrative incompetence, the Dean of Humanities meandered into the room. "'Bout time you showed up" teased the Chair of the Philosophy Department. "If you had taken any longer, my colleagues in crime would have overthrown the administration, burned our state charter, and mellowed out on the rubble." This comment eased the tension in the room, , and verified the dean's impression that she had a difficult task in hand. "I apologize for being late" replied the dean. "I had a call from the president that I just had to take – you know how she is when she gets an idea in her head; she just can't wait to share it." The department heads murmured in agreement and the apology seemed to ease their bruised egos, except for the Chair of the English Department. "Come, come Dean. Let's get on with it. I have better things to do than sit here exchanging *pleasantries. What is all this falderal about academic program planning? What does the administration want from us now?" "That's a wonderful question!* Let me share with you this magnificent opportunity our school has to obtain new students, additional faculty, and more resources through academic program planning. Once I've explained the eight-step process and how we are going to involve the students, alumni and faculty, I'd appreciate your input and invite you to become part of the planning process." The dean knew that she had a long road ahead of her and that this was the first step in the journey.*

Specifically, WHO Does the Work on Developing an Academic Plan?

The academic plan is a fluid and living document. It is a process that contains several sub-processes. As we have indicated earlier, the elements of a college or university academic plan come from a wide variety of places, many off-campus. Yet the responsibility for creating an effective academic plan is that of the individual college or university, especially the academic side of the campus. We believe that academic planning should start at the level of the provost, vice president for academic affairs, or vice provost for academic affairs, and then move down through the school or college deans to department chairs, and finally to the permanent faculty.

Presidents and chancellors, along with governing board members, certainly have a stake in academic planning activities, but we do not believe they should be directly involved in the planning process itself. While we recognize that on many campuses, the president or chancellor holds the title of "Chief Academic Officer," these individuals oversee the activities of the entire campus and should not diminish their broader responsibilities to oversee the development and maintenance of the academic plan. The role of presidents and chancellors, along with governing boards, is to review, advise, reject, or approve the plan that comes from the academic side of the organization.

The Role of Academics

The provost, academic vice president, or academic vice chancellor – for simplicity's sake, we will refer to this role from now on as that of provost – should have a clear vision of the general mission of the college or university from association with the on-going academic program. We further assume that the provost is a standing member of the institution's strategic planning committee, and has full knowledge of the planning which takes place there. This puts the provost in the unique and strong position of seeing the direction of the campus from both the administrative and academic sides. From this perspective, the provost can then set a direction that takes both elements into account. In particular, the provost should take the initiative to test the academic program mix with the findings of the institutional strategic plan.

While they do not have the broad perspectives of the provost, deans do have the best view of the state of the academic structures and programs within their schools or colleges. As a group, the provost and deans comprise a solid knowledge base of what is present in the academic program of the college or university, the state of the components of that program, and a fairly thorough knowledge of where program components are headed. This is the first major group to begin to draw conclusions about the academic program and the way in which it fits with the campus strategic plan. Assuming that politics can be kept to a minimum, and that objectivity is the central decision-making modality, this group can and should make strong suggestions about how the institution should begin to move to create a better match between the strategic plan and the academic plan. This is also the group most responsible for overseeing the process of program review, which we discuss in the next session. This important component of departmental planning, overall academic planning, and an important part of strategic planning has a central function in establishing standards and measuring quality in the primary activities of the college or university's central mission.

Deans form the next group of those in charge of the academic planning process. Each dean should be an expert on the types of programs that are offered at the college level, and should also be confident of the quality level of the programs the various departments offer. The dean, in concert with department chairs, should have a good idea of weaker programs, stronger programs, growing programs, declining programs, and the reasons for each.. This group can contribute a large amount of data regarding discipline status, which is one of the fundamental building blocks of the academic planning process.

Department chairs and departmental faculty form the last major segment of those involved in academic planning. Clearly these are the people who have the most intimate details of the states of their disciplines, as well as the place of their college in the University. Their input is extremely important in the academic planning process, but it can suffer from a couple of realities:

1) Departmental faculty are so immersed in their own disciplines, they seldom have much appreciation for other disciplines, even those that are somewhat related; and

2) Departmental faculty are naturally protective of their own activities, and may not be forthcoming.

Through this description, we've tried to indicate the structural process in academic planning. The procedural process is more complex, as shown in Table 7.1 below.

Table 7.1
Planning Process for Academic Planning

Provost	Step One ⟶
	• Provost shares general planning guidelines with deans
	• Deans share general planning guidelines with chairs
Deans	• Chairs share general planning guidelines with faculty
	Step Two
	• Beginning at the faculty level, each group works with each other to develop data sets and clarity
Chairs	Step Three
	• Faculty submit proposals to chairs
	• Chairs present a unified plan to deans
Faculty	• Deans submit unit plans to provost
	• Provost approves and moves the plan to the institutional level
	• OR Provost renegotiates the plan with area out of sync with the balance of the plan

As the table suggests, the academic side of the academic planning process involves several levels as well as several iterations of various components of the plan as it becomes better solidified and more directly a part of the institutional strategic plan. In a collaborative environment, each level of the academic ladder contributes its own knowledge base and coordination to the entire process. Negotiation must be part of this process, since no single person or group will have complete knowledge.   If the participants in this process are able to create an effective academic plan based on clear, objective, and reliable data, then the resulting academic plan should better define the tenets of the institutional strategic plan itself and   serve as a link to academic side of the college or university. Administrative, support, and governance consideration may then combine to create an effective strategic plan.

The Role of Program Review

Program Review is one of the most important parts of academic planning.   When done properly, the activities of program review fit perfectly into both the strategic planning and the academic planning processes.

Program reviews, now a part of the institution's outcomes assessment process, are the traditional approach to program planning and are, in many cases, mandated by the institution's state and regional accrediting bodies (Barak and Breier, 1990: Conrad and Wilson, 1986). A recent search of the ERIC Database revealed 359 articles dealing with program review in higher education, with articles on specific college's program reviews (Keene State College, 1998; Ecker, 1994), surveys of institutions (Barak, 1982; Mets, 1995), and a survey of the literature (Satterlee, 1992).

Program reviews have taken on a heightened importance since institutions have come under intense scrutiny and criticism, and have been used to respond to public pressure for accountability. The heightened interest in college program review is due to a widespread interest in improving educational quality, as well as the need to respond creatively to financial constraints and external expectations for accountability. Current program reviews have also been designed to aid in decision making about resource reallocation and program discontinuance. (Conrad and Wilson, 1986).

Program reviews have generally operated as feedback control mechanisms (Dubrin, 2003): that is, they compare college and industry program standards with program outcomes and then correct for deviations after they have occurred.   A good example would be administering an English proficiency exam as an outcome measure at the end of the senior year and then modifying the college's writing program based upon the results obtained from the test.   The new program may correct problems stemming from the old program, but are of little assistance to those students who have already graduated without appropriate writing skills.

Benoist (1986) warned that given the focus on past practices, program reviews must become an integral part of program planning for the future. In order for program reviews to morph into programming planning, program reviews must become part of a continuous improvement process (Hugenberg, 1997) by creating real-time feedback loops that allow faculty and administrators to impact the learning process before students' completion of a program.

According to Conrad and Wilson (1986), academic program reviews draw on one or more formal evaluation models--goal-based, responsive to stakeholder needs, connected to program decision-making, or connoisseurship/ expert judgment)--with the underlying objective of defining quality in four different perspectives: the reputational view of expert judgment; the resources view, focused on effective and efficient use of human, financial and physical assets; the outcomes view, or program quality measured by faculty and student performance;, and the value-added view of what the student has learned. Regardless of the evaluative method employed, three characteristics of effective program reviews are that they are systematic, regular, and comprehensive (Ewell, 1983).

Yet one must understand that program review is not everything that goes into academic program planning and vise-versa. Most of what goes on in standard program review is concentrated only in one department or discipline area, and is not coordinated with the activities of the rest of the campus. Without these broader campus linkages, program review may well improve program quality in individual departments, but it cannot create the bridges or linkages that are essential in the strategic planning process,.

Nonetheless, program review generally has exactly the types of activities that make it a natural partner with overall academic planning. Table 7.2 below shows some of the characteristics of program review typical of many American colleges or universities.

Though the characteristics in Table 7.2 include a section on implementation, we caution that program review itself still does not necessarily create linkages to the broader academic community. While this set of characteristics does call for fit, it still relies on other elements of the academic superstructure to create, analyze, and potentially change those relationships. Program review generally focuses on single departments and disciplines; nevertheless, the process of program review and the resulting conclusions tell us a great amount about the status and role of individual departments, a valuable addition to academic planning itself.

Table 7.2
Program Review Characteristics

- **Analysis**: Identify the strengths and weaknesses of the department
- **Goal Setting**: 5-year and annual goals for continual improvement
- **Resource Identification**: Identify how available resources will aid in allowing department to attain their goals
- **Participation**: Identify all departmental faculty members and show how they are involved in the self-study, including its recommendations
- **Student Assessment**: Inclusion of student outcome assessment data as well as other feedback including surveys, interviews, and focus groups
- **Annual Updates**: Scheduled reports that show progress or changes
- **Implementation**: Demonstration of how the departmental plan fits within the academic plan as well as the institutional strategic plan (UNC, 2000)

The activities of program review are outlined in Table 7.3 and show a typical method of setting up, going through, and then evaluating the process.

Table 7.3
The Process of Program Review

- The Office of Academic Affairs notifies a department of the timing of program review
- The dean will meet with the unit or department to solidify a schedule and develop criteria
- The unit or department will begin its self-study
    - The unit with gather assessment data for the past several years
    - The unit will select its internal program review team and review
    - The unit will review data (assessment, program, staffing, etc.)
    - The dean will select an external reviewer to survey the unit based on questions provided by the Office of Academic Affairs

- The external reviewer will make her/his report
- The unit will respond and prepare a report that lists
  - Issues raised by the external reviewer
  - Continuous improvement goals that will provide a better fit between the unit, the institutional mission, productivity, and quality
- The department or unit will submit the report to the dean for approval
- The dean will submit the report to the provost for approval
- The provost will submit the report to college or university governance for approval
- The unit begins its next program review cycle providing annual progress reports to the provost

This schema of program review contains several elements that can incorporate it solidly into the academic planning process as well as the strategic planning process. Through direction from the provost and deans, the incorporation of unit or departmental planning into the academic plan should be synchronous. Neither the provost nor deans should allow the unit or department to ignore its place within the larger academic plan, and should structure the review to assure a good fit. Further, as the completed review goes through the approval procedures there will be ample opportunity to test it against the college or university strategic plan. In keeping the unit within these frameworks, all three elements should work well together and result in a unified direction for all parts of the campus.

A brief word on assessment: accurate and reliable data about the unit's operations over the previous few years is one of the key considerations in the effectiveness of program review. The review needs to contain accurate assessment of learning, research, and service. In many cases, the review team must use surrogate measures, such as surveys, interviews with alumni, and interview with employers and other service area constituents to try to measure something as abstract as learning. In other cases hard data may be available, such as the results of exit exams, research outcomes, and measurable elements of service. Regardless, the institution must be willing to fund an assessment process with appropriate assessment measures in order to assure the effectiveness of this process.

Program Review Limitations

Ewell (1983) felt that program reviews could go wrong in three ways: in the use of data; in the conduct of reviews; and in whether and how the results are used. The fallacies involved in each of these three areas are discussed, including the single indicator fallacy, the perfect data fallacy, and several kinds of false assumptions and comparisons. Further, Ewell was concerned that reviews focused too much on traditional measures of efficiency and inputs rather than program outcomes.

Most important, Skolnick (1989) described some of the ways in which a system of program evaluation works to suppress diversity, innovation, and nonconformist approaches in the search for knowledge. He particularly questioned the appropriateness of a total system-wide application of the connoisseurship/expert model. These impressions were echoed by Seymour and Fife (1988), who felt that program innovation and change was quite slow since the program review process evaluated existing programs and suggested only iterative changes at best. Since innovation is important in program development there is a need to overlap innovation planning in organizations with strategic planning and program evaluation. They suggest improving the review process of developing new programs by creating and maintaining a climate for innovation, bringing innovative people into the institution, developing a selective strategy, and developing the means to look outward.

Programs need to be treated not as givens to be tinkered with only during the review cycle but as commodities or products that could be modified, added or dropped from a college's offerings as needed. This new thinking about program review emulates a zero-based approach to program review where "every program, new or old, had to justify its existence and "each and every expenditure, each year" (Birnbaum, 2000, pg.52).

The Role of Campus Administrators

As we stated earlier, the role of presidents, chancellors and governing boards is to review, advise, reject, or approve the plan that comes from the purely academic side of the organization. Assuming that these are also the people who are most actively involved with the college or university strategic plan, their major responsibility is then to test the academic plan against the strategic plan to make certain that there is a natural and easy fit between the two.

While administrators may not have the information they need to fully understand the state of academic disciplines, and must rely on faculty members ultimately to inform them adequately, they should be in a better position to understand the needs of the service area. Governing boards in particular should be comprised of individuals who represent a large segment of the service area, have a deep interest in the success of the college or university, and have influence with major external resource providers. As a group, the governing board should be a powerful ally in being able to determine how good the fit is between campus and community. In both their advising as well as in their approving/disapproving capacities, they can gather data of community needs which can then be shared with the academic side, They can also react to academic initiatives from across the college or university, and provide valuable insights as to the timeliness, need, and potential effectiveness of those initiatives.

Presidents and chancellors become important links among the academic functions of the campus, the governing boards, and many elements of the service area's other major stakeholders. Judging just how much of a president's or chancellor's time should be devoted to internal and external concerns is one of the more crucial decisions presidents make. When balanced appropriately, however, this person provides databases and linkages that can clearly benefit the academic planning process. Once determined, the president or chancellor can then facilitate a link between external and internal constituents that can allow the academic side to benefit.. Such benefits include research possibilities for both faculty and students; greater interest and involvement of campus activities by external constituents; information generation and sharing; field laboratory experiences; building and cementing service area relationships; and new resources for the campus.

Altogether, the administrative side of the college or university can be an invaluable asset in creating community links, and provide a significantly valuable service which should aid the academic planning process. Within the framework of the strategic plan, the administrative element should be effective in creating an effective fit between it and the academic plan.

When Should Departments/Schools/Colleges/The Entire CampusStart the Academic Program Planning Cycle?

Most colleges or universities have their departments go through the review process on a fixed schedule, usually five or seven years. Academic program planning, however, is something that must be ongoing; it is not on a cycle so much as a continuous process. It may be that the provost will create a schedule of activities that fill out a year's calendar, and may repeat that schedule each year. Yet since academics are not static changes in many areas of the academy occur all the time, and awareness of innovations and changes in disciplines is something faculty members, department chairs, deans, and the provost must be on top of all the time.

The clear value of identifying a cycle is that activities tend to be standardized and certain things happen each year on a regular basis. So while there might not be any easy answer about the appropriate course of an academic program cycle,, institutions should make a decision to do campus-wide academic planning and then implement it

In terms of timing, we recognize there are potentially two different situations: those campuses that are not doing formalized academic planning, and those that are. For those not planning but beginning to see the value of a formalized academic program, ,perhaps because they see the need to augment their strategic plan with the wisdom that flows from the academic planning process, they need to plan-to-plan. A plan-to-plan might be begun in the spring, when people across the campus are finishing out the current year and aware of both problems and opportunities they are experiencing. The provost, president or chancellor, strategic planning officer, and faculty leaders can use this time to determine the best method of beginning a formalized academic planning process. During the following summer, when much of the campus is empty and the pace of life is slower, this group could put processes and policies in place so that when the fall term begins the first cycle of planning is launched. This is not meant to be an absolute best method for beginning planning, but a brief account of how a plan-to-plan schedule might come together. The point is that campuses wanting to begin a formalized academic planning process need to develop a plan to plan.

For those colleges and universities that already have a formalized planning process, the key would be to begin to work more closely with the strategic planning process to assure alignment between the two. Any cycle adjustment that might be necessary to accommodate both processes would be well worth the effort.

What are the Steps Involved?

What we describe now is an institution-wide process of developing an academic plan based on the guidelines identified above. This approach assumes that the college or university either does not yet have a formalized academic plan or that it wishes to reengineer its process. It combines the basic models we developed for academic planning along with program review in creating a more holistic approach to planning combining academic planning, the principles of program review, and strategic planning. The steps involved are listed out in Table 7.4 below.

The importance of academic planning calls for actions as dramatic as a **campus-wide initiative**. As we have stated,, while the academic side will be most involved with academic planning it still impacts all other parts of the campus, so it is a good idea to make sure that the entire campus is aware of the process and how the process may impact them. This should allow other campus groups such as the institutional strategic planning committee to begin to build appropriate linkages so that their activities do not begin to diverge from the activities of the academic planners.

The actual kick-off of the academic planning process should begin with the **campus-wide charge**, something that he president or chancellor would fashion as a way of showing the high level of importance of the process. This charge should be followed by the provost, who would begin to outline the steps the academic side of the college or university intends to follow in first creating and then implementing its overall plan. These charges should challenge the faculty to vigorously test their programs. Are they relevant? Are they up-to-date? Are they leading-edge? Are they in demand--and how can this be determined? Do the programs fit the mission of the college or university, and do they fit the needs of the service area? The charge should also include developing methods of assuring high quality as well as procedures that insure continual improvement. The charges should empower the faculty to openly question what they teach and how they teach it. Finally, these charges need to inspire rather than threaten, and be a basis upon which all departments and disciplines can build academic programs supportive of the college or university.

Table 7.4
The Steps in the Academic Planning Process

Step one: the campus-wide initiative
Step two: the campus-wide charge
Step three: the mid-level charges (schools or colleges)
Step four: the departmental commitment
Research phase
a).   Library
b).   Internet
c).   Interviews
Analysis phase
a).   Establishing validity
b).   Establishing reliability
Resource review phase
Decision phase
Proposal phase
Step five: mid-level review, coordination, testing, and consolidation
Step six: campus-wide review, coordination, testing, and consolidation
Step seven: governing board approval and resource commitment
Step eight: incorporation into the campus strategic plan
Step nine: creating of cyclical review and revision

Based on the campus charges from the top administrative and academic officers, deans further clarify the process through the issuing of **mid-level charges, in which** the programs for assessment, evaluation, and recommendations for continuous improvement will be made more specific. Deans need to work in concert with each other as well as with the provost in this step so as to continue to assure common purposes and direction. However, this is also the point where deans begin to differentiate the characteristics of their schools or colleges, and begin to tailor the process to be more discipline specific. Planning for a college of music and fine arts is going to be different from that of a college or arts and sciences or school of medicine.

At this point the individual departments begin their plan-to-plan, and form their own **departmental commitment** to the overall academic planning process. As would be true of program review, one of the first major activities needs to be data collection. The two major areas of research are in areas of educational delivery and/or research, and outcomes.

It is interesting to note how many different ways faculty members teach, and the differences in what they teach. This is one of the beauties of academic freedom, and nothing in academic planning should challenge academic freedom. However, it is useful to test what is taught and how it is taught, because professors, instructors, and even researchers may suddenly discover better methods of inquiry or instruction as well as new avenues for understanding the discipline better. This example, along with a general description of the organization and methods of operations of the department, are important explanation to how the department performs.

Outcomes data is also important. As we suggested in the discussion of program review, the accumulation of outcomes data can be both easy and hard. It is certainly easier if the department already has several standardized measures in place which are used on a continual basis. For departments without developed assessment techniques and appropriate measures, this requirement could be daunting. For either group, however, department members need to develop and use assessment tools that are both valid and reliable. They must be able to create data bases that accurately describe the effectiveness of the learning process in their department with measurable and comparable results. They need to be able to show areas of success they can build upon, as well as areas of concern they can begin to improve.

In the **research phase**, there are several areas where good data collection can occur. Library data is one source, especially examples of what other institutions measure and how they measure it. The library is also an excellent source of establishing databases such as placement rates of other institutions, for example, in either the job market or graduate school. The **Internet** continues to be a growing source of diverse, but readily accessible databases and can provide quick knowledge in terms of up-to-date developments, popularity, and usage in many academic disciplines. **Interviews** with current students, alumni, employers of graduates, community leaders, as well as state leaders and industry leaders can all provide very valuable information in regards to the needs of the service area and the department's effectiveness in meeting those needs. Other good sources for obtaining outcomes data include **exit exams**, performance on **entrance exams** and **employment rates**.

The next phase for departmental academic planning is the **analysis phase**. Accumulating data and then organizing it for analysis will always prove to be an arduous process. While information overload is always a threat, particularly for faculty who have other agendas, the department does need to hit a happy medium where it believes it has adequate data on which to make decisions, without having either too little or more than is useful. At this point, the analysis begins. Establishing both the **validity** and **reliability** of the data is important here. The department needs to be confident that it is looking at information which is objective, reflective of the actual state of affairs, and not mere speculation. When the department members feel confident of their data, they can then begin to interpret it. The results of the analysis could be what everyone expects or it could contain a fair amount of surprises. Regardless, the results should be something that the department can believe and act on from that point.

The **resource review phase** is next. Through an understanding of the resources already contained in the department-- (faculty, researchers, staff support, facilities, annual funding levels, unencumbered funds, foundation funds, grants, and endowments--, the department can begin to put together its proposal for the departmental academic plan. With input from the levels of the dean, the provost, and perhaps the rest of the administration, departmental planners should have a good idea of the prospect for additional or diminished resources.

The **decision phase** occurs when members of the department have all the facts in front of them, and need to begin to decide what they can and cannot do to support excellence and continual improvement. Very few, if any, departments will be able to do everything they want, or even what they need to do, so the decisions they reach may well be sub-optimal and heavy with compromise. Reconciling the opportunities and realities of external and internal circumstances on a basis of what is best for all involved is a painstaking and time-consuming event. Yet it is crucial, and the results will shape the department for years to come.

Finally, departmental planning moves to the **proposal phase**. The planners prepare a report that contains the significant findings of its research, analysis, and decision-making activities and then sets forth its best assessment as to the best course of future activity. This needs to be a formal report, well documented, and equally well conceived.

Step five is the **mid-level review**, where deans coordinate the plans of the various departments in the school or college, test them against the tenets of the original academic planning charges and then consolidate the plans into an entire school or college plan. It is possible the dean may see problems at this level   requiring that some of the departmental plans be sent back. However, once the dean determines that the sum of the parts is acceptable the plan should be sent on..

Step six involves **campus-wide review**, first by the provost and possibly the president or chancellor. Here the purpose is to coordinate, test, and consolidate the overall college or university academic plan. The developing academic plan must be tested against the strategic plan. It must be clear that both plans complement each other, without conflict   If this cannot be done, then it is up to both the people who have developed the academic plan as well as those who have developed the strategic plan to go back and work out the differences. Only when both plans coincide should the plan move forward.

Step seven is **governing board approval and resource commitment, taking** place at step eight, when the academic plan would is formally **incorporated into the campus strategic plan**. Rowley and Sherman (2001) clearly identified resource allocation as the single most effective way in which colleges and universities can implement their strategic plans. This is true in the process we describe here as well. Once the governing board is confident enough in both the strategic plan and the academic plan, they then should fund them accordingly. This, along with the high level of participation that has characterized the academic planning process so far, should leave little doubt that both the academic plan and the strategic plan should become widely accepted policy, very soon operational..

Finally, step nine is the creation of a **cyclical review and revision process** that continually tests the academic plan in place. Just as Rowley, Lujan, and Dolence stated (1997), the planning process is not an event but a process. It doesn't end when the governing board has approved the final plan or when administrators and academic leaders put it into place. It must always be subject to testing and revision. Unlike program review, which might occur only over a period of years, the academic plan doesn't have the luxury of failing to address emerging needs. The academic planning process must be fluid and flexible enough to recognize new opportunities as well as new threats, and be in a position to make changes. Departments should be an integral part of this process, issuing annual updates both on what is happening in the disciplines as well as what must be done to meet continuous improvement goals. Simply, this process of review and potential revision must become a part of the central culture of the campus.

Does the Learner Have a Role in the Academic Program Planning Process?

Thus far we have not talked much about the role of those outside the academic structure of a college or university. We have alluded to a role for graduates and alumni in the data gathering phases of academic planning, but have given no particular role to learners as a group. The importance of the learner is undeniable in understanding the major purpose of a contemporary college or university. Learners are why the institution exists. Should they then be involved in developing the academic plan they will benefit from over their tenure within the institution?

The answer is yes. While they can provide little in terms of new information about the disciplines, they do have a growing role in helping educators understand both what they need to learn and what they need to do with their learning. Older, the so-called non-traditional students normally have a solid idea of what they need to learn, so their participation in interviews, focus-groups, and surveys is obvious. Yet the more traditional entering freshman too has a good idea of what he/she needs to learn in order to be successful in the world following graduation. The general growth of technology, the ease with which we get news, the shrinking of the world through improved transportation and communication and the popularity of media such as the Internet, all create maturity levels and knowledge bases which make incoming freshmen different from their predecessors. Gathering data on what this group of learners think and need should be a significant component of the overall academic program planning process. Then the learner becomes not just a consumer of the college or university's academic products but a partner in the school's effort to assure higher levels of relevance and excellence.

How Should We Teach?

ଔ Chapter Eight Cଜ

So, What's Wrong With the Lecture?

"*Jonathan, what did you think of old man Smith's lecture on ancient Greek philosophers? I caught myself napping several times through his comparison of Thucydides, Plato, and Aristotle, especially during his diatribe on Plato's just man. I thought that taking an eight o'clock was a mistake but I never thought that I'd have a professor that would so easily lull me back to sleep! Why couldn't the university find us someone more entertaining and exciting for an early morning class? The topics really interest me, but we never get a chance to discuss this material in class . Why are we learning about the philosophers and their thinking if we can't talk about them?*"

"*Yeah*" chimed in Tom, another student who had overhead Jack's comment about Dr. Smith's class to Jonathan, "*I took his class last year and all he did was read from his old notes, write unreadable comments on the blackboard, scratch his beard about every five minutes, and talk about Aristotle's conception of the unity of the state as association versus Plato's oneness. What's that gibberish all about? And by the way, his lectures haven't changed in twenty years and his tests are based on those notes. I bought his lecture notes off a senior so I really aced his exams. I'll sell you my copy as well as a copy of an old exam - he rarely changes the questions.*"

Jonathan was not listening. The moment his classical philosophy class was mentioned he went into a deep trance, the same trance he would go into each and every day during his first two weeks of class. Jonathan decided that since the course grade was dependent only upon his grades on his midterm and final exam, and that attendance wasn't mandatory (or even taken), his time was better spent either sleeping or surfing the net and he would never again attend a class lecture. Since he got nothing out of the lectures why would he bother attending? And anyway, Jonathan, an expert net surfer, had found several websites that were chuck full of information on classical philosophy and were far more interesting than old man Smith. Several sites had detailed notes, papers, and old exams – in fact he found one fraternity site that had Smith's three last exams on it!

"*Jonathan, are you listening to me?*" Jack queried. "*Sorry, Jack*" replied Jonathan. "*I was just thinking what a waste of time and money Smith's class is.*" "*I know*" responded Jack. "*I just hope that all of our classes in the future do not turn out like this one." "They won't, I promise" retorted Sal. "Not all of the faculty teach like Smith. Some classes are really quite interesting and a lot of fun. However, there are other professors like him. I'll be happy to tell you who they are and what they teach so that you're not stuck with them in the future."*

The Lecture as Practiced in Higher Education

In employing the most effective methods available to educators and learners today, we begin by examining the most common knowledge transfer method, the lecture. The lecture method of teaching is often the primary tool college and university educators have used to facilitate the learning process. This is historical, and it is traditional. Professor and instructors are familiar with it and are comfortable using it. Yet there is growing evidence that this method of educating is not as effective as many believe. Pascarella and Terenzini (1991) tell us that while the lecture can demonstrate some effectiveness in the transmission of factual information, it is much less effective in dealing with cognitive issues where critical thinking and problem-solving skills are needed. Kember and Gow (1994) have suggested that the lecture method, by itself, is insufficient to meet the needs of the modern college and university learner.

Rowley, Lujan, and Dolence (1998) have suggested that there is little teaching preparation for today's professors and instructors other than the example of their own teachers and mentors, who, in most cases, employed the lecture method. Other authors agree with these conclusions to a greater or lesser degree, but the central point here is that it is fairly well accepted that the lecture method of transferring knowledge is not always the most effective pedagogy instructors can use. In concert with lecturing, or in a setting where the lecture method is not used at all, other methods of instruction might be more effective.

These studies should be especially interesting for those engaged in higher education. By its very nature, most graduates will engage in work that is highly cognitive-process-oriented, dependent upon the success of critical thinking, and fully reliant on effective problem-solving skills.

More importantly, successful learning occurs when the learner is actively involved in the learning process. Unfortunately, the lecture is a passive method of knowledge transfer, and may not provide the learning methods that are most useful to management learners and other business learners as well. If these observations are correct, then management and business educators should seriously look at the propensity of business school educators to use lectures as their primary method of teaching. Perhaps educators and administrators need to expand the scope of teaching and learning methods made available in order to support more effective alternatives.

Unfortunately, there is little to suggest that the vast majority of college and university educators or campus administrators are either abandoning the lecture method or actively trying out other methods. Also, it is interesting to note that on many campuses, the lecture method has been institutionalized. For example, at the university of one of the authors of this book, the architecture of the college of business features almost exclusively fixed seating auditorium style classrooms. At the time of the reopening of the building, this seating was heralded as making sure that no student was ever more than 3 places away from the lecturer. While that sounded good at the time, and was an improvement over the long rows of moveable seating where some students could camp out in the back of the room virtually unnoticed for the entire length of the semester, as other styles of transferring knowledge become known the very architecture of the rooms made it extremely difficult for professors and instructors to move away from the lecture. These conditions exist on many campuses.

It is not our intention here to suggest that the lecture method has no place in higher education today. As we identified earlier, Pascarella and Terenzini (1991) have stated that the lecture can demonstrate effectiveness in the transmission of factual information. We agree and contend that in those courses where basic facts or principles are the focus of the course, the lecture could well be the most effective method of transferring such information. It's when one goes beyond the teaching and learning of principles that we suggest the lecture begins to lose its effectiveness, and other methods may well prove to be more useful.

Why Haven't We Changed Our Approach to Educating in Colleges and Universities?

A number of other teaching and learning methods exist that at least promise higher levels of effective managerial and business education. These include case analysis, experiential exercises, technological and non-technological simulations, groupware, group and cooperative learning projects, field assignments, student debates, joint professor/learner research projects, multi-media presentations, the use of executive professors, and virtual classrooms.

These alternative methods provide professors and instructors, as well as learners, with an expanded variety of learning tools that can enhance the educational experience. Just as with the lecture method, these choices do not fit all circumstances either. Educators need to understand the underlying assumptions of each method, and choose the one most appropriate method for the particular design of a course. For example, experiential exercises are designed to provide learners with a practical experience that demonstrates a given principle or method at work in a particular situation by having learners explore, act out, or simulate actual situations involving theory and practice. This method seems to work well in a course on organizational behavior, because learners get to experience constructs such as motivation, leadership, communication, and group dynamics by actually engaging in several different approaches to each. Further, case analysis might not be as appropriate or as effective in this course as it might be in a strategic management course, where experiential exercises might be much more problematic in achieving the objectives of the course.

Another important difference in the state of the classroom today from the state of the classroom ten years ago is the growth of technology. However, in a way, this has also helped to mask the problem, not necessarily solve it. For example, PowerPoint slides are now common; the ability to access the Internet in the classroom is growing; and the ability to offer on-line chat rooms, testing, grading, and assignment submission is increasing. Most formal uses of these tools, however, seem to be built more for lecture than for alternative settings. Textbook publisher-provided PowerPoint slides, for example, very often are colorful, sometimes animated, easy to manipulate and easily linked to Internet connections, all in a lecture mode. If professors or instructors wish to use advances in classroom technology for alternative methods, they must usually design those uses on their own. Fortunately, many educators are developing technology for alternative uses, and we would hope that the proliferation of these methods will become more and more available to management and business educators through applied journals, conferences, and workshops in the near future.

What's Behind the Popularity of the Lecture?

The lecture is perhaps the most pervasive method of teaching in the world today. Its roots come from the nature of the academy itself

– a place where knowledge was created and defined and then shared with others. This sharing was done in at least two ways; by writing it down and by telling about it. Thus the lecture was born. A major presumption with the lecture is that the person giving the lecture is the expert, and those who listen are not. The lecturer is the active person in this exchange, telling, showing, or demonstrating knowledge that she/he has while the student is the passive person, listening, thinking, absorbing, and trying to develop understanding of what he/she is hearing and observing.

Within this description lie several pros and cons about the use of the lecture as a teaching tool. The pros:

- The lecture is led by an expert providing access to her/his knowledge base and understanding
- The lecture is easy for both instructor and student
- The lecture is familiar to both instructor and student
- The lecture is economically a cheap method of transferring knowledge, as many are given in large classrooms, others are recorded or even televised for larger groups)
- The lecture is organized and relatively easy to follow
- The lecturer is recognized as fully in charge and easily directs the class

The cons:

- The lecture can be boring and repetitive
- The lecture does not engage the student nor does it assume the student to be a learner
- The lecture assumes the student is ignorant and must be taught
- The lecture does not permit high levels of interaction or the opportunity to challenge the material being presented, especially in larger classroom settings
- The lecture follows a prescribed schedule and curriculum base
- The lecture has been found time and time again to be the least effective method of conveying knowledge to learners

In looking at our own doctoral preparation, little was made available to us in terms of developing good teaching techniques. One of us remembers being told to walk around the room as much as possible and avoid standing behind the lectern. The other remembers being told to use as much humor as possible to keep students' attention. In talking with colleagues, we find that very few if any of our fellow professors and lecturers have ever been taught how to teach. As a result, most of us teach as we have observed which has been overwhelmingly the lecture method.

Do Professors and Instructors *Really Care* About Their Teaching Methods?

We believe that most professors and instructors really do care about their teaching effectiveness, but are essentially unaware of better methods of teaching. Much of this comes from the simple reality of walking into a classroom and realizing you're alone, in charge of what will take place in that classroom. Traditional students sit patiently and wait for the professor or instructor to lead them through the material. There is no committee of other instructors who will back you up or provide other types of supports – it's just you and the students. And most professors and instructors do the best they know to make the situation successful. Here, success is defined as getting through the class, covering all the assigned material, determining course grades, and surviving the course evaluation questionnaire.

This is the model of what the classroom experience is like for many professors and instructors, and it has been this way for literally hundreds of years. The model that most professors and instructors depend on to tell them how to conduct themselves in the classroom is the same one their own professors and instructors used. We do not fault those who use the lecture based on these assumptions; if there are no other models available, no other models would be used. Yet researchers have consistently found that the lecture is the least effective method of transferring knowledge used in most colleges and universities in the U.S., as well as around the world today.

Fortunately, there are alternatives to the lecture method and throughout the second part of this book we will examine several of them, hoping to provide some insight on a method which could prove to be the most effective methods of transferring knowledge from expert to learner. It's just unfortunate that many professors and instructors don't know about them. If they did, at least they would have the opportunity to choose between methods and, for those who truly want to be more effective in the classroom, the result of their choices could change classroom dynamics dramatically.

What about faculty development programs? Don't they improve teaching? In some cases yes, but in many other cases no. There is no central model that provides individual campuses with knowledge about what development opportunities are best, or which ones can produce particular outcomes. As one examines the components of faculty development from one campus to the next, there is no central theme, no common goals nor specific objectives which provide a uniform way of delivering higher levels of excellence or continuous improvement. Each campus makes its own decisions about faculty development.

Another major problem with many programs of faculty development is that they tend to be on the lower end of the priority list in terms of how college or university resources are used. The tenuous notion that professors and instructors are experts and already know how to educate will often cause governing boards and campus administrators to shy away from funding significant faculty development activities.

There are campuses, however, where the wisdom of supporting faculty development exists. One can visit several good examples on the Internet. In most of these, one can see the concern for effective learning, the use of the term "learner," and a series of workshops, conference opportunities, and other resources that aim to improve the knowledge transfer process. It is obvious these campuses have recognized the importance of continuously training faculty members to be more effective and have put resources behind those efforts.

One very interesting site is that demonstrates this expanded approach is that of Western Michigan University (http://www.wmich.edu/teachlearn/). The site includes a listing of several major faculty development resources, along with articles and examples of improved teaching methods. In one article on the site, Saunders and Werner (2002) describe a blended approach using a variety of teaching methods which has demonstrated remarkable effectiveness. They write,

"Only a blend of methods and approaches can produce the richness and achieve the desired learning outcomes. What is interesting is that 73% of our learners felt that our blend was a positive experience despite experiencing minor technical problems. They told us they preferred a blend of in-class learning and e-learning over straight in-class learning, thus supporting the conclusion that was reported in the 2000 Benchmarking Service report."

They go on to describe several different teaching methods used in their blending approach. These include 1) problem-based learning, 2) collaborative learning, 3) activation of previous knowledge, 4) demonstration of new knowledge, 5) application of new knowledge, 6) integration of new knowledge into the learner's world, and 7) assessment of the learning process and learners' progress. We will describe several of these methods, along with others in subsequent chapters.

But Aren't the Learners in Charge of Their Own Education Anyway, and Isn't the Use of Any Pedagogical Method Irrelevant?

This is a view shared my many professors and instructors. The rationale goes this way – "students come to college to learn and want to learn. They pay to learn. This kind of motivation is all that is necessary – look at all the successful people who went through college under the lecture method and did very well. Therefore, as long as the content is there, any method of delivering the knowledge base should be sufficient."

Then one can retort, "Motivated for what?" Are all college students motivated to learn or are some just motivated to graduate? Aren't the methods that professors and instructors choose to convey knowledge a factor in motivation? If the lecture method is the least effective method of transferring knowledge, the implication is that there are other methods that are more effective. The real bottom line here is that colleges and universities must seek to provide the educational bases that can best serve their learners, and then seek ways that make the knowledge transfer experience as effective as possible. If we know, then, that some methods are better than others, what is the rationale behind not seeking the best methods of providing meaningful and effective learning experiences?

We believe that a common motivation among college and university students is to prepare to be successful in life after college. They divide themselves into interest areas, or majors that indicate what knowledge bases they believe will best prepare them to do just this. The programs that we offer and the methods we use to teach must conform to the highest intentions of the academy by providing the education needed by society to grow and prosper. Putting the burden of learning on the student regardless of the weightiness or irrelevance of that burden is both unfair and unethical. On the contrary, we must seek to find the best methods of knowledge transference available, be prepared to discover even newer and better methods, and be willing to support the process with the resources of the institution.

Is it Better to be the "Sage on the Stage," or the "Guide on the Side?"

Gibbons, et al (1994) along with others described a paradigm shift that occurs when a teacher decides to move from the role of a "Sage on the State," to that of a "Guide on the Side." These two different approaches to teaching speak to two fundamentally different beliefs about the role of both the instructor and the role of the learner in the overall transfer of knowledge in an educational setting. This discussion is also an additional challenge to the lecture method in that it develops the methods of the two different approaches and strongly suggests that one method is better than the other.

What is the Difference between "Mode 1" and Mode 2"?

Gibbons (1994) and others have proposed that the learner has changed over the past several years from a passive collector of knowledge to a more active participant in the educational process. He has suggested that there are essentially two different approaches to delivering education based on this emerging model, and has labeled them Mode 1 and Mode 2. Table 8.1 outlines the characteristics of these two leaning approached.

These two modes of learning seek to deliver education to the learner, but do so based on two different philosophical views. We might best refer to Mode 1 as the traditional approach and Mode 2 as the alternative approach. Both form the backdrop of the discussion we present throughout this article.

In business and management education, field research, applied research, and theory building demonstrates that the knowledge base is constantly growing. This is good. The second part of the issue, however, is in many ways more troubling. As retiring President of the Academy of Management Huff (2000) suggested, while the academy may continue to lead the new economy in epistemological development, applied research is much better accomplished outside the academy by groups and firms closer to the realities of today's organizations than are the researchers found on most college and university campuses. While she also suggests approaches that attempt to reconcile these differences and improve management education, she also acknowledges that U.S. research institutions are not likely to leave their roots. These observations mirror the Carnegie Report of the 1950s, which also called for strong disciplinary research in American higher education.

Table 8.1
Mode 1 vs. Mode 2 Learning Philosophies
(Based on Gibbons, et al, 1994)

Mode 1 Learning	Mode 2 Learning
•Instructor is the *Sage on the Stage*	•Instructor becomes the *Guide on the Side*
•Dependence on the lecture method	•Instructor and learners become a team in the learning process
	•Leaning is focused on the world where graduates will work, not the academic world
•Students are "sponges"	•Material is holistic
	•Instructors and learners research/learn together
•Knowledge is highly laboratory-research oriented, highly specialized, reductionistic	•Applied research is valued as a partner to basic research
•Knowledge base is often fragmented and homogeneous	•"How" and "Will it work" are the centers of classroom and research activities
•Knowledge base is empirical, present and past oriented, objective, and impersonal	

In an earlier presidential address to the Academy of Management, Hitt (1998) stated that not only do the changes in today's economy change *what* we teach but also impact *how* we teach. Though his discussion focused on the impact of technology in the classroom, he also suggested that we consider some Mode 2 attributes, as suggested in Table 1 above, which include group learning, applied research validated by use and which is more responsive to consumer demand. So while it is reassuring to hear leaders in our field call for change in both the curriculum base and the methods of teaching, it is also disappointing that there is currently so very little literature in management and business education that tries to provide alternatives beneficial to both the academy and the learner.

What is the Role of the Educator in the Classroom?

Mode 1 requires a pedagogical setting that is significantly different from Mode 2. This significantly changes the role of the educator in the classroom. Preparation is different, approach is different, methods of instruction are different, and the view of the student is different. The educator is the one in charge in the use of either modes, but the activities and predispositioning are entirely different.

It may sound insignificant, but one of the major changes that must occur is in the view of who the student is. We believe that the term itself is significant. A student, by definition, is one who learns from those who can teach. The implication is that the student is passive in the process, that the educator is the active individual in the transaction because the educator is the expert and is sharing her/his expertise with others. This is one-way communication, in which the student absorbs knowledge that the educator has decided to share. Feedback is normally accomplished through testing, and the result of the entire experience is a grade, a mark that signifies the educator's assessment as to how much the student has learned.

Now, consider the term learner. A learner is someone who is specifically seeking knowledge. This makes this person much more active in the process, but also much more directed. If a student attends a class because he/she needs the class to fulfill a predetermined core of classes leading to a degree, this person has little to no expectation for the course curriculum. The learner has expectations for what she/he is hoping to learn from the curriculum and is much more interested in both the content and quality of the experience. The learner knows that he/she needs the knowledge the educator is making available, and wants to both understand the knowledge as well as be in a position to use it. To achieve these goals, the learner will want to engage in active two-way communication, be in a position to question elements of the curriculum to achieve greater understanding, and may well push the educator beyond the basic curriculum to solidify the learning experience. As such, the educator is placed in a position where she/he may well also be a learner and along with the target learner will engage in joint investigation and explanation.

Feedback is more complicated, because in this type of a learning environment, standardized tests (especially multiple-choice exams) don't particularly fit well; the knowledge base that the educator and learner are building is fluid and developing. Other methods such as portfolio building and analysis seem much more appropriate here as a means of viewing accomplishments and then evaluating the learning process. It is possible here that the educator and learner can decide on the course outcome together, whether that be the eventual assignment of a letter grade, a pass-fail outcome, or other achievement indicator. This is possible because in this Mode 2 approach, responsibility for learning is shared, and who knows better than the learner whether or not the learning goals were achieved?

Adopting methods for learning that allow for this type of interchange is essential. Experimentation; individual, joint, and group research; field investigation; presentation of findings; and practicing the behaviors taught in the curriculum are all objectives of a new pedagogy. In this type of setting, the educator may well find that lecturing is a waste of time, that his/her time is better spent working directly with learners to test the knowledge base that comes from the course texts, library research, and electronic research and instruction. This is a clear example of how to move the "sage on the stage" to the new role of "guide on the side."

For the educator to get to this mindset, some form of intervention is needed. Faculty development is a term that has a variety of meanings. While one might assume that the term refers to an activity that allows faculty to gain new skills and elements of knowledge, how individual institutions address this issue vary greatly over the thousands of institutions within the academy. One good example comes from the University of the Highlands and Islands (UHI), headquartered in Inverness, Scotland (Rowley, 1998). A relatively new university, UHI not only understands the importance of training faculty members to educate learners in the most effective environment possible, but does so on a continuing basis. UHI's approach is to actively involve the learner in all phases of the educational process, both during the formal degree process and later as associates in a life-long learning program, challenging traditional course offering schedules and even curriculum content in helping to assure that each learner gets exactly what she/he needs. This customer-focused approach is difficult for many already-established colleges and universities to embrace, and is not a model we recommend for campuses other than those which have the capabilities, philosophies, and faculty in place to go in this particular direction. Regardless, this example does represent what an institution can do with faculty development if it defines the term in such a manner. During an interview with several senior administrators at UHI, one of the authors was told that UHI is committed to spending 10% of its revenues on faculty development.

This represents yet another problem with the non-uniformity of faculty development. The resource base of each institution often does not allow for such significant investment in faculty development. In many American colleges and universities the demands upon the resource base are prioritized, and many institutions have not valued faculty development as highly as   others.   We would hope, however, that through academic planning many colleges and universities might change their valuation of faculty development and realize the important of treating the faculty as a growing resource.

What is the Role of the Educator in the Laboratory?

The term laboratory can refer to many different settings on a college or university campus.   The laboratory is not simply a place where research scientists conduct series of experiments and are heavily funded by outside grant providers.   The laboratory is anyplace where scholars and learners test knowledge.   In a Mode 2 environment, the laboratory can occur in any location where learners seek to extend their developing knowledge by actively testing it against reality.   This can be in the classroom, the dorm room, over the Internet, in the library, in formal laboratory facilities, but, most importantly, in the rest of the world.

The role for the educator here is that of guide and collaborator..   Clearly, most doctoral-qualified faculty members are familiar with laboratory research.   Many continue to work in the laboratory throughout their lives as they discover and test new knowledge.   Some have graduate assistants who work with them in designing experiments, running tests, and drawing conclusions.   The graduate assistant in this setting is very much a learner together with the principle researcher, and learning occurs as the laboratory work unfolds and as results begin to become apparent.   Regardless of its physical nature, the laboratory is a proven setting for creating knowledge that extends the base of both the researcher and the assistant in a very effective and meaningful way.

What we suggest is that the same type of relationship that exists in the familiar laboratory setting with graduate assistants is one that should be carried the undergraduate classroom as well.   In a Mode 2 approach, the educator can use the laboratory as a major pedagogical technique for helping learners at any level of the higher educational experience become researchers, analyzers, and conveyers of new knowledge for classroom use and beyond.   Further, this mindset also helps prepare the learner to be a life-long learner and provides the learner with a set of valuable tools which will help throughout life

One might ask, is the undergraduate capable of doing primary research in the laboratory?   We believe the answer is a resounding yes, but are also mindful of the variety of maturity levels   reflected in learners in today's college and university populations.   For the learner who comes to college to be a student, it may be difficult to get into a mindset of being excited about exploration and learning. Perhaps others have come to college for some specific programs, such as engineering, business, pre-law, or pre-med. Many of these students seem to have difficulty getting excited about areas of learning outside their main discipline interests. The authors have had many students express their displeasure at having to take general education courses in poetry, languages, or art when they want to learn a business discipline. Sometimes it get even more focused than that when a business management major questions why she/he has to take accounting or marketing.

Dealing with the student who does not particularly want to be a learner makes the job of the educator more difficult. However, we also believe that part of the role of an educator is to excite students to become learners. Involving less motivated students in the investigation of the educator's discipline might well pique their interest, and help them get more excited about learning beyond their parochial goals. As an example, one of the authors recalls taking a class in Shakespeare to fulfill a general education requirement during his undergraduate years. He took the class because nothing else was open that sounded more appealing. Yet, the professor of the class turned out to be a director in the annual Colorado Shakespeare Festival and had class members act out the parts, just as if they were part of the actual stage experience. This involved immersing learners in the stories behind the plays, what Shakespeare was thinking or trying to say, and how a director is faced with a myriad of challenges in interpreting what he felt Shakespeare was trying to do. This was fascinating, and not only did the author take a second semester of the course but he has enjoyed Shakespearean plays ever since. Here the student became a learner, and it was the educator who was able to inspire the transformation.

This example of laboratory work is but one of many ways in which the educator can share the primary facility used to master the discipline directly with learners, involving those learners in the knowledge building process. Maturity issues aside, it is probably a very good idea that faculty members assume that all learners can be motivated to get involved with their disciplines and the courses they teach. As in the previous section, we believe that faculty development programs can be extremely helpful in helping move faculty members into a new frame of mind that will benefit themselves as well as their learners. This is another reason why it should be part of any academic planning activities.

What is the Role of the Educator in the Office?

The responsibilities of any faculty member includes being available to learners through establishing specific office hours. Different campuses have different views of office hours – it might be part of a person's academic responsibility or part of that person's service responsibility. Regardless, a faculty member is required to be available at specific times to perform a variety of duties related to being a member of a faculty. In a Mode 2 approach, office time is very important because this is the greatest opportunity for the educator and the learner to interact in a relatively private environment, free of the social norms that occur in the classroom, the level of shyness a person may have regarding asking questions or making comments in class, or any one of the things that can prevent a learner from getting individual attention.

While nearly every educator will have office hours, different educators use them in different ways. Some faculty resent having to be there at regularly scheduled times, while others honestly are not comfortable dealing with learners (or students) on a one-to-one basis. In a Mode 1 environment, the office may appear as a sort of holy-of-holies where the student is allowed in only to ask straightforward questions. It may be a study, where the professor retreats to read and reflect; and the intrusion of a student may be greeted with a look of disappointment or worse. Some faculty members force students to make specific appointments and then treat those appointment times as inflexible, while still other faculty members regard the office as the only place to interact with students outside of the classroom.

In a Mode 2 environment, the educator's attitude toward the office significantly changes. Not only is this a place where the faculty member can meet individually with a learner to help solidify the learning process through an open dialogue and a sharing of ideas, but this can also be a place where problems are solved, ideas are generated, and where learning is extended. The atmosphere of a casual office can overcome the formality of the classroom and allow both educator and learner to get deeper into the issues of understanding. This can work with individual learners and even small groups.

To help achieve this outcome, the educator should be somewhat concerned about the atmosphere of the faculty office. By placing furniture in certain arrangements, different atmospheres result. For example, if the faculty member's desk is placed so that the faculty member sits behind it and faces learners who either sit or stand on the other side, a barrier exists. If, on the other hand, the desk is pushed back to the wall and the faculty member interacts with students without a barrier between them, the atmosphere is immediately more inviting and less formal. Some faculty members decorate their offices with easy chairs, colorful prints or pictures on the wall, different lighting and perhaps music playing in the background. These examples show that the faculty member wants to make the visit to the office as pleasant and inviting as possible. The learner should feel at ease, and should also feel that the conversations which occur there will be as open and easy as possible.

In a Mode 2 environment, the office is not necessarily confined to the assigned space provided to the educator by the college or university. There are clearly good reasons why a faculty member should have a college-provided office space and maintain scheduled office hours, but the faculty member has many other opportunities to extend availability. For example, the Internet and e-mail are devices an instructor can use to be more available to learners. An open policy that a learner can e-mail a professor at any time and that the professor will get back to the student within 24 hours is an example of how today's educator's can use technology emanating from the exploding Information Age to increase contact with learners.. Further, the ease of using the Internet and programs such as Blackboard allow input and feedback regardless of the physical location of either the instructor or the learner.

We understand that lawsuits are common and causes for lawsuits may be frivolous, so educators must protect themselves from situations where something could happen that might compromise them. For example, it is probably always a good idea to leave the office door open when talking with learners. It is probably a good idea not to meet learners away from the campus on a one-to-one basis, regardless of sex. It is probably not a good idea for educators to call learners late at night. Yet while we recognize that both educators and learners need to be prudent in their dealings with each other, prudence permits openness and interactivity. By creating and maintaining a professional attitude, educators and learners can interact in an environment that is exciting and supportive of the learning process, and both should benefit from those exchanges.

This chapter has begun to present several of the questions we believe academics need to ask about bringing the curriculum into the classroom in a more effective manner. While we are critical of the overuse of the lecture, we still recognize that there are occasions and circumstances where it is appropriate. However, we also want to open the thinking of educators to an educational environment where new methods of teaching, new directions in knowledge development, and differing attitudes can make a significant difference. We believe that all faculty members are basically motivated to be good teachers, and all really do want to be successful in the classroom. What we are saying is that the faculty member has choices, and the more the academic planning process can do to help elucidate those choices, the more effective the academic plan will be. In the next several chapters, we will examine several specific classroom options.

Pedagogical Alternatives

Jonathan had come home for his first Thanksgiving, and although he enjoyed his freedom living away at school there was nothing like coming home to a meal cooked by Mom, especially for Thanksgiving. The family was gathered around the table, chowing down on turkey, stuffing, fresh garden vegetables, and mom's famous mashed potatoes – of course, covered in gravy-- when Jonathan's parent decided to take off the gloves, and ask him about his classes at the university.

"I know that you're a freshman in college Jonathan," said his father, "so I would be quite interested to hear about your classes. How are they going? What do you think of the topics?" "Yes, dear" his mom interjected. "I'm dying to hear about your impressions of the campus, your classes, and your teachers. It's been over 25 years since your dad and I attended college and we're wondering what college life is like."

How does one answer a question like this, thought Jonathan. College life is just the way it is. "Well Dad, Mom, It's like this. You get up every morning, you go to class, you eat your meals, you go back to the dorms, you study, watch TV, listen to music, surf the net and yes, even party." "Then I guess college life hasn't change much since you and I were in school" his mother commented to his father. "Well, perhaps, honey," His dad replied. "But we didn't have the internet to play with, or that noise your son calls music to listen to. Yes, I guess college is the same old same old." Yet they both could not be further from the truth.

What Jonathan wasn't telling them was that, in his political science class, students were reading their assigned texts and partaking in classroom discussions. They were also working in the on-campus public interest organizing group, collecting data through telephone surveys for the upcoming elections. He also didn't mention that his introduction to college class not only involved role-playing exercises and in-class experiential exercises but also a community clean-up event sponsored by the university. Furthermore, his math class was purely computer-based, using multimedia presentations and computer-assisted instructions as well as Internet think groups to assist in homework assignments. All work was e-mailed to the instructor and returned with comments the next day. His introduction to business class was using a group-based computer simulator where student groups competed to make pet robots; every member of the group was responsible for

151

making at least one decision in each round of the game. His English class was in a room with linked computers where students could easily read each others' works, make comments in writing including correcting grammar, and then have the modified work shared with the class as a whole. Only his philosophy class was traditional in nature, and it was the only class in which he did not actively participate.

Yes, Jonathan did wake up, go to school and then go back to the dorms. But the learning environment of the 21st Century in no way mirrored the educational environment of his parents.

A Wide Variety of Ways to Learn

In the last chapter, we challenged the broad use of the lecture method of educating. While we do not repudiate the method altogether, and do recognize that there are certain circumstances where the lecture does serve a useful purpose, we indicated that the lecture method should never be the only pedagogical tool instructors and professors use.

This chapter looks at several alternatives to the lecture method. It is not exhaustive, as new methods seem to reveal themselves on a regular basis, but we do want to provide a description of alternative methods which have gained support in several segments of higher education. For each, we provide a basic description, a brief example of how the method may be used, and some pros and cons of each. In this discussion, we do not wish to imply that each of these pedagogical methods is a panacea in itself, or that any one can be a complete method of learning. Blending these methods, moving from one method to another, and even using different methods with different classes are all possibilities. There are no hard and fast rules here. Instructors and professors should feel creative and seek to find the one or two methods that appear to best fit the material, the learner, and the instructor.

Experiential Exercises

Experiential exercises put the learner into a hypothetical or real-world situation where the learner must make decisions that simulate what might occur in the world outside the classroom. These can occur with individuals, but more typically occur in groups. Instructors normally choose an experiential exercise to coincide with a particular course topic and allow learners to work through it with minimal input.

An example of this might be a sociology class going through an exercise that simulates a series of culture clashes occurring when a group of international students is assigned the task of choosing food for an international banquet. The learners have to discover what the preferred foods of each ethnic group are, as well as any food taboos which might exist. If the assignment is to come up with a menu that everyone can eat and enjoy, the learners must do a significant amount of research, interact with each other to increase their understanding, work together and submit their results for analysis, either by the instructor or perhaps the class as a whole.

Experiential exercises are activity events where interaction among learners is significantly increased. Learners must often define many of the variables of the exercise, and take initiative in organizing themselves. Learners apply the material to a simulated real-life decision-making scenario and should gain some insight into the phenomena the course instructor is trying to teach them. Yet such exercises are contrived. They are controlled exercises which usually lead to single conclusions. There is seldom connectivity between experiential exercises, and while they may demonstrate single points, they generally do not examine all of the eventualities that can occur in a real world setting. Regardless, many instructors who use experiential exercises in their classrooms see great benefits in their application, and are able to supplement the gaps with other materials that bring the entire classroom experience meaningful.

Use of Technology in the Classroom

One of the exciting advances in higher education is the advent of significant technological tools. Unfortunately, most technologies are quite expensive and unless there is a major dedication on the part of campus academic planners to find and allocate resources to provide technology, as well as to continuously maintain and update it, many campuses cannot take advantage of the technologies that are available.

There are two parts to the technology component, hardware and software. Hardware that supports classroom use includes some or all of the following items: campus mainframe computer; campus or school mainframe computers; local area networks; extra area networks; computer-linked projection systems; smart classrooms equipped with computers, VCRs, television connections, Internet connections, ELMO projectors, and overall visual projection systems, laptop classrooms where every seat has a set up for learners and the instructor to work on lap top computers. Some of these classroom contain links between the laptops so that the instructor can see what each learner is working on from a central monitoring station; group smart classrooms, where groups of students work on projects at 3-5-seat stations and use their group computer to make reports to the rest of the class through a centralized control point; distance learning rooms equipped with both sending and receiving television devices; computer labs for learners; and computer interfaces for faculty members to work on-line with other faculty members or with learners. And there is much more coming.

The software portion of the technology component is even more exciting. Many companies around the world are developing educational software packages that make the learning experience more fun, more involving, timely, and highly effective. For example, there are certain software packages that allow chemistry students to conduct experiments with highly toxic or volatile chemical compounds through the computer without the risk of actually handling these compounds or creating hazards for themselves or their colleagues. Further, the software available and becoming available reaches into every segment of the learning community and provides instructors and professors with leading-edge teaching tools to help them be more effective. At the Open University in England, much of the activities which occur on its central campus in Milton Keynes, England involve creating technologically driven learning tools to support the University's over 200,000 distance learning students.

The Internet is becoming more and more useful as an educational tool. While the Internet contains an incredible amount of trash, it also contains a growing stock pile of useful information which can enhance both the in-classroom and out-of-classroom experience of learners. This trend should continue and become more important in the future.

The pros of the growing use of technology in the classrooms include the increase in interest level it can provide and the wealth of materials which bring classrooms more dramatically into the world outside the textbook. Technology can help take the edge off lecturing and provide a sense of reality not seen up to this point. Another advantage of technology on the college or university campus is the continuing digitizing of campus libraries, the increase of contact through e-mail and teleconferencing over the Internet, and the growth of the virtual classroom, where students can assess class materials, text book support, research bases, and even other group members at any time of the day or night.

On the other hand, technology is expensive and constantly changing, so it will continue to be expensive. This means that not all campuses or classrooms can take advantage of the wealth of educational opportunities technology provides, and this can hurt the learner. Technology can also become more of the classroom experience than the learning it is supposed to support. Glitzy, flashy, colorful, and entertaining, technology can overshadow the lesson, so instructors and professors who are able to use a variety of technology need to be certain that they understand it and can adapt it so as to enhance the learning experience.

Distance Learning

Learning away from the classroom is becoming more and more popular. Distance learning can occur with technology aids such as television or Internet access or through the postal service. In a reference to the Open University in the last section, we note that while it does create learning materials high in quality, content, and appeal, nearly all of its distance learning is done through the mail. CD-ROMs, books, videos, and audio tapes are sent to students who then complete the material on their own and then return assignments. The Open University maintains a number of centers around the United Kingdom where learners can go to get help, and each course is concluded with the traditional British testing system.

Blackboard and the Internet Classroom are two technology-driven methods available to any college or university> Using them it is possible to create and run on-line courses to serve off-campus learners. A large number of campuses are becoming involved with these programs, particularly where they see the ease of taking standard classroom materials and putting them on-line to serve both campus-enrolled students and those who are not. Unlike the Open University offerings which allow the learner to learn when convenient, most on-line classes are held on a schedule and require learners to tune in when the class goes live. In some locations, however, the technology is beginning to allow on-line access during real time for the learner so that the learner can be engaged at convenience. So far, however, these classes are rare.

The great advantage of distance learning is that it allows learners from a wide area to be involved with college classes without the need to be physically present. This opens up higher education to a broader audience, a real need of the emerging Information Age. It also allows the college or university to grow its programs, increase revenues, and develop new course delivery methods that help keep the disciplines fresh and alive. Further, they tend to provide the institution with a reality check in terms of matching its offerings to the demands of learners from a wide area within the general service area. If no one wants to take a course, it might be a good sign that the course is not appropriate to the service area, as we discussed in an earlier chapter.

The disadvantage of distance learning is that there is very little face-to-face contact between instructor and learner. There is also little to no group contact. While this might not be a negative factor for certain courses, it could be a major factor in others. Such classes also normally require added support personnel, creation of dedicated transmission and receiving facilities, and a training program for instructors and professors in the program. All in all, however, distance learning, especially based on the growth of learning technologies, appears to be a growing phenomenon in higher education.

Team Research and Learning

Another alternative method of teaching is through team research and learning. Many colleges and universities have discovered the advantages of cohort groups, which are groups of learners who take many of their classes together, study together, and perhaps live in the same dorm. Roskilde University in Denmark has created an entire curriculum around the concept, and has gone so far as to have faculty offices in dorms to help assure that cohort groups have easy access to professors. While most American colleges and universities would not be willing to mover faculty offices into dormitories, cohort group learning is nevertheless catching on..

In a cohort group learning community, learners self-select or are assigned a group of other learners who have expressed interest in a common educational goal. They follow a schedule that puts all of them in certain courses together, whether all or a few.. The learners then schedule time when they can all meet together and go over assignments, reading comprehension, or generally discuss the classes and the class material. They help each other understand, and then support each other in getting over the difficult parts. For classes where cohort groups exist, the teaching style includes the incorporation of the cohort experience into the structure of the overall class. Group projects, group research, and group presentations can all flow naturally from this type of learning.

There are lots of pros to group learning and group research. Since many learners who enter college are just out of high school and away from home for the first time, cohort groups can provide a feeling of family and comfort which helps the less mature learner adapt more effectively to the social and academic worlds of higher education. By supporting each other's learning, each learner learns even more and understands the material at a greater depth.

There are few cons to cohort learning, other than the ability of the college or university to create a system which supports it. Normally there need to be faculty and staff assigned to the cohort program to administer, organize, provide outside assistance with social and academic problems and to evaluate when the cohorts are working well or are falling into trouble. There is some expense in this, and if it is not clearly spelled out as a goal of the academic plan the money may not be there.

Professor-Learner Joint Research

We have briefly discussed the potential for instructors and learners to work together in conducting research. This is hardly a new idea; graduate students have been graduate research assistants for many years. What we encourage here is to broaden the approach to include the undergraduate student as well.

The instructor or professor would need to be willing to work with an undergraduate student to do some original research. This could involve an element of library research on the part of the undergraduate, but could also involve the learner in writing a summary of the findings or even part of the analysis. This probably works best with a limited number of students--the authors have problems envisioning a class of 500 each doing research with the professor and receiving personal attention throughout the process--but the potential for adding to the learning and the excitement of learning increases for both the professor and the learner.

The benefits certainly include the expansion of learning for both instructor and learner, but go much deeper. One of the things the learner is learning here is how to learn. Joint research implies that there are unsolved questions and opportunities to explore the elements of knowledge. While this is the pattern of a professor's life, it is probably a new experience for the learner. Instead of having knowledge determined by others and then imparted impassively through classroom experiences, the learner is now engaging in the discovery of knowledge and will be asked to organize it so it can be shared with others. More importantly, in learning to learn, the learner develops a skill that will serve for life. This is a crucial need in the emerging economy of the Information Age, and learners who have been able to develop this skill will be well-set to take advantage of that new economy.

There are risks with this approach as well. There is a potential ethical problem for the instructor or professor who takes the research students produce and then go on to have it published or presented at scholarly meetings without giving adequate credit to the contributing students. Another issue is that not all research is appropriate for active research by undergraduates. One might think that studying atomic fission in a physics class is not the best place to play with radioactive elements to see what will happen. Overall, however, where the opportunity presents itself, instructor-learner research opportunities hold a great deal of promise and hold benefits for both the academic and the learner.

Case Studies

Case studies contain stories of real-world events containing the elements of actions or outcomes which demonstrate the points the case writer wants the reader to learn. Instructors have available to them a wide range of cases, which allows them to make the points central to the course design. Perhaps best known is Harvard University's School of Business, where the case method has caught on and is a common pedagogical tool found even in departments outside of business. Here is a typical example of a case used in a class. In a marketing class, an instructor might use a case to see how a large retail chain first grew to national prominence, and then failed when an up-start competitor was able to take away huge chunks of market share. The learner is probably familiar with the company, and may also know that the company has fallen on hard times. The case identifies many of the root causes for failure and then allows for a broader class discussion of causes and effects. The instructor can then also tie these lessons to ideas from the text, book or from other parts of the course. This method is widely popular as a teaching technique, both in colleges and universities as well as in professional learning environments.

There are basically two types of case studies: prepared, and live. Prepared cases are written by case writers who have studied a particular company or phenomenon over a period of time. In the case of an organizational example, the case writer will present a history, allowing the reader to get a sense of the nature of the organization, its founders, its culture, and its function. This is usually followed by descriptions of key personnel, landmark events, financial analyses, product or service descriptions and an ending circumstance. Most case writers also prepare teaching notes for the instructor that outline what the writer felt were the salient points of the case.

Live cases are not as structured. For example, in a strategic management class, the instructor asks the learners to come up with their own case; go out on the Internet and find a company they are interest in and that has a strong website that provides company information; begin to accumulate data on the company in line with the elements of the strategic planning model the instructor is using in the class; and to periodically share these findings with the rest of the class as they build their case over the course of the term. This can be done in a technology-free classroom or in a technology-rich classroom such as the smart group room we described earlier. Regardless, the point is to have students create their own cases, learn for themselves the strengths and weaknesses of the company, analyze the pattern of strategic events that occur in the company and then make a recommendation based on both the facts they have gathered and the central points of good strategic management which have come from the rest of the classroom experience.

Scripted or live, case studies helps learners see real examples of real world phenomena, analyze why conditions are as they are, and then apply the knowledge they gain from the class to form knowledge bases helpful in future live events. Pre-written cases may be contrived to help the writer demonstrate specific points, where live cases tend to have no preset points to make at all. Regardless, each method challenges the learner to look at real world situations, think about them, and learn from the experience.

Case studies are, however, necessarily confining. Pre-written cases may get stale. And even live cases tend to concentrate on a single phenomenon rather than developing a sense of the larger context. They also tend to be prescriptive, and in the real world what works for one situation doesn't necessarily work for another. So the challenge to the instructor is to continuously broaden the context and treat case examples as true for that case only, with only limited inference from a single example to the state of the rest of the world.

Problem-Based Learning

An intriguing alternative method gaining credibility is Problem-Based Learning (PBL). In this portion of this chapter, we focus on PBL because it is not as widely known as the other alternatives we identified in the previous section. Also we believe it offers some particularly effective techniques in helping upper-division learners gain mastery of the subject matter they are studying.

Beyond being another alternative, PBL is also a different philosophy of learning. Here responsibility shifts from the shoulder of the professor or instructor to a combination of both the educator and the learner. Certainly one could argue effective learning has always been dependent upon the qualities of the educator as well as the qualities of the learner; PBL doesn't seek to change the inherent qualities of either party in the educational process. It seeks to change the philosophy, and believes that as one result, improved quality will follow.

PBL is a relatively new method of knowledge transference. The Faculty of Health Sciences initially developed PBL in the late 1960s at McMaster University in Canada (Barrows, 1996). They developed this approach because of the university found that their students were disenchanted and bored, "saturated by the vast amounts of information they had to absorb, much of which was perceived to have little relevance to medical practice" (Pg. 4). They also recognized that medical students were much more enthusiastic and motivated when working with patients and engaged in problem solving (Spaulding, 1991). Based on these observations, they developed a technique that shifted the focus of medical education from a predomination of facts and figures to real-life problems, student-led research, and problem-solving experiences.

Other medical schools picked up this change of curriculum, including Michigan State University and the University of New Mexico as well as schools in Australia and the Netherlands. While medical schools have been the major academic groups to adopt the technique, over the past several years, PBL has broken out into other areas of the campus. In the 1980s, the University of Hawaii was the first U.S. university to attempt to institute PBL campus wide. Many American schools have since adopted PBL in various segments of their campuses, including Harvard University (Barrows, 1996).

The University of Maastrick in the Netherlands provides a good contemporary example of a successful campus-wide approach. Here, supported by national educational policy of the Dutch government, PBL is the singular approved method of providing instruction throughout the campus. Learners become familiar with PBL with their first class experiences and work within this common framework until graduation. Further, departmental funding and faculty rewards are keyed to the success of PBL applications in their classrooms. Interestingly enough, it is the university's school of business that is regarded as the leader in both initiating and delivering PBL.

In 1995, a group of state and federal policymakers and in educator met to discuss and evaluate the quality of undergraduate education in the U.S. (About Teaching, 1995). They concluded that today's college and university graduates need to possess specific characteristics of quality performance. These are:

1. High levels of communication skills, computational skills, technological literacy, and informational abilities that enable individuals to gain and apply new knowledge and skills as needed,

2. The ability to arrive at informed judgments: that is, to effectively define problems, gather and evaluate information related to those problems and develop solutions,

3. The ability to function in a global community, having a range of attitudes and dispositions including flexibility and adaptability, ease with diversity, motivation and persistence. These might include, being a self starter, ethical and civil behavior, creativity and resourcefulness and the ability to work with others, especially in team settings,

4. Technical competence, and demonstrated ability to develop all of the above to address specific problems in complex real work settings, in which the development of workable solutions is required.

PBL seeks to address the development of these characteristics in the learners it affects. PBL is a process that allows students not only to draw upon their existing knowledge base through emphasis, but also seek and acquire relevant information to supplement and strengthen their knowledge base. Stinson and Milter (1996) suggest that the basic tenets of PBL are that:

1. Learning outcomes should be holistic, not divided by narrow disciplinary boundaries,

2. Problems should mirror professional practice,

3. Problems should be ill-structured, and

4. Problems should be contemporary.

In implementing PBL, it is important to keep in mind that the roles of the faculty, learners, and the environment will need major restructuring. PBL begins with providing learners with an ill-structured problem. Instructors assume the roles of coaches, providing learners guidance and counseling in channeling their thought processes. They become managers and facilitators of the learning process. Learners assume the roles of active problem solvers, decision makers and meaning seekers, allowing themselves to learn. PBL challenges learners to generate their own strategies for defining the problem, identify information necessary to evaluate the problem, gather additional information necessary to totally analyze the problem situation, and compare and share the various strategies generated by others that are involved in the process. Thus, PBL situations continuously challenge learners determine what information is needed, where and how to obtain the information needed, how to manage the information obtained in evaluating the problem situation and how to share the organized knowledge and information with others engaged in problem solving. Due to the ill-structured nature of the problem, learners are challenged into divergent thinking modes. Since there is no one single correct method of addressing the problem, the approach to problem solving involves multiple perspectives and higher level of thinking.

PBL Methods

PBL is an educational philosophy and methodology in which the course instructor, often a person called a tutor, creates a learning environment where a real world scenario drives learning. In a module of learning, the instructor follows the following steps: establishing goals and priorities of learning for the class; translating the goals and priorities into learning objectives; developing and posing a problem that requires learners to acquire a knowledge base through self-learning; designing and conducting assessments of learning the objectives; evaluating assessment findings, and using the results for decision-making. These steps are a full cycle of the learning process. PBL encourages the instructor to decide what objectives are to be achieved from the learning task, create and assign the problem, and to assess whether the objectives have been achieved.

The nature of the problem requires learners to conduct both group and individual research to learn new information and knowledge that will help them understand and work through the problem. Group work is one of the methods of PBL, and the learning groups develop their own theories and identify learning goals.

Finkle and Torp (1995) state that Problem Based Learning is a curriculum development and instructional system that simultaneously develops both problem solving strategies and disciplinary knowledge bases and skills by placing students in the active role of problem solvers confronted with an ill-structured problem that mirrors real-world problems. The use of a genuine ill structured problem provides a driving force for learning, as the posed problem predetermines the reason for acquiring new knowledge. This need to solve a problem fosters and motivates learners by allowing them to learn within a meaningful context.

Another important method of PBL is that it gives learners more and more responsibilities in achieving their own education and in becoming increasingly self-reliant and unregimented, and more importantly, less dependent on their instructors for their education. Instead, instructors act as guides. For example, they normally provide learners with a list of tasks to be carried out during the learning process. These tasks include:

- determining whether a problem exists
- understanding the problem through brainstorming and articulating an exact statement of the problem
- identifying the information already known and needed to evaluate the problem
- identifying resources that need to be used to gather information regarding the problem at hand
- evaluating the problem through outlining and categorizing the variables and/causes
- determine/establishing learning goals from analyses in relation to existing knowledge, and
- summarizing relevant findings amongst the group members.

PBL Characteristics

There are a number of specific activities that PBL uses in supporting the learning environment of learners. These characteristics of PBL include:

- learning through group meetings
- being "learner-oriented" by implying that learners determine what is to be learned and what is to be done to accomplish this learning,
- students determine how to accomplish/complete the various tasks assigned,
- students determine what books to read and what literature and resources to consult for task completion, and
- learning occurs as the task is being completed.

These characteristics are similar to the characteristics described in the previous chapter by Gibbons et al (1994) as "Mode 2" knowledge creation and learning. The advantages for learners include improved ability to work in groups, developing applied research skills, taking responsibility for the learning process and developing ownership of the knowledge and skills they generate. While Huff (2000) suggests there may be some downside to this form of educational process, such as moving away from science and being too pragmatic, she also recognizes that these types of methods are far more timely, more practical, and more democratic than traditional academic educational methods.

Goals of PBL

When practitioners properly administer PBL, they begin to see that learners seek to become more familiar with the existing knowledge base, and as a consequence, learners acquire and retain new knowledge at a much better level than otherwise happens. Learners attain knowledge through the development of learning goals. These goals include the ability to analyze relevant problems using the existing knowledge base, developing an effective personal learning strategy, learning to analyze different problems and identifying various information needs, using various theoretical underpinnings and viewpoints in conjunction with a problem, and sharing and expressing the knowledge learned with others. Additional outcomes of learning using PBL include, learning to use a variety of information sources, learning to summarize the relevant findings, learning to formulate and discuss ideas and findings with others, learning to work in groups, and learning leadership skills in conducting group meetings.

Issues of Implementation

Before instructors can implement Problem-Based Learning into a learning environment, they need to understand that PBL has its own particular preparation requirements. Since the major elements in the PBL process include the problems, the learners, the faculty, the environment itself in which the process is to be implemented, and the constant and continuous interaction/feedback between all of these components, a great deal of up-front planning and development is essential.

Preparing the Problem. The problem posed needs to be a reflection of the real world. Learners need to believe that the congruence of the problem with what is actually going on beyond the walls of the college or university is realistic and relevant. Equally important, the problem needs to reflect currency with existing business practices rather than historical ones. The problem should engage learners in such a way that they feel challenged to understand the situation. Further, learners must be able to learn from each other's experiences and be able to generalize from the specific problem situation to develop more rigorous knowledge and understanding.

Preparing the Learners. The learners engaged in PBL need to possess certain basic readiness to take on the responsibilities for learning. This includes being competent enough to answer questions such as "what are we supposed to do", "how do we do that", "tell us what you want and how we will do it" and "show us how to get the information". In essence, the first thing that needs to happen for the learner is an exercise that will help the learner learn to learn.

Preparing the Instructor. This is perhaps the most influential element of PBL. There needs to be a total paradigm shift in the thinking of the educator. The instructor needs to trust in the abilities of the students. In moving the responsibility for learning away from the educator to the learner, the instructor takes on several roles, becoming 1) a CATALYST for learning rather than a PERFORMER; 2) a GUIDE rather than a JUDGE; 3) a LISTENER rather than a TALKER; and 4) a FACILITATOR rather than an ENFORCER. We recognize that these are characteristics that may not be comfortable for traditional college and university faculty members. Because of the nature of academic preparation, faculty members normally develop extremely specialized set of skills in very narrow subject areas and are not comfortable delving into other non-areas of expertise (Rowley, Lujan, and Dolence, 1998). In order to be successful in teaching in a PBL classroom, however, instructors need to work in a highly collaborative manner with learners and with other faculty members in creating a more multidisciplinary environment. The paradigm needs to shift from the thought processes of recognizing Marketing, Management, Finance, MIS, or Production problems to Business problems.

Preparing the Environment. One of the strategies for helping make PBL a success is for entire college faculties to adopt the concept throughout the curriculum. This requires that faculties challenge the traditional practices of instructor-driven classroom practices, including performance evaluation measures, examinations, quizzes, and special project requirements. In developing a more learner-centered environment, business faculties should be willing to alter traditional practices to accommodate learner-driven performance measures of task determination, goal setting, and task completion modalities.

Mentoring for learners is far more important in PBL than in traditional teacher-student environments. It is important constantly to provide learners with feedback and encouragement as they start taking more and more responsibilities for their own learning. The role of the instructor then becomes one of helping learners seek their own answers for the questions they themselves pose. Basic learning is significantly enhanced as learners seek and gain additional knowledge on their own.

Conclusion Regarding PBL

In order to provide the most effective educational experience for today's learners, colleges and universities should expand their methods of knowledge delivery in order to more adequately address the diverse need of today's learners. Fortunately, there are an increasing number of modalities which provide a variety of different approaches to learning. These allow professors and instructors to choose a method that can help them oversee the delivery of courses in the most effective manner.

Though it has its roots in schools of medicine, PBL is proving an exciting alternative in other parts of the campus, including the business school. For those who teach business or management courses, PBL provides an opportunity to move from a passive learning situation to a much more active learning environment, where learners take a large amount of responsibility for their own learning and engage in research, interpretation, group discussions, and projects in a manner that makes the material come alive in a very meaningful way. As a stand-alone approach, or in concert with other methods as we have identified throughout this article, professors and instructors can use PBL in those courses or subjects where application is more important than the learning of facts.

However, in order for PBL to be effective in the classroom, certain learning conditions need to be right.

- Learners need to have a basic understanding of most of the concepts and principles of the subject matter.
- Professors and instructors need to understand the concept of the ill-structured problem and then design modules for the PBL experience.
- Students need to understand the nature of this type of learning and be willing to take responsibility for setting their own learning goals for learning.
- Once learners are divided into groups, the instructor ,or tutor, acts as a catalyst to enhance the learning process.

- Coaching encourages and fosters learning.
- The focus of the exercise needs to identify problem-solving techniques and not necessarily specific outcomes or solutions within the ill structured problem format.
- Learners need to have access to information that will aid the learning process and expand their knowledge bases.

With these conditions in place, instructors and learners can begin to experience the material in a learning environment that depends on discovery and participation. Learners can deepen their enjoyment of learning as they build skills that they can use, not only in the classroom but in the business world as well. This is a clear advantage of this type of learning and is a solid reason for professors and instructors in business and management studies to consider adopting the method for their classrooms. Finally, Wilkerson and Gijselaers have suggested that, regardless of the differing application modes, PBL learning can be characterized by at least three common features (1996). These are:

1. PBL is student-centered. Learners play a role in determining what will be learned and how. Learners are active participants in the process by actively engaged in inquiry and collaboration.
2. In PBL Instructors become facilitators rather than disseminators of information, observers rather than actors. They act as coaches rather than active players providing constructive feedback to the students and challenge the students to excel, and
3. In PBL, problems serve as the initial stimulus and framework for learning and are introduced early in the learning process. The problems are ill-structured, multidisciplinary, and meaningful. They require skills in analysis, synthesis and evaluation. They provoke, puzzle and surprise. (pps 101-102).

In supporting the development and use of PBL in the management and business education of today's colleges and universities, it is useful to examine the similarities and differences between PBL and more traditional or classical approach to classroom education. In classroom lectures and discussions, normally it is the instructor who identifies the topics that need to be covered and also outlines the nature and the extent of the coverage. The topics are preset and the content delivery is instructor-driven. In this approach, the learner is passive to the process. In the PBL approach, the instructor is still responsible for setting the general direction of the class, but allows learners to develop topics that are personally of interest. Learners are allowed to go as deeply into the material as they wish. Here, the learner is active in the process.

In the case approach, another popular method of knowledge transfer, the instructor chooses business examples that he/she hopes will bring together course concepts and knowledge within a predefined applied setting. There are two different uses of cases – case incidents and entire case studies. Case examples are always helpful, regardless of the setting, because they help elucidate the material and make it seem more real.

Full case studies, however, can be problematic. Here, one clear positive of the method is that learners do focus more on the application of concepts. However, this is too often done so in a dated and segmented fashion. Unfortunately, unless the professor or instructor is able to up-date the case, this particular method of exchange of information may do little to improve the critical thinking skills of learners. Use of live cases, those learners choose and develop themselves from library research or from the Internet, can prove to be an extremely significant method of making case study more effective. In PBL, case development, research, analysis, and discussion is all learner-centered, meaning that the instructor provides the format for case study, not the case itself, and relies on the student to develop and take responsibility for the material.

Group learning is another popular educational approach found in more and more classrooms today. However, McCorkle (1999) reports that several researchers have identified a number of problems regarding group learning. These include free riding/social loafing, inadequate rewards, skills and attitude problems, transaction-costs problems, integrative learning problems, poor product quality, lack of individual innovation, pacing of the project workload, and not enough timely feedback to improve the quality of work. The role of the teacher in the traditional or classical teaching scheme is to set up the framework for learning to occur by a highly structured set of subjective criteria and ensure that learning takes place through lectures, discussions, examinations, and presentations that finally translate to a grade. Unfortunately, many of the activities in the classroom are driven by the letter grades that result from student activities. Whether actual learning has taken place is a highly debatable and an important area of concern.

Moving the Paradigm from Teaching to Learning

Dr. Schwartz felt like he was sitting on a pincushion which was surrounded by a fiery pit of molten lava as he sat for his tenure review. As an assistant professor in the English department he knew that going for tenure was going to be a demanding process, however, he never expected that the school-wide rank and tenure committee would act like the Spanish Inquisition. He knew that he would be grilled on his publication record; that was to be expected since his publications were numerous but in second and third tier academic journals. He was fully prepared to defend his work and had several letters from outside reviewers praising his research. Yet the committee brushed over this material, in fact paid lip service to the entire topic of research. What the committee kept harping on, to Dr. Schwartz's amazement and dismay, was the area of course development and instruction. Dr. Schwartz was brought out of his revelry by a question from the chair of the committee.

"Dr. Schwartz, would you care to explain to us why your course outline for the Basic Writing II course, the class students take before they take the English proficiency exam, is never the same from semester to semester? The committee finds it rather curious that for such a basic required course, a course that you must have taught for at least six times in the four years you've been at the university, you could not find a suitable instructional methodology?" There was murmuring amongst the faculty committee members. The chair must have hit a real sore point with the committee, thought Dr. Schwartz, and I better have an appropriate rejoinder.

"Perhaps I misunderstood your question" started Dr. Schwartz. "But I do not comprehend what the problem possibly could be with my changing my outline, from semester to semester to accommodate both changes in my field and changes in instructional methodology and technology. Perhaps you could clarify exactly what points in my outlines you and the committee have problems with?"

This answer, as Schwartz quickly realized, did not sit well with the committee. "Listen here, Schwartz", commented the representative from his own department, English, "and we'll get straight to the point. The proficiency exam never changes in scope and in nature and our faculty and students expect that your writing course will prepare them to take the exam. How can you meet that objective with a course that changes in instructional methodology and sometimes even in content? Don't you realize that a student who fails your course the first time and

169

retakes the course with you again may walk into an entirely new course structure?" Committee members seemed to be nodding their heads in agreement with this last comment and Schwartz saw his hopes for tenure fading fast.

"Another thing," chimed in another member of the committee. "We've noticed that you have your students run the class. They apportion out the readings themselves, collect and evaluate each others' homework, run a virtual chat room, and even lead discussions on assigned readings. We are quite interested in what you do to ensure the quality of their work and how you then evaluate your students' performance."

This hit a raw nerve in Dr. Schwartz. The principle of academic freedom provided him the right to use any instructional method he deemed appropriate as long as he achieved the department's objectives. "Wait a minute" snapped Schwartz. "If my course outlines and my instructional methodologies are so erratic and erroneous, how come my students' passing rate on the proficiency exam is consistently higher than the overall mean score for the college? If I'm doing something wrong, wouldn't that show up on the exams?" The committee's response to Schwartz's outburst was silence.

Something was wrong, very in wrong in fact, but it had nothing to do with Schwartz's students' passing rates on the English proficiency exam. What Dr. Schwartz didn't realize was that his instructional style of continuous improvement, instructional incremental change, and student involvement did not fit in with the strategic and academic plans of the university; plans that focused on consistency and reliability, rather than innovation. Dr. Schwartz never did receive a direct answer to his question ... nor did he receive tenure.

Which Methods of Delivering Education are Best?

Many faculty members can distinctly remember hearing an academic dean, when questioned about quality faculty instruction, state that, "I can't give you any details but I know good teaching when I see it." At first this might strike the reader as a rather strange statement for an academic dean to make for one would hope, given that most academic institutions pride themselves on some modicum of instructional ability, an academic dean should be able to operational strong teaching. As the leader and administrative head of the academic unit one would also hope that the academic dean would and could lead by example when it came to academic instruction: that is, be able to not only elaborate on the attributes of a first-class teacher but be able to demonstrate in the classroom those same characteristics.[1] This would provide the dean instructional academic credibility, a particularly important commodity if it is necessary for the dean to develop and lead faculty training sessions on instruction and assist junior faculty in these endeavors.

There are certainly other reasons one would expect an academic dean to be able to describe in great detail excellent instruction in great detail. Many smaller colleges and universities, as well as some larger institutions, require that the academic dean conduct classroom evaluations of non-tenured professors and those seeking promotion. If a dean is going to assess an instructor's teaching abilities, then one would hope that the dean would also be familiar with the criteria, the specific evaluative variables, associated with the evaluation.

Second, some colleges and universities even require their academic deans to teach one course per semester or per year. The rationale for this is that the deans will become closer to the student body in their academic area as well as keep current in instructional issues.

Third, based on the litigious nature of our society, one would expect that such an open-ended, non-specific statement by the dean about teaching would open the floodgates for law suits. Faculty members denied promotion or tenure, based upon the dean's negative recommendation, would be quite apt to sue -- and their lawyers would have a field day with this dean on cross examination, particularly if the dean's evaluation was harmful concerning a faculty member's instructional ability.

Fourth, the statement also seems both elitist and haughty. Who is this person who can, by merely watching a faculty member teach for perhaps twenty minutes or so, declare whether good teaching is or is not occurring in the class room? More importantly, why should we take this person's word for whether this instructor is competent or not if the person cannot provide us an adequate explanation of competency itself?[2]

---

[1] Frederick Taylor's concept of the functional foreman – the manager is a master in every task that his or her subordinates perform (Taylor, 1947).

[2] McGregor's (1960) major criticism of most appraisal systems is that superiors use subjective measures of performance including the subordinates' attitudes and personality traits.

Educational Delivery as an Art

The dean's statement about teaching sounds strikingly similar to those one might make about art, music, film, and theatre; "I know good ___ when I see it, but I can't explain it. Or, good ___ is in the eye of the beholder." The dean's statement then, purposely or otherwise, treats teaching and all methods of educational delivery as an art form, that is, an unlearned skill that draws on intuition and subjective judgment (Webber, 1979).

Taking this analysis to its most illogical conclusion, if teaching and instruction are merely forms of art then all academic deans need to do is to hire talented faculty and let the faculty do their own thing. This laissez-faire approach assumes that faculty as professionals will keep abreast of both instructional innovations and content changes in theirs fields, and will always be at their best in the classroom.

Kerr (1975) in his classic article on motivation theory noted that "society hopes that [university] teachers will not neglect their teaching responsibilities but *rewards* them almost entirely for research and publications … rewards for good teaching usually are limited to outstanding teaching awards … punishment for poor teaching also are rare" (pg. 772). Kerr concluded that, given the numerous rewards for publishing, and the ease in which one can document excellent research over exceptional teaching, faculty will invariably spend their time performing research rather than course and instructional development and renewal. Skill in educational delivery systems alone will not suffice unless coupled with the motivation to keep current in the field. "Skill (art) without knowledge (science) means stagnancy and the inability to pass on learning" (Webber, 1979, pg. 6).

Educational Delivery as a Science

Teacher education is one of the oldest fields of college instruction. Many comprehensive and small liberal arts colleges and universities started their august careers as Normal schools; postsecondary institutions dedicated to producing primary and secondary school teachers. As a field of study, education also has a very long and well tested body of knowledge, with the most notable early work of Campbell and Stanley (1963) on the experimental designs of teaching and research crossing over into many other social science disciplines.

Early research on instructional methodologies seemed to focus on the general utility of each instructional technique. For example, Smith and Bourgault (1976) found that the case study approach was advocated as an instructional technique for the relevance and motivation it provided, while the lecture and group study approach focused upon the behavioral objectives that must be met by the instructor. Carroll, Paine, and Ivanevich (1972) evaluated and rank-ordered nine different instructional techniques in terms of specific learning attributes including knowledge acquisition, attitudinal change, problem solving, inter-personal skills, participant acceptance and knowledge retention.

This search for empirical evidence supporting a one best method of instructional delivery for a particular learning objective[3] was the irrational extension of the scientific method. That is, through science it was assumed that researchers could discern the best teaching technique to employ for any situation, and, with the right training and instruction, any teacher could learn to employ these instructional delivery techniques. Teaching as a science also implied that faculty members were empty, malleable, and interchangeable vessels that could be dumped into any course in which they had the academic credentials for, and with training, perform admirably. Whether the course for which they had 20 or 500 students, involved straight lecture method or internet instruction, required field work or quantitative research approaches, any professional instructor could handle the instructional task.

Perhaps this was what the academic dean was referring to, assuming that the phrase "what he saw" referred to the product of instruction and not the instruction itself. A one-type-fits-all approach to instruction – will we all use the same syllabus, the same text, the same exams, the same techniques for the same course? – reeks of a production line mentality (Block, 1995) and does not allow for individual differences in terms of preferences and abilities (Hoerner, 1998). One's teaching approach is as much a function of personality, style, and attitude as it is of course topic and learning objectives and so a purely scientific approach must be tempered to allow for distinctions amongst instructors. Differing instructors must be allowed to teach the same course differently, not only because of issues of academic

---

[3] See McClenney (1980). Described an empirical model to increase instructional productivity and suggested alternative instructional methodologies be utilized by community colleges.

freedom, but because dissimilar instructors may produce comparable learning outcomes using divergent instruction delivery systems.

The focus of attention of the science of education has shifted from evaluating the process of instruction (how one teaches) to the result and impact of instruction, the outcomes – actual learning. The academic dean may not have been far from the truth when he stated that he could not describe good teaching since good teaching has to do with whether the student learns, not how the teacher has taught (Banta, 1999).

Educational Delivery as an Art and a Science

Outcomes assessment integrates the knowledge-base of the field of education and instruction through scientific methodology and rigor, with the overall purpose of supporting institutional self-renewal and continuous improvement. It is the task of the institution to develop an outcomes assessment methodology that maximizes the use of the institution's current data and information while producing results that yield a net benefit to the institution (Middle States Association of Colleges and Schools, 1996).

Yet there is also an art or skill in outcomes assessment. Webber (1979) indicated that "knowledge (science) without skill (art) is useless, or dangerous (pg. 6)" and, in outcomes assessment, making the connections between program and course learning objectives, teaching methodologies, outcome assessment instruments, and instructional improvement require cognitive skills (Middle States Association of Colleges and Schools, 1996).

As discussed in earlier chapters, Banta (1999) suggested that societal and market forces are changing expectations for higher education by: (1) a change in focus from teaching to learning; (2) the need to base teaching credentials on demonstrated competence; (3) a demonstration of the value added of higher education; (4) the need to deliver workforce training; (5) the use of technology in instruction; (6 and) the needs of the community.

Outcomes assessment opens the discussion about instruction from the learner's perspective. Hoerner (1998) found that matching instructors' teaching styles and instructional technology with student learning (using a Myers-Briggs psychological type questionnaire) produced positive learning results. Other articles dealing with the need to match learners with instructional methodologies include Krank (2001), Bernauer (1998), Dart and Boulton-Lewis (1998), and Zeegers (2001).

Pratt (1997) argued that, given this new orientation towards instructional outcomes, college faculty evaluation policies, procedures, and criteria would have to be altered. Colleges would now have to accentuate the substantive and de-emphasize the technical aspects of teaching, focus on outcomes over process, and include strategic concerns for institutional use of evaluation data. He recommended evaluating three aspects of teaching: planning, execution, and results, and he stressed the need to establish criteria, data sources, and the nature of the data.

Learner-Centered Educational Delivery

Outcomes assessment raises another issue concerning educational delivery systems, that of the role of the learner in the instructional process. The irony of the statement of the academic dean who knows good teaching when he sees it is in the context of learner-driven instruction, is that good teaching may involve no actual teaching by the instructor at all. One of the authors of this book remembers being evaluated in his undergraduate business capstone course by a fellow instructor who taught finance. The evaluator was appalled to find the faculty member seated in the back of the class while his senior business students ran discussions sessions on assigned readings, field research and business cases. The evaluator was perplexed as to how "anyone could learn anything" in the class if the instructor was not lecturing on the assigned material and conveyed his feelings during the evaluation debriefing. The response given was succinct and to the point: "Is it important how I teach or what my students learn?"

"The best way for a student to learn a well-defined and recorded body of knowledge is to teach it to [other] ... students who would [then] be evaluated ... on how much they taught rather than on how much they learned" (Ackoff, 1994, pg. 214-5). This rather radical notion bring us back to the cornerstone of academic planning that we described in Chapter One, that is, the role of the learner in the educational process.

Guffey, Rampp and Masters (1998) attempted to make a case for employing andragogical rather than pedagogical instructional methodologies to solve the learning problems of low skilled students. They believed that, in order for learning to become a felt need, students must be actively engaged in the learning process. "We agree with Rogers' thesis and suggest that a hallmark of adulthood is learning to take responsibility for one's actions. Methods of instruction in which the teacher is the center of the process and the disseminator of knowledge do not call on the learner to take responsibility. The learner becomes captive of the processes, procedures, and biases of the teacher. Approaching education from a teacher-centered perspective is tantamount to saying that the learner cannot behave as an adult" (pg.s 428-9). This paradigm shift produces a learner who views learning, not as an accumulation of facts, but as a method of solving real life problems, problems that are relevant to the learner.

According to Dunlap (1997), if learning how to learn (Ackoff, 1994) is the actual value-added benefit provided by an academic institution to any student, then creating lifelong learners is the primary educational objective. Lifelong learning skills need to be developed if educators intend for their students to stay current in their fields. Staying abreast of new innovations, research, techniques, and information is a prerequisite for successful decision-making and problem-solving on the job. Instructors need to become facilitators and mentors for learners by using instructional methodologies – collaboration, reflection, student autonomy, and intrinsically-motivating actualization – that help students develop the cognitive and self-directed learning skills needed to remain competitive in an ever changing professional climate, such as collaboration, reflection, student autonomy, and intrinsically-motivating activities.

No Single Instructional Delivery System is Best

With the need to actively involve the learner in the educational process, and the need to tailor instructional methodologies to fit the needs and learning styles of the learner, it is apparent that no one particular instructional method – lecture, case method, role play, problem-based field work, etc. – or one specific instructional delivery system, such as Internet instruction, will meet the needs of all of the institution's learners. Then how is a college or university to decide which instructional methods to utilize, and invest in both in terms of physical and human resources?

Guidelines for Delivering Effective Education

Guidelines, also known as policies, are defined as a set of instructions that provide the decision-maker advice, assistance and support when making a determination as to a specific course of action to follow (DuBrin, 2003). Unlike rules, guidelines allow decision-makers the discretion of varying from the guidelines if the situation so calls for it. With this understanding, we present the following guidelines for selecting education delivery systems.

Delivery Systems Must be Tied to the Institution's Academic Plan and its Support Plans.

In Chapter Two, we defined the academic plan as the plan that addresses the multiple roles of the academic community (learning center, spiritual center, career center, fitness center, entertainment center, and living center) and the relative mix of those roles in the context of the mission and strategy of the institution. We also noted that the academic plan can be broken down into four types: academic program plans, faculty development plans, administrative support plans, and learner service plans.

The institution's educational delivery system cuts across the academic program plans, faculty development plans, administrative support plans, and learner service plans in that it is the transformation process that nurtures student learning. For example, an educational delivery system based predominately upon classroom instruction must have the physical facilities and space in which to hold classes in; must recruit, train, and develop faculty with excellent platform instructional skills: must have a system for managing classroom allocation by instructional needs and class size, and have support personnel (advisors, counselors, tutors, mentors) to assist students in the selection of the proper courses to take and in their ability to learn through classroom instruction, such as study skills and taking notes. If this type of institution were to try to add a virtual component to its instruction, all of the supporting plans would have to be modified in order to accommodate this change, whether they are the related to computer LAN systems with the in-house capacity to on-line instruction, faculty trained to use on-line instructional software, student enrollment tracking through on-line registration systems, or student access to computers with internet connections.

There must be a clear fit or alignment of the educational delivery systems employed by the institution and the academic plan and its component plans or the institution will send very mixed signals to the learners in the system, the faculty, and staff of the institution.

For example, one of the author's institutions, one that delivers education predominately through classroom instruction to traditional day students, wanted to bolster classroom utilization by offering more courses during the evening and over the weekends. Surveys of current students, especially the adult learners, indicated that there was some interest in an evening program and this finding was echoed by research dealing with local businesses' employees. The institution decided to introduce an evening program and guaranteed that certain degree programs, business, accounting, and liberal studies, could be completed by taking only evening courses. A college course management matrix was developed, based upon these three degree programs that detailed which courses in the student's degree programs would be during which semesters at night. This matrix was distributed by the academic dean to the department chairs with the expectation that the matrix would be adhered to.

The program failed miserably. First, department chairs could not or would not schedule certain required courses during the evening sessions due to historically low enrollments at that time period. Secondly, many faculty members believed that three hour evening classes were counterproductive and would only agree to teach evening courses that met twice a week. Evening students, on the other hand, did not want to come to campus twice a week unless they could take two separate classes. No administrative offices were opened after 5 PM, so students who wanted to go to school in the evening could not register in the evening nor receive academic advisement. Lastly, many student services, such as the book store, had minimal service in the evening and students were forced to either go off-campus or use these services during the day. Simply stated, this daytime college did not have an academic plan to accommodate evening students and the evening program was bound to fail since it did not include support plans dealing with academic programming, administrative support services, faculty training, and student services.

Delivery Systems Must be Tied to the Institution's Strategic Plan

The strategic plan of the institution, continuing the discussion we began in Chapter Two, defines the college's market position and its role in the marketplace, with the role being defined through the college's competitive advantage and its strategic approach to the market. An institution's delivery system must first be based upon the institution's distinctive skills and competencies: that is, its teaching methodologies should be derived from the instructional skills and expertise of the faculty. According to Peters and Waterman (1982), an institution should "stick to the knitting" (pg. 294) by doing what it does well and by focusing on those centers of instructional excellence already present in the institution. For example, one cannot expect a computer-illiterate faculty to embrace web-based instruction unless one is prepared to train and reward the faculty for employing this instructional methodology. This action may in fact be counterproductive, since it may turn excellent lecturers into mediocre web facilitators.

Not only should the educational delivery system fit the instructional skills of the faculty, the delivery system must also fit the mission of the institution. Two year and local community colleges tend have as part of their mission statements concerns for access to education, what Rowley and Sherman (2001) called consumer-driven concerns. Their missions are defined in terms of affordability, catering to those who are academically-challenged or have more remedial educational needs (Guffey, Rampp and Masters, 1998), or have scheduling needs, or who are first generation college attendees.

Community colleges have a narrower focus than public comprehensive universities since they serve a smaller student population. Their educational delivery systems tend to be somewhat mixed in that they serve several populations whose needs vary from traditional classroom instruction, to evening and weekend classes, to distance and web-based instruction, co-operative education, and, at times, contract learning. As compared to public comprehensive universities, such as the University of Texas at Austin, Penn State University, and Miami University, community colleges have smaller classes taught by full-time faculty members, provide more academic and advising support, and seem to be more learner friendly. From a strategic perspective, community colleges are more consumer-driven than comprehensive universities for those students who desire personalized instruction and who do not want classes in large lecture halls.

Several institutions' educational delivery systems are so unique that it is their competitive advantage in the marketplace. We have already described two unique educational delivery systems, such as those of Union Institute and University, and Empire State College. Rowley, Lujan and Dolence (1998) described several other institutions and institutional consortiums that offer web-based degree programs. Excelsior College in New York (formerly Regents College) offers a distance learning model of education where students may earn credit by examination, courses through other accredited institutions, distance education, and training evaluated by the American Council on Education (http://www.excelsior.edu/ec_howit.htm, 8/29/2002).

Privately owned Capella University in Minneapolis, founded in 1993, is a regionally accredited online university that offers courses, certificates and degree programs, including MBA, doctorate, graduate and undergraduate degrees in business, technology, education, human services and psychology. Capella University has more than 5,000 learners using "e-learning" and innovative curriculum designed to create a virtual campus. Capella redefines the higher education experience for non-traditional learners, thereby offering an accessible and flexible education program that allows technology to remove the barriers of time and place (Carpella University, 2002).

As we also discussed in Chapter Two, a college's strategic approach refers to the relative activity or aggressiveness of the institution in the marketplace. Proactive academic institutions will embrace new instructional delivery systems, while analyzers will wait to have the proactive colleges make mistakes in working the bugs out of the new systems before they adapt it themselves. Defenders will continue their current method of instruction, regardless of market changes, and will change only if a new methodology is imposed by government agencies or accrediting bodies or if the change supports their current delivery systems. Reactors will not have an academic plan that addresses educational delivery systems and will haphazardly, at best in response to change.

There are numerous examples all of these differing types of strategic behaviors about educational delivery systems in the marketplace. One of the authors distinctly recalls the president of his university, when asked by the faculty about the use of Internet instruction, responding that the university would never move to virtual instruction since, as a teaching institution, the value-added for the student was classroom instruction and face-to-face contact with faculty. This defender strategic approach would have made inordinate sense except that the university was simultaneously decreasing the number of courses and sections being offered in an attempt to increase student/faculty class ratios and trying to strong arm faculty into using web-based instruction, becoming more provider-driven.

The university went so far as to have the information technology office setup up certain department's courses on the net (via WebCt) without permission from the faculty teaching the courses or training of the faculty on the instructional software. More importantly, the university never surveyed its student population to determine whether web-based instruction was desirable or not or at least which segments would desire it. The university, in fact and in deed, was far more reactive in nature in terms of this educational delivery system then it was defender. It is interesting to note that our prior two examples, Excelsior College and Capella University, are good cases in point of an analytical and proactive approach to the market in terms of the use of internet instruction. Capella is clearly proactive in that its entire instructional format is Internet instruction. Excelsior, on the other hand, incorporated internet communications into its program but has remained steadfast by not offering any course instruction over the net.

Delivery Systems Must be Tied to the Basic Educational Philosophies and Ideals of the Campus

The heart of the strategic plan is the vision that the institution has of its educational system, what Mintzberg (1987) would call its perspective or the way in which the institution views its role in the field of education. Rowley and Sherman (2001) have used the terms provider-oriented and consumer-oriented to describe the two differing worldviews that educational institutions possess regarding their students. "Being *provider-oriented* refers to the disposition of the institution to follow a more traditional academic approach (internally driven) ... being *consumer-oriented* refers to the disposition of the institution to follow a course that is more cognizant of market needs and market demands in designing its research agenda and curriculum base" (pg.s 31-32). Institutional philosophies are not black and white. These orientations form the end points of a continuum of educational philosophy towards learners. As discussed in chapter 1, three educational paradigms emerge (university-focused, consumer-focused, community-focused) from this continuum and form the basis in which the institution's teaching and learning strategies are developed.

It is clear that certain educational delivery systems are more provider-driven than others. The straight lecture method, for example, with the sage on the stage telling students what is knowledge is far more provider-driven than the faculty directed discussion method, which is in turn more provider-driven than student directed discussions. A continuum of instructional techniques can be constructed with faculty-driven instruction on one side, student-driven instruction on the other, and faculty/student collaboration at the center. It is possible to compare and contrast instructional delivery systems with the university's overall educational philosophy and determine the relative fit or alignment between them. Misfits (Miles and Snow, 1984) or misalignments (Kotter, 1978) will lead to ineffective instruction and have systemic side effects.

The introductory case at the beginning of this chapter highlighted what may happen when a misalignment is present. Dr. Schwartz utilized a far more student-driven, collaborative approach to course instruction than his colleagues on the rank and tenure committee and the mismatch resulted in Dr. Schwartz not receiving tenure. Faculty need to understand the range of acceptable instructional techniques and the social and economic support for more student-centered teaching in order to meet institutional expectations for quality instruction.

More importantly, misalignments send mixed and confusing messages to the marketplace. Students who are attracted to an institution that proclaims a family atmosphere with personalized instruction and caring faculty will be completely distraught if that institution operates large classes with adjuncts or teaching assistants, assuming the adjuncts or teaching assistants see their role as purely instructional. Furthermore, institutions that embrace student-centered or collaborative instruction as their core value yet offer students traditionally structured programs with required courses and only in-class or on-site instruction will find they have lower student enrollment and retention.

Delivery Systems Must be Tied to the Resource Base of the Institution

Course and educational delivery systems development and implementation, especially those that involve the use of instructional technology, require resources. Faculty members must be given the time, the training, the tools and the equipment necessary to develop the desire mix of instructional methodologies and must be rewarded for their course and curriculum development efforts. Faculty also must be properly oriented to the type of instructional methods the institution wants to employ and given a rationale for how these systems fit with the mission and values of the institution.

Since most institutions have very limited resources and low reserves, resources act as a delimiter to the more labor and technology intensive instructional methodologies. The institution must make conscious choices as to how it will invest its assets in order to meet its learning and educational objectives with the understanding that the institution may not be able to offer certain modes of instruction. Constrained resources require that the institution focus its educational distribution system and not offer all modes of instruction to all types of learners.

Since faculty members are the developers and implementers of the institution's educational delivery system, the strategic plan must set aside resources to educate the educators and support on-going faculty development. Faculty members must feel that course development plays a vital function in the mission of the institution. The way to reinforce those impressions is through the utilization of both extrinsic and intrinsic systems that focus on excellence in instructional development and course instruction – this may also have contractual implications. For example, one of the author's union contracts had to be modified to account for field work, team teaching, courses with enrollment over the designated class size, distance learning, and off-campus instruction. Ironically, the same contract allowed faculty to reduce teaching load by one course per semester if they opted to perform research.

Delivery Systems Must be Tied to the Research Arm of the Institution

The university must, in a systematic fashion, collect and analyze data not only on external and internal conditions but more explicitly on the changing educational delivery systems available in the marketplace and those being employed by competitive institutions. Although faculty may perform this function individually, and for their areas of expertise, it is paramount that the university understands the breadth of instructional techniques available to it and its competitors. Centralized data collection and storage on instructional techniques must be executed.

This information is vital to the strategic and academic planning processes since these delivery systems provide for market opportunities and defend against potential competitive threats in the form of alternative distribution channels that could be employed by the institution or its rivals.

Learning: A Research Mentality

Regardless of the particular mission or philosophy of the institution, all academic institutions are devoted to learning. By definition, then, they are devoted to research. Learning is not only the absorption of a body of knowledge, the encoding, filing, and storage of data, and the ability to answer questions and solve problems. "Problems are seldom *given* ... they usually have to be *taken*, extracted from complex situations. Problems are not out there waiting to be taken, they are abstractions extracted from reality by analysis" (Ackoff, 1994, pg.s 201-2).

Learning as Problem Formulation and Resolution

The fundamental attributes of learning is for the student to be able to formulate and answer questions based upon knowledge derived from primary and secondary data sources. The learner must first determine what is the problem or problems to be solved by gathering and examining prior literature on the topic. The learner must then determine whether enough data has been collected and analyzed in order to phrase a question or whether further research is necessary (Dubin, 1969).

Once enough information is gathered, the learner must examine the key facts and try to isolate symptoms, indicators of the problem, from the problem itself. For example, a business student examining a firm's profit and loss statement might note that the firm has been running at a loss. The loss of funds, liabilities exceeding revenues, is not the business's operating problem but an indication that the learner needs to examine the firm's cost structure and the firm's unit sales. The student might then identify operating inefficiencies or low sales as the possible moderating indicators, and would have to dig into the specificities behind these factors to determine the causes for these inefficiencies or these losses. The firm's operating system would have to be defined and explored, not only by examining the pieces of the system and how they fit together but also how the system interacts with the firm's operating environment (Ackoff, 1994).

Once the learner has defined the system in which the problem resides, the next step is to develop an educated guess as a possible solution and explain how the proposed solution would change the system and solve the problem. This would include signifying how the symptoms (i.e. profitability) would be impacted, with perhaps predictions to the direction and strength of the changes in the symptoms.

Once the problem is defined within the context of the system, the learner constructs a methodology for testing the proposed solution to the problem, using data gathering and statistical and/or qualitative techniques to test the solution, and determines whether the proposed solution would provide the desired results. The learner would note the limitations and weaknesses of his or her findings and decide whether the current suggested solution or alternatives possibly delineated from the analysis are viable or whether other possible solutions need to be tested (Lyons, 1965).

Although the above description of learning as research presents the scientific approach or method to learning, we are certainly open to phenomenological research as another learning approach. "Phenomenological research seeks essentially to describe rather than explain, and to start from a perspective free from hypotheses or preconceptions. The purpose of the phenomenological approach is to illuminate the specific, to identify phenomena through how they are perceived by the actors in a situation. In the human sphere this normally translates into gathering 'deep' information and perceptions through inductive, qualitative methods such as interviews, discussions and participant observation, and representing it from the perspective of the research participant(s)" (Lester, 2002, pg.1).

Dedication to Mode 2 Learning Styles

Whichever research method the learner employs, scientific or phenomenological, academic institutions need to inspire their faculty, their staff and their learners, to nurture life long learning, that is. Knowledge changes over time but the ability to obtain knowledge and employ wisdom to solve problems is eternal. This devotion to creating an independent, self-motivated, and self-directed learner must be incorporated into the strategic and academic plan. Otherwise the institution is paying lip service to both the learner and the educational process.

ɛɔ Chapter Eleven ᴄ੪

Tying It All Together in a Strategic Context

The deans were all gathered for the mid-year luncheon scheduled by the President of ABC University and the Vice-President for Academic Affairs to go over the new program offerings that were being proposed for the university. The president knew that all the deans were working very ardently and arduously with their department chairs and faculty to create innovative programs, the president wanted this opportunity to showcase their progress and to lay the ground work for taking these proposals as a package to the board of trustees. The president also hoped that by asking each dean to discuss their progress with the other deans. This would serve as a motivator for the less committed and/or successful deans.

Several of the deans had already discussed their programs with the group. The Dean of the School of Business had proposed that, given the university's unique location and the education industry's increased demands for doctoral degreed business instructors, that the School offer a Ph.D. in Business Administration. Since the School of Business was AACSB accredited, its doctoral program would be quite traditional. The Dean of Natural Sciences in conjunction with the Dean of Education, on the other hand, had proposed that the university take advantage of in-house expertise in oceanography and marine sciences. They also wanted to develop an off-campus living center which would include student housing and food facilities, traditional classrooms, and a fully operational mariner and aquarium. The aquarium would be open to the public and would feature educational programs for local school children run by the college students. The Dean of the Social Sciences had also proposed a very ambitious program which would be interdisciplinary in nature, involve a series of international experiences with an internship at each location, and would be based upon the notion of social and economic justice. Experiences might range from working in the Ecuadorian rain forests to working with a small business in Moscow. The program would employ individualized learning agreements comprising the student's entire educational program.

Other deans, including the Dean of Humanities, were still in the planning phase and had only a rudimentary outline of their proposed programs. They were less than forthcoming as to when their proposed programs would be ready to present and listed several reasons why they felt that they needed more time, resources, and information. More importantly, they needed to convince their faculty members of the need for program planning.

The vice-president was pleased with what she had heard from those deans who did offer program specifics. Each plan was well researched and based upon the competencies of the individual schools. Each plan expanded their program offerings and allowed the university to tap a population of students normally did not have access to. Yet the president's demeanor, which the vice-president had learned to read early on in her academic career, indicated that the president was not at all pleased, in fact he seemed downright incensed!

During a five-minute break, the vice-president cornered the president to see if she could discern what was wrong. "Something's just not right" the president replied. "It's not that certain deans were unable to present their proposed programs today, I can live with that and I understand their problems. But I know that something is amiss and we've overlooked something – it is like having an itch you can't scratch."

"Don't worry about it" replied the vice-president. "If it is that important I'm sure that it will come to mind." "You're probably right", responded the president. Yet the president's first impression was absolutely correct – something had been forgotten, or even worse, never considered in the first place.

In this scenario, the president seemed disturbed about the deans' presentations of their proposed academic proposals yet could not vocalize the cause of the disturbance. The deans had done exactly what the president had requested back in the situation in Chapter One. They developed new programs which they believed would add enrollment to the college either by proposing programs that would tap into their current customer base or creating innovative programs that might attract new students to the college.   Besides the obvious cost considerations -- a major consideration since the university was experiencing negative cash flows -- and the need to demonstrate that revenues derived from these programs would surpass costs, the real question was to isolate what was missing from either the content of the proposals or the process in which the proposals were developed?

As we described in Figure 2.7 in Chapter Two, academic program planning is subsidiary to academic planning, which is in turn complementary to strategic planning. Academic program planning, as explained in Chapter Four, is a portfolio of courses and program offerings available from the institution and includes both prioritization of those programs and the relative expectation of new program development over time.   From a collaborative standpoint, that of a learning community, learners and other key stakeholders should be included in the creation of the program plans in order to ensure that the process works for all participants.   As we noted in Chapter Five, there needs to be a campus-wide initiative and charge, a set of guidelines to help schools and departments within those schools determine the scope and context of their academic program plans within the overall academic plan and the strategic plan of the university.   The program planning is a top-down, bottom-up planning process.   Last, as we discussed in Chapter Ten, educational delivery systems, or the way in which information is imparted to the learner, are components of the academic program plan and must be tied into the strategic plan and vision of the campus.

So, one might ask, where did the president's approach to program planning go wrong?

Academic Program Planning Starts with Strategic Planning

Academic program plans are developed to enact the institution's strategic and academic planning.   Otherwise, the academic program mix and the institution's strategy will be both unintended and haphazard.   The President of ABC University never addressed issues of competitive strategy, such as low cost or differentiation.   A market approach – whether the proposals are provider, consumer, or community driven – was cast aside as were distinctive competencies, and institutional vision, and mission.   As a result, the academic deans created academic programs in a strategic vacuum.   There was a complete disconnect between what the University was, who it served, and how it served them.   The university's mission, the university's competitive advantage, the university's distinct strategy and its centers of excellence, and the university's resource base were all disregarded along with the academic program planning process.

It is not surprising, then, that the president was concerned with the deans' proposed programs.   There was never a discussion as to how these programs strengthened the university's competitiveness or added to the university's program portfolio.   These programs could have been proposed for any university, by any faculty, for any set of new learners. The critical issue for the president to address is whether these programs fit into the institution's current strategy, require a change in strategic position, and/or require resources and skills not currently available at the university.

What Should the Strategic Plan say about Academic Content and Pedagogy?

Looking at the case of contemporary colleges and universities, it should be evident that the strategic plan must encompass more then just the strategic positioning of the institution and its competitive approach to the marketplace. Academic content and its support services must first be tied to the institutional mission and the learners included in that mission. For example, one of the authors teaches at an institution which is a liberal arts college where non-traditional, interdisciplinary and applied programs (such as the psychology of biology, environmental science, education, creative writing) have much larger enrollments than the traditional programs (such as psychology, art, chemistry, philosophy). In particular, interdisciplinary science programs constitute over 60% of undergraduate enrollment at the institution.

This has caused something of an identity crisis for the institution and its faculty members. Are they members of a liberal arts college which just happens to have centers of excellence in interdisciplinary areas or are they members of an interdisciplinary college, heavily focused in the sciences, which also possesses some traditional programs? Although these statements may seem as if they are two sides of the same coin, they represent differing philosophies and values. Conflicts arise in faculty-wide meetings since these differing perspectives impact every part of campus life from the core curriculum to capital investment. Is a new library more important than a new marina?

More importantly, the two definitions of the institution denote contrary strategic market positions and differing approaches to program content and pedagogy. If the college were to emphasize its nontraditional, interdisciplinary programs in its mission and through its academic plan, the college would be positioning itself as a proactive differentiator, that is actively seeking students who subscribe to a nontraditional educational. The college would also be developing more innovative educational delivery systems in order to add value to the learner's overall educational experience. Since most learners, even in the 21st century, are seeking more traditional degrees even though they may be very applied in nature, the college would be focusing its marketing and educational efforts on a small group of learners, a market niche, and putting its resources into investments which yield notoriety in course and program content and delivery. Such a school might hire world renowned faculty who are experts in their fields, offering field and international experiences, or become a theme college – perhaps a greening college. There would also be a limited number of competitor colleges since the programs offered would be of such a specialized nature as to preclude mass duplication since there would be so few students in total to garner. This reduces the number of new entrants.

The Strategic Perspective is Crucial in all Aspects of Academic Program Planning. Rowley and Sherman (2001) would categorize this college as a specialty college and note that these colleges and universities tend to be one-dimensional. Their academic programs are quite limited beyond the specialty areas. "For [some] colleges and universities [which are] deciding to become specialty colleges and universities ... developing a unified culture is one of the major stumbling blocks ..." (pg. 51). The high to moderate risks associated with this strategy are tied to the popularity of their offerings and to the institution's ability to quickly react quickly to market changes through program modification and development. Inflexible colleges, colleges with a high percentage of tenured faculty in specialty areas, may find it "extremely difficult to close down particular schools, fire tenured faculty members, ..." (pg. 51).

The alternative approach would be for the college to de-emphasize its specialty programs, becoming either a comprehensive university by offering a plethora of programs in order to attract a large array of students. Or perhaps it might become a small college offering a narrower grouping of programs with more emphasis on teaching than the comprehensives. Given this college's particular resource base and enrollment of under 5000 students, however, the only alternative left is the small college option. Small colleges' competitive advantage include that "they usually provide a tremendous amount of interaction among administrators, staff, faculty, and students" (p. 45) and appeal to the student who wants smaller class sizes, instruction by full-time members of the faculty, personal attention, and participation in on-going research.

This is an alternative differentiation strategy than those employed by specialty colleges since it is not the programs which attract students to the college but the college's friendly and tailored learning environment which is focused on students' non-academic needs. In business management terms, specialty colleges invest in program development as their products while small colleges invest in their processes, primarily the delivery of services to the student. Small colleges tend to be more defensive in nature: that is, they tend not to develop new programs and try not to attract new types of students but rather "do an excellent job of recruiting – seeking out students who will blend very well into their culture and then providing them with the attention and services that they will need to perform well within that culture" (pg. 47).

Unlike specialty colleges, small colleges "have a relatively small faculty whose primary discipline has been broadened to include related disciplines, in which the faculty may have little training (for example having a professor in marketing teach courses in management and finance) [and] resources ... are woefully undersupplied and sometimes even antiquated" (pg. 45). The high risk associated with this strategy lies in small colleges' lack of resources, their inability to employ economy of scale in course instruction, the heavy dependence on consumer-driven enrollment, and their need to have excellent enrollment management skills.

The Need for a Clear and Decisive Mission and Strategy. The college needs to have an agreement among the faculty as to the mission of the institution and the pedagogical values affiliated with that mission, so that it can translate its strategy and academic imperatives into specific course instructional methodologies.

For example, in the above college the interdisciplinary faculty and those who teach in specialized programs value experiential learning – cooperative education, internships, travel courses – and alternative modes of demonstrating competency in a course of study using in-house challenge exams, life experience credit, external credit-based examinations. The more traditional members of the faculty, those who teach in such majors as English and history, value the classroom experience. If this college were a specialty institution, the faculty experts in their fields would determine the relative merits associated with specific pedagogical techniques including the alternative modes of instruction. Given the large numbers of students in the specialty programs, these faculty experts would constitute a dominant coalition to determine the overall pedagogical approach of the institution as these techniques would enhance program instruction and visibility. On the other hand, if the focus were on maintaining the traditional liberal arts elements of the college, then the faculty as a whole, not the experts in specialty areas, would determine what constitutes appropriate instruction; given the currently faculty this would be predominately classroom instruction.

The President of ABC University, in the opening case, has put the cart before the horse. Before he can ask his deans to develop academic programs he must first work with them to help define the mission of the institution as derived from an analysis of the market conditions in which they are operating in and the particular competencies of the institution. The mission can be defined in terms of the relative consumer orientation of the university, the needs of the learners addressed by the university and the roles of the faculty. Once the mission is defined, in the context of the organization's marketplace and distinctive competencies, the president then must work with the deans to iron out a grand strategy for the university as well as its strategic competitive approach.

It would have aided the deans' program development if the president could have described the college's current program mix using Figure 4.5, The Academic Program Planning Matrix. This would have clearly delineated which learning centers are or are not being addressed as well as the faculty's roles in implementing those programs. The focus of the discussion would be on whether the current program mix fairly represents the current mission and takes advantage of market opportunities, and ask such questions such as whether faculty members and other resources are properly deployed in light of the mission and those opportunities. Once the current situation has been analyzed then the deans, with guidance from the president and vice-president, can either determine how best to pursue growth in enrollment and the appropriate programs and educational delivery systems to employ.

Academic Pedagogy Must be Tied to the Learner the College or University Serves. Programs must employ teaching techniques which meet, if not exceed, the expectations of the learner who enrolls at the institution. For example, students who enroll in a small college have the expectation of being in small classes taught by full-time faculty, where the faculty member is personable, approachable, and knows the learner's name. Students in specialty colleges, on the other hand, might expect to be taught by the experts in their field of specialization, with the focus on cutting-edge learning with state-of- the-art theory and practice.

A university that chooses to recruit traditional students must serve the needs of those learners from an instructional perspective. Classes need to be offered on campus, during reasonable times, which minimize evenings and weekends and allow students to have a full residential experience while allowing time for clubs, sports, part-time work. Resources must be focused upon providing a comfortable classroom environment, augmented by technology in order to enhance the quality of instruction. This includes funding for faculty instructional development.

The reality is that there are very few true traditional students. Most students who graduate from high school are comfortable with both traditional lecture-method instruction as well as non-traditional forms of instruction, such as group projects, field case work, co-operative education, and distance learning. But they may also have special interests and needs that may preclude them from being traditional day students such as having a full time job. Given the university's mission and its core competencies, the institution must be able to determine its relative breadth of pedagogical techniques and related support services. For example, a college that wants to offer an evening program for its adult learners must be able to offer its entire breadth of core course at night, as well as advanced courses in those majors that it would offer as part of the evening program. This will require not only having some of the full-time faculty teach in the evening, maintaining access to such academic support services as registration, tutoring, advising, food services, and computer labs.

In order to ensure adequate services and quality faculty instruction, certain colleges have compartmentalized (Galbraith, 1973) their nontraditional programs – that is, made them separate, stand-alone programs with their own faculty and their own administration. This has worked well for Marist College's evening program and Dominican College's weekend program, in that each has selected faculty who are comfortable teaching adult learners and who are cognizant of adult learner needs. Travel courses and programs, international experiences, exchange programs, co-operative education and honors programs may be operated independently.

The view of the modern Information Age learner, as we described in Chapters One and Two, requires that institutions not only understand the individualized learning needs of each particular student, but that the college deal with the larger issue of the learner's desire for certain pedagogical approaches which may or may not fit the university's mission and/or skill set. The university must be prepared to meet the challenges posed by these new learners and dedicate the resources necessary to properly serve them, or yield their market position to institutions that will.

We are not suggesting that every college or university embrace every pedagogical approach desired by students nor are we saying that colleges and universities should ignore market trends and hide behind tradition and past practices. What we are advocating is that every postsecondary educational institution needs to address these issues and determine what it can and, more importantly, cannot offer students in terms of instructional options. Porter (1985) notes that trying to be all things to all people, especially in those areas where the institution does not have the resources or competencies necessary to provide adequate service, is a formula for disaster. We also suggest that institutions with limited resources stick to the knitting (Peters and Waterman, 1982), that is, do what they know and do what they do best. Institutions that try to shift their missions by offering new pedagogical approaches without the proper planning and economic support will find that they serve new learners badly while losing the learners that they currently serve. One of the authors of this book, for instance, observed that his institution's attempt to offer an evening program failed not only because of the lack of academic and administrative support for the program but also because many traditional day students, who did not want to take courses at night, were in fact forced to take night courses in order to graduate in a timely manner. This led to a drop in retention and ill-will among the daytime students.

Communication and Coordination are the Keys to Successful Academic Program Planning

Having an academic program plan derived from a broader academic plan which was in turn developed from the university's strategic plan is a difficult task. A tremendous amount of coordination is required to flesh out derivative plans clearly tied to the mission and strategic approach of the institution. How can such coordination actually take place?

Essentially, formulation of program plans requires that the college develop a communication system reducing task uncertainty and ensuring that everyone in the planning process understands their responsibilities and has access to needed information. Institutions can accomplish this by either increasing the speed in which the organization can process information or reducing the amount of information required by an individual to create his or her portion of the program plan. Organizational communications can become more effective by either redesigning the organization's structure or by changing the work processes in which the academic plan is formulated (Galbraith, 1973; 1977). Figure 11.1 below depicts the options available to an institution designing its communication system.

Reducing Information Need - Creation of Slack Resources. The term slack resources refers to providing individuals or planning groups with additional or extra time and/or capital resources which allow them to perform their tasks more efficiently. This approach to program planning allows for problems and errors in the planning process by reducing the level of performance required by those who construct the plan. The intent is to accept the inherent tradeoff between the costs associated with organizational changes and what might be needed to increase information flow.

Figure 11.1
Design Strategies for Effective Communications[1]

	Structural Change	Work Processes Change
Reduce Information Needs	**Creation of Self-Contained Tasks**	**Creation of Slack Resources**
Increase Information Processing	**Creation of Lateral Relations**	**Investment in Vertical Information Systems**

In the case of ABC University, the president could have allowed some of his deans additional time and resources in which to develop their proposed programs. This may have allowed those deans to complete their work as the other deans could included a competitor analysis by determining which schools offer similar programs. Resource lists and enrollment projections would also help.

Reducing Information Need - Creation of Self-Contained Tasks. Another way to reduce the need for lateral or vertical communication in program planning is by the creation of self-contained tasks. This method changes the structure of the organization by creating independent operating units, elsewhere called strategic business units, which possess all of the resources necessary in which to perform a task or function. There is no need for coordination between academic departments, or between academic departments and administrative services, since all of the instructional and service needs of the student are provided within that one unit. All the resources and information are available within the unit in order to develop the

---

[1] Adopted from Jay Galbraith (1973), p. 15.

program plan, and units have the authority with which to develop and implement academic programs.

The inherent weakness of this is duplication of effort inherent in providing similar services within different operations, such as each unit being responsible for offering all courses, including core courses. This creates a diseconomy of scale: there are few cost savings associated with serving more students, since these students may require the addition of faculty, staff, and classrooms. Examples of this type of structure include the separate colleges within a university system, the Weekend College at Dominican of New York, and the Friends World Program at Southampton College.

The President of ABC University allowed his deans to act autonomously in developing their plans with their faculty. However, it is clear that they do not have the authority with which to move forward in the implementation of their plans. Their authority to plan may not be recognized by a reticent faculty, since they had to report these plans to the president and vice president who in turn would have to seek approval from the board of trustees. A self-contained structure, however, may work for several of the proposed programs (such as the marine living center and the abroad programs) if the university does not want to capitalize on its existing faculty and administrative services pool or if the university wants to differentiate these programs from its more traditional offerings.

Increasing Information Flow – Vertical Information Systems (VIS). The college can purchase systems which permit it to process information more quickly while not overloading the college's capacity to process that information. This investment should increase the ability of the person or committee formulating the academic program plan by collecting information at the source and directing it to the person or persons who require it the most. VIS may be as simple as increasing the rate in which information is sent to academic program planners or may be as sophisticated as providing an on-line, real-time database for access to all internal planning documents as well as external information on the marketplace.

Many colleges and universities have offices of institutional research whose sole task it is to gather, organize, and disseminate data about the institution and its marketplace. These offices may use mainframe or intranet systems to provide a broad access base and allow program planners, regardless of their location, access to this critical information. Secondly, the VIS may also allow program planners from differing schools to share their planning information, comment upon each others' work, and conduct virtual meetings.

The President of ABC University could have employed a VIS to check on the progress of the deans, and offer guidance. The president and the provost would have known which deans had made progress and which had not. This would have allowed the president and the vice president the ability to provide assistance and support. The deans could also use this system for communicating with their chairs and their faculty, synchronizing these subordinates' activities.

Increasing Information Flow – Lateral Relations. Lateral relations, the creation of a secondary, supporting organization structure, moves the information and decision-making down the organizational ladder by creating bridging mechanisms between departments, divisions, and schools as well as between academic units and administrative units. The coordinating mechanism can range from direct contact between two academic planners in differing departments, to formalized liaison. Linking pin, or integrating roles, to the development of a committee and/or a cross-functional work team are also possible (Fujishin, 2001). The greater the need to coordinate actions between the institutional units, the more sophisticated the coordinating mechanisms will be.

Most colleges and universities already use lateral relations through their committee structures. These coordinating mechanisms seem to work fairly well at bringing disparate parts of the institution together, performing many of the integrative functions of the university: enforcing academic standards, curriculum development, outcomes assessment, awarding promotion, and tenure. Planning committees tend to be the norm at most academic institutions for coordinating program planning and seem to be an acceptable way or communicating and organizing academic program planning.

Referring back to our opening case example, the president could have organized the deans into a program planning committee and empowered them to work together to develop a comprehensive academic program plan that would have included every school in the planning process. This would have allowed all schools to collaborate, which had already occurred in one case through direct contact, while the planning committee decided whether other schools might need to propose new programs given the strategy of the institution and the institution's limited resources.

The Communication Strategy Must Fit the Strategy and Mission of the Institution, Including the Role of the Learner. Different communication strategies imply differing approaches to learners -- consumer-driven, provider-driven, or community-driven --

and may not fit well with the institution's overall strategy as a low-cost provider or as a differentiator as suggested in Table 11.1 below.

Table 11.1
Aligning Communications, Learner Orientation, and Institution Strategy

Communications Strategy	Learner Orientation	Institutional Strategy
Slack Resources	Provider	Differentiation
Self-Contained Tasks	Consumer/Community	Focused Differentiation
Vertical Information	Provider/Consumer/ Community	Low Cost/ Differentiation
Lateral Relations	Provider/Consumer/ Community	Differentiation

By using slack resources, the institution has the ability to add cost, resources, or time to program planning and make it easier, although more costly, for program planners to formulate and implement their plans. Since the cost involved in this communication issue does not directly solve the communication problem by speeding up the process of communicating, the cost attached to this action adds to the basic costs involved with program planning without offsetting cost savings for future planning processes. Institutions competing on low cost may find that they must pass these planning costs onto their learners through higher tuition which in itself may produce a competitive disadvantage. Differentiated institutions have a greater leeway in absorbing these costs, as the difference between their revenues and expenses is much higher than their low cost counterparts; they may well find that their students can absorb these costs given their relative price insensitivity.

Self-contained tasks allow the program planners to make decisions with their separate operating units. It also allows the planners to deal directly with their learners' needs and tailor-make their academic programs. Because these are stand alone units, the opportunity exists to invite learners into the program development process and to create a community of learners independent from the mainstream university's operation. Union Institute and University (Cincinnati, Ohio) treats each doctoral student's program as a self-contained unit. The university experience, as determined by the student's learning agreement, is unique for each and every student, with the unit determining whether the student has met the developed program requirements.

VIS, also referred to as management information systems (MIS), may add a tremendous cost to the university in the short run if they opt for fairly sophisticated computer equipment. But it will inevitably reduce the cost of planning in the long run, which is a low cost provider strategy. This is not to say that differentiators would not employ such a communications tactic. In fact they would if they believed that the additional information or the speed of gathering it would allow them to better understand and address the needs of their particular learners. The difference is that low cost providers will look for the most efficient VIS which meets their program planning needs, those with the least cost, while differentiators will opt for more costly systems that may provide greater flexibility and capacity to meet future needs. The deployment of the VIS and the question of access will, however, will be determined by the institution's learner orientation.

Lateral relations add cost to the communication system by supplementing machine power with people power. People augment the reporting and computer-based systems of the institution through formalized networking. This allows differentiator institutions to have their program planning specialists in each unit interact with one another, perhaps creating new and innovative programs that share elements from each unit. Again, the level of the involvement of the learner in these networks will be a product of the college's philosophy concerning students.

Many colleges have students sit on academic committees, including program planning, yet this does not necessarily lead to a more community-based planning system. The varying roles that these students take on such committees -- figurehead, spokesperson, or negotiator -- will determine their relative value to the committee and the college's learner orientation (Mintzberg, 1975).

The New Paradigm Revisited: Learner-Focused Education

"Let's get this meeting started, shall we? Thank you for your attention. As you all know, today's meeting has been called to discuss the proposal by the English department to implement contract learning for their Master's Degree in Writing program. Would the representative of the English department kindly provide us a short overview of the proposal?"

"I would be more than happy to," responded the representative. *"The English department has perused several nontraditional models of education, including Empire State College, the University of Phoenix, Walden University, Nova Southeastern, Bellevue University, and Excelsior College. We have decided to shift from a traditional, menu-driven and credit-based program of instruction to a program that combines competency-based testing and contract learning. Admittance to the program will still be based upon a formula which includes GRE scores and undergraduate grade point average, but it will also include writing samples, interviews--by phone, e-mail or in-person--and a resume. The admissions committee will be comprised of five individuals: a faculty member, an alumnus, a current student, an admissions counselor, and a local writer. The decision of the committee can be challenged by the applicant with the Dean of Humanities arbitrating the decision. You have all had a chance to read the proposal, so if you have any questions I'd be happy to answer them."*

"I have a question," requested the representative from the philosophy department. *"On page six of the proposal, there is a discussion of the assessment instruments to be employed once an applicant has been admitted but has not yet entered the program. What specific methods of assessment will be employed?"* *"Although not described in great detail,"* countered the representative of the English department, *"the testing instruments have both quantitative and qualitative components. Secondly, an accepted student's writing portfolio will also be evaluated by at least two faculty members .... "*

The Dean of Humanities, an ad hoc member of this curriculum committee, sat silently admiring the work of the committee. The members were well prepared, civil to one another, and actively engaged in a discussion about a significant new program for the university and the School of Humanities. They were committed to working with the faculty and administration to strengthen the School of Humanities.

The English Department proposal was a good case in point. The committee reached out to local writers, alumni, current students and faculty, and developed a cutting-edge proposal that included many of the ideas from each of these groups. They had even started their own listserv, which aided in soliciting feedback from distant writers and alumni.

Yes, the student and alumni committee for curriculum development had exceeded the Dean's expectations. The committee was quite successful in making substantive academic program changes. If the Dean could now figure out a way to get some of her own senior faculty to act with such team spirit and enthusiasm, her life would be complete!

Why is Learner-Focused Education so Important?

Throughout this book, we have emphasized the need for a more consumer-based orientation in devising the college or university academic plan. One might argue that, in fact, colleges and universities really do this anyway – research is done to satisfy some need, often the need of an off-campus partner, such as the government, technology companies or medical and pharmaceutical companies. Isn't this being consumer-oriented? Of course it is, but this isn't the heart of our concern.

But doesn't the university provide major service to the community through both free advising as well as paid consulting? Certainly, members of the academic community are regarded as experts to whom many community groups and organizations, as well as community businesses, turn to for trustworthy advice.

Certainly then, the argument continues, we are not suggesting that we don't care about what students learn, or that we don't provide an education that our students need and will set them up for a lifetime of success. Are the authors suggesting that? To this, we reply that yes, we do have a problem with what we teach and how we teach it. Throughout this discussion, we have offered a set of arguments that directly suggest that in the interchange between instructor and learner, the instructor needs to form a deeper understanding and appreciation for the needs of the learner.

We do not believe that instructors and professors are somehow malevolent in their approach to the classroom. This is clearly not true, and hardly our contention. Rather, we reject the central myth of higher education, which over the history of the academy has spawned a stereotyping of the classroom instructor as all-wise, unapproachable, and the only brain in the room. We have tended to ascribe to the instructor something like guru status, a position of reverence and even awe which has fostered the notion that the professor knows everything, the student nothing, and that it is the responsibility of the professor to enlighten. It is this perception we attack.

The modern classroom is populated by an instructor who knows a lot but not everything, not even in his/her own field of expertise. The instructor is joined by a group of students, to whom we refer as learners, who know something but are there to learn more. In identifying a gap between present knowledge and perfect knowledge, both instructor and learner should engage in the creation of a social contract: that each will help the other to better understand the material and make it applicable to the world beyond the classroom.

The Learner Drives the Learning Process

There is clearly a responsibility on the part of the instructor to provide the information that the learner is there to obtain. The central question then becomes, "Does the learner know what she/he needs to know?" The answer to this question is that it depends. Especially in a general education atmosphere, many learners question why the college or university require certain courses to obtain a degree, when what they really want is encapsulated in their major course of study. What about the motivation to learn here? Do the learners know what they *should* get from these courses complementing their major course of study? The authors will not try to argue here against a well-rounded education as being important for every college and university graduate; we agree on the importance of this. Our concern is rather that the reasons for requiring courses are often not shared with the learner. As professors ourselves, we understand the importance of a quality liberal education. All learners with college and university degrees should write well, be excited to read and be informed; appreciate nature and science; have a sense of history; be able to understand and use complex mathematically-based systems, especially in a technological world; have a basic understanding of human behavior and interactions; and be aware of the business world they will enter into after graduation. Yet this reasoning is more implied than related. Learners come to be educated but are passive in the process until they begin to understand that higher education is really interdisciplinary experience: appreciating Shakespeare helps the physics major better understand the roles of art and music in the world.

By including the learner in the purpose and design of the learning process, educators move learners from passive to active. Once informed, the learner can then become motivated, perhaps even highly motivated, able to relish all the opportunities found in a college experience. Once motivated, the learner becomes involved and contributes to not only her/her own learning but to the learning experience of everyone in the classroom.

The Academy Can Learn from the Learner

We have suggested that the institution needs to seek input from its service community. Does the individual learner have a role in this input function? As it turns out, yes, the learner does. Providing there are choices of other colleges and universities within the service area, the informed learner goes to the institution which meets her/his needs. This means that while no single institution could or should try to be everything, each can develop its centers of excellence, publicize them, and then appeal to those learners in the area what can most benefit from its programs.

As an aside, we want to comment on the role of student evaluations and how they should inform the institution of the needs and wants of the learner. Frankly, neither of us has yet to find a course evaluation instrument which honestly measures whether or not a learner has achieved the level of knowledge to which he/she was entitled. Most course evaluation forms tend to be popularity contests, ask questions for which there are much better sources for answers (for example: "Did the course have an ethics component?" – a question that is better answered by a reading of the course syllabus), or set up the instructor for punishment or reward during annual evaluations. Yet this is a marvelous opportunity to get honest feedback on the learning experience from the learner's point of view. We urge academic program planners to consider designing a feedback form that answers substantive questions about the learning which has occurred, to develop questions that challenge the substance and method of the course as opposed to the aesthetics. With this type of a survey, then yes, the learner would have a meaningful input on the material related in the classroom.

What are the Barriers that Might Hinder Implementing a Learner-Focused Planning Process?

The role of tradition, history and culture, as we have suggested above, can be a major impediment toward moving toward a more learner-focused process. It is hard to take a large faculty with a provider-centered orientation and transform it to a consumer-focused teaching corps. It is hard to overcome a proud tradition, to say that we are now leaving the Industrial Age and entering the Information Age, and that we should abandon traditional practices.

Change is always difficult. For denizens of the Ivory Tower change has always been internally created rather than something that others created and we adapted to. Academic freedom, intellectual inquiry, laboratory research, and providing a quality education are honorable aspects of the traditional academy. In such a proud environment, of course change is going to be a difficulty program to sell.

Other barriers are taking paths of least resistance and muddling through difficult times. As largely independent contractors, college and university professors believe that they hold their positions based on what they know, and what the institution believes they are capable of achieving in the future. This semi-autonomous relationship tends to bring with it a detachment that suggests "regardless of what the college wants to do, it really won't affect me – and if they try, I'm tenured, and I will wait it out." While the tenure system is in place primarily to protect academic freedom, more and more regulatory and governmental administrators question the value of tenure. It tends, they believe, to establish an entrenched group of arrogant faculty members resistant to meeting the needs of a changing society.

While regulators and governmental administrator may express frustration with faculty members and tenure, they also create a barrier to change by controlling resources. Particularly is this true in state colleges and universities, as change often comes as bureaucratic nightmare. Private institutions are not immune. Alumni, grant providers, national governmental funding sources and other stakeholders often make substantive change extremely difficult. We do not suggest that these stakeholders actually prevent colleges and universities from being more learner-oriented; instead, they tend to only support existing programs which have demonstrated success on one level or another, and they make it very difficult for such programs to make major structural or philosophical changes.

Most colleges and universities survive despite themselves. There is a plethora of colleges and universities around which do not provide good teaching, research, or service – but survive anyway. They defy the marketing imperative, and plod along on a decent endowment base, state support, or creative accounting. These skew the field, and suggest that higher education will survive on sheer inertia, regardless of the challenges. So why change?

All of these barriers exist, but none should triumph.. More than survival defines a successful or quality academic program. This is the clear challenge to the academic planning process, and why it is inextricably tied to strategic planning. No one is guaranteed a successful future, and this includes colleges and universities. The better institutions of the 21st Century will be those which have seen the needs of their service areas and have overcome any and all barriers to meeting external needs.

How Can We Ready the College or University for Learner-Focused Planning?

We believe that the most important thing colleges and universities can do is engage in substantive faculty development programs. As we discussed in earlier chapters, we firmly believe that today's instructors and professors really do want to be effective in the classroom, just as they seek to be successful in their research and service activities. The issue is that most instructors teach based on the models from which they themselves learned, primarily the lecture. How do these people learn new methods? How to they test their classroom presence to assure that they are the best that they can be? How do they move from being the "sage on the state" to being the "guide on the side?" The best answer is an institution-wide commitment to substantive faculty development programs.

The academic plan needs to address this issue squarely and honestly. It is not enough to assume that doctorally-prepared instructors and professors know how to teach and do it well. Very few doctoral programs do this, hence the reliance on the mentor process. Instead, the academic plan needs to help faculty set its own academic direction. Institutionally-supported faculty development programs can help align these two forces, and insure a learner-focused orientation.

Including administrators and learners in the change process will solidify the overall process of academic planning.. Administrators need to understand the direction of the academic plan, its motivations, drivers and intended results. Learners need to feel that they have a right to participate in their own education, that they will be the big winners in helping to create an educational environment based on active instead of passive learning.

It would be a mistake not to bring the reward system into this discussion. Psychology, sociology, and organizational behavior all tell us that people respond best when they see benefits for themselves. This is one of the reasons why we have a problem with colleges and universities which expect faculty members to provide for their own faculty development, expending the teacher's own resource base to benefit the institution. A college or university which values its faculty resources will invest in them. Altruism is great, but when a college or university expects altruism from its faculty to save resources the institution misjudges the motivations and dedication of its most important institutional resource. The motivation for change *should* instead originate with the employer because *the employer will benefit* from the result. Rewards can inspire and motivate. If the academic plan recognizes and uses this basic principle, it can help create a significantly improved faculty resource and, hence, a significantly improved academic program.

Implementation – The Real Test of Academic Program Planning

Rowley and Sherman (2002) noted that the formulation of a good plan, whether it be a strategic or academic plan, is only the first part of a successful planning process. Program planning implementation, putting the academic program plan into action, "is the ability to forge {subsequent} links in the causal chain so as to obtain the desired results" (Pressman and Wildavsky, 1973, p. xxi). This definition of implementation requires that goals and objectives are developed as part of the plan. These goals may be institutional in nature, or for individual schools or departments, or deal directly with learners' needs..

Nutt (1992) indicated that the key features of successful implementation include recognition of the need for a change. Change agents must take charge while key managers commit to the change, and change agents gather and disseminate information while offering credible ideas and solutions. There needs to be involvement at several organizational levels, and it must be understood that success is gradual. Unsuccessful implementations seemed to be marred by disagreements over the need for change, lack of leadership, process failures such as poor formulation, option generation, and evaluation, and the use of unilateral approaches.

In the next section we will examine some of the factors related to academic program implementation.

Implementation: Planning Components

The seeds of failure may have already been planted through the program development process. Academic programs must have face validity by seeming to meet the needs and desires of the learner, and include methods for implementing and evaluating the program while also offering a budget of expenses.

Goals and Objectives. Program goals and objectives include those that address such issues as financial success of the institution and the program,, productivity expressed by number of   graduating students, competitive position,, faculty and staff development, employee and student relations, technological leadership, and public and professional responsibility (Pearce and Robinson, 2000). For these goals to become meaningful to the institution they must be quantified and measurable, prioritized, flexible, motivating, appropriate to the mission of the institution, achievable (Pearce and Robinson, 2000) understandable, and acceptable (Barnard, 1938).

Policies, Procedures, and Rules. Colleges and universities should develop plans to directly support the academic program planning process. These usually entail the development of program guidelines, or policies, with operating procedures and rules. Policies should include a set of guidelines that assist administrators, faculty, and staff to make decisions, but also allow for discretion.   Direction is provided, though the individual is left to make the decision on his or her own.   A good example would be the waiving of a course requirement in an academic program by the chair of the department.

Rules, on the other hand, are expectations of behavior and are usually associated with negative consequences for breaking them. For example, students must maintain a certain academic average in order to be in a particular major; if they do not maintain that average they may be disqualified. Procedures are a set of rules which assist in carrying out a task or function, and must be accurately followed in order to complete the requirement.

Scorecards and KPIs. A relatively new method employed by the business sector to operationalize specific strategies is the Balanced Scorecard, attributed to Kaplan and Norton (1996). This approach requires that institutions list their objectives, their measurement instruments of those objectives, their specific targets, and their initiatives for four key performance areas: finance, customer, internal business processes, and learning and growth. Dolence, Rowley and Lujan (1997) proposed a similar methodology for colleges and universities based upon the concept of key performance indicators (KPIs), as we discussed in Chapter Six. They observed that KPIs can be developed for the institution, the school, the department, and even for a course, and suggested that KPIs may be employed at the program level as well. They also indicate that KPIs usually deal with academics, enrollment, administration, resources, campus support, facilities and information technology.

We suggest developing objectives and KPIs for each proposed program based upon Figure 4.5, The Academic Program Planning Matrix as shown in Figure 12.1 below.

Figure 12.1
Key Performance Indicators and Program Planning

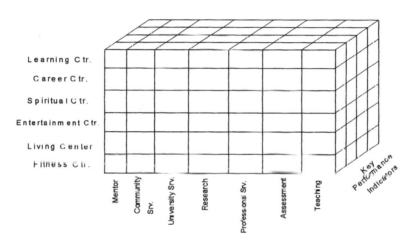

Budgets. Budgets include the allocation of time, energy, and resources. Budgets also determine the relative importance of a program, since budgets indicate the availability of resources for program implementation. Budgets are also expectations of performance, since they indicate the institution's commitment. An academic program without a budget is similar to a government program without a separate budget request: unless the department or school has the inherent resources to implement the program it is very apt to fail.

For example, several years ago, one of the authors was asked to develop an academic journal for his school of business. This was an exciting proposition because the journal was to include works of the full-time and adjunct faculty members as well as students, and juried works from other institutions. When the Dean of the School of Business was asked what type of budget was allocated for the publication and what time would be made available for this project, the Dean reaped what he had sown; he offered nothing and received nothing in return.

Implementation and Change

The earlier definition of implementation also implies that implementation is a change process. Mourier and Smith (2001) asked 210 North American managers about the change process and about why change processes succeed or fail. They developed ten propositions concerning organizational change:

1. Approximately 75% of all major change efforts fail to meet the needs of key stakeholders.
2. Change is driven by internal and external factors.
3. Change usually involves more that one type of change.
4. Change is usually categorized as reengineering, culture change, and restructuring.
5. Change is most likely to succeed with discernible support at the top, when employees understand what they have to do, and when adequate resources and provided.
6. Change is most likely to fail when driven by poor or conflicting leadership.
7. Failure to change is most often due to lack of planning and clear goals.
8. Change succeeds when supported by top and middle management.
9. Successful change is measured by financial, operational, and customer satisfaction data, while unsuccessful change is measured by opinion data.
10. Critical factors affecting change are common to most organizations. Change, and the forces that drive change, need to be considered as factors that impact the success or failure of implementing an academic plan.

External Factors. Academic program plans are not developed in a vacuum. Academic plans should be developed relative to the needs and demands of the external environment of the institution. Program planning should also address general market conditions – political, economic, environmental, social, and technological – as well as such industry-specific factors as competitors, suppliers, buyers, consumers, substitutes, and entrance barriers (Pearce and Robinson, 2000).

Many colleges and universities define their external environment by their key stakeholder groups: specific competitors, accrediting bodies, funding agencies, alumni, creditors, the local community, the general public, high schools and community colleges, unions, professional associations, philanthropists, potential students, learners' parents and/or significant others, and learners' employers (Rowley and Sherman, 2001). "These stakeholders push and pull the college in different directions (Lewin, 1951a, 1951b) and may have interests that run counter not only to each other but perhaps even to the mission of the institution" (pg. 214).

The importance of each of these groups is relative to the resources that these groups control and the need of the institution for them. French and Bell (1999) and Pfeffer and Salancik (1978) suggest including the more critical stakeholders in the program planning process inducing or co-opting their assistance and support.

Colleges and universities, however, cannot please all of their stakeholders all of the time and must be prepared to alienate certain interest groups based upon the needs of the institution. For example, Southampton College changed the format of its public radio station from a mix of classical and jazz to straight jazz based upon a survey of listener preferences and listener focus groups. A small percentage of listeners were outraged, withdrew their financial support of the station, and wrote critical articles for the local press. Once the bad press blew over, however, the station's listening audience dramatically increased, as did its external financial support.

Internal factors. New programs or modifications to existing programs may require changes in the institution's (or school or department's) structure, skill set, operating systems, leadership style, shared values, staff and strategy (Peters and Waterman, 1982; Rowley and Sherman, 2001). Flexibility or adaptability, as suggested by Galbraith (2002), becomes a very critical component of the implementation process, both at the program and more macro levels of the institution. The more subsystems which are frozen and cannot change, the more likely that program proposals that call for dramatic change will fail, regardless of the institution's best intentions.

Rowley and Sherman (2001) noted that an institution's ability to change is dependent upon its strategic approach to the marketplace, what Mintzberg (1987) called its market perspective. Certain institutions are quite proactive in the marketplace – that is, they "compete mainly by creating new products and services that establish new markets, or market niches, and take advantage of perceived opportunities" (Rowley and Sherman, 2001, pg. 96).

Prospectors are first movers or pioneers. They have very fluid operations, can alter their subsystems quickly, empower their employees, and are very consumer-oriented. They also have a tremendous capacity to learn (Slater and Narver, 1995) and are willing to question assumptions and preconceived notions held about the institution and its environment. They enliven organizational renewal (Katz and Oblinger, 1999).

Based on this description, one might think that small colleges, given their relative lack of hierarchy and long chain of command, would exhibit prospector tendencies. However, there are numerous other factors besides size that affect the change process, such as tradition/values, politics, and propensity to change; see Yin, Heald and Vogel, 1977). These may inhibit even small colleges' ability to take advantage of market opportunities.

Defender colleges, on the other hand, are predisposed to disregard the marketplace, since they have already established themselves in their markets with either high quality programs or low-cost operations. "Successful defenders usually focus on continuous improvement of the product processes to create greater operating efficiencies and better service delivery, or continuous improvement of the product or service to increase product-service quality" (Rowley and Sherman, 2001, p.97).

These strategies are associated either with public institutions because of their relative cost advantages, research institutions with large endowments and grants and/or excellent reputation, or specialty colleges occupying niche markets including internet and distance learning institutions. These institutions make changes incrementally rather than radically, and tend to err on the side of caution. They operate in rather stable market segments and already serve a fairly captive group of learners due to their low price or unique program offerings (Harrison, 1987).

Some institutions choose a middle of the road strategic perspective, that of an *analyzer*. These colleges and universities "try to maintain a strong [market] position in their key product- market but also try to grow their operation by expanding into related markets" (pg. 99). As second movers or followers, these institutions learn from the mistakes made by their prospecting counterparts by offering superior programs--better service, quality and educational delivery systems--or similar programs at lower costs. They tend to enter new educational markets with superior instructional technology and/or superior resources like better physical plant or lower tuition, and try to leap-frog over the prospectors. Analyzers can come from any market segment of the postsecondary educational market, but must possess traits and characteristics associated with both prospectors and defenders.

The last strategic perspective, *reactors*, is in fact not a perspective at all. "Reactors are usually dysfunctional organizations in that they have no clearly defined or deliberate strategy. Their strategy is emergent at best and imposed by the marketplace; they respond only when forced to by environmental pressures" (Mintzberg, 1987, pg. 100). Change is haphazard and unintended with decision-making best described as muddling through (Lindbloom, 1959).

Institutions in this category survive by the benevolence of other institutions and/or the quirks of the marketplace. They inhabit markets and market niches abandoned by prospectors, defenders, and analyzers, and are always fighting merely to survive.

How institutions react to and process change is a critical component of the academic program planning process. For example, defender colleges and universities, regardless of the available opportunities for new students, will employ internet instruction far more slowly than their prospector or analyzer complements unless they perceive this technology as directly impacting their current learner population. Institutions must consider their market perspective when developing academic program plans.

Resistance to Change and Program Implementation

Resistance to change can occur at the individual, group, subsystem, and system level, and may require intervention strategies in order to assist the program implementation process (French and Bell, 1999). At the individual level, Hersey and Blanchard (1993) noted that in order to overcome resistance to change, the program plan has to address the subordinate's level of readiness to change.

The lowest level of readiness, outright resistance, requires the use of coercive or connection power. The program plan must provide those individuals responsible for implementing the plan the ability to *tell* the employee what needs to be done. That is, the plan must provide the implementers adequate punishments in order to motivate employees to avoid the punishment or provide them access to those who can punish.. This power base should be employed as a last resort, since it tends to alienate.

The middle levels of readiness, compliance, require that the plan and its implementers *sell* the change to employees either through reward systems, legitimate authority, or charismatic/referent power. Employees conform to the changes because conformity is either in their own best interest, they are being told by their boss(es) to do it, or out of the desire to please their superiors.

The highest level of readiness, commitment, utilizes *participation* and *delegation* in order to obtain the employee's willingness to execute the plan. This process occurs by providing easy access to the program plan, and having employees educated as to the purpose and goals of the plan. Employee dedication is also accomplished through expert power, the recognition that those who were involved in the development and implementation of the program have the requisite skill and knowledge.

Change at the group level requires that the academic program plan identify the group or groups impacted by the change. A determination must be made as to whether the group will outright resist change or negative groupthink, according to Janis (1983), be thrown into internal conflict based upon the change (Brown, 1983) or embrace change. Dyer (1977) recommends that team building exercises be conducted prior to implementing the academic program plan in order to make "order out of chaos and conflict" or "overcoming unhealthy agreement" (pg.s 84, 93). Inter-team conflict may also occur if the plan impacts more than one academic unit and may require inter-team building and third party consultation (Walton, 1969).

Some changes may impact whole subsystems or the entire institution. Subsystem changes required by the academic program plan necessitate an examination of the short-term, mid-term, and long term impact of the new programs. These analyses range from immediate cause-effect influences on the subsystems to subsystems alignments and the overall adaptability of the subsystem and the organization as a whole (Kotter, 1978). Subsystem misalignments and subsystem inflexibility may become resistors to change, and hinder the academic program implementation process. Regardless of where resistance to change emanates, the academic program plan needs to identify and address that resistance if the plan is to be successful.

Academic Responsibility, Strategy, and Program Planning

It is our fervent belief that the academy has the responsibility of delivering academic excellence to its learners and therein serving both the profession and society at large. This responsibility includes the institution's identifying its mission and role in the industry (comprehensive, research, specialty, small, or community colleges), its orientation towards its students (provider, consumer, community), its competitive advantage (low cost, differentiation), and its strategic perspective (prospector, defender, analyzer, reactor).

More specifically, we also believe that the academy has the responsibility of serving the learner in an excellent manner, that is, creating centers of excellence that maximize the faculty's role in the delivery of services to the students. The role of academic program planning is to develop an holistic perspective on the learning process as it impacts both the learner and the institution.

We have a commonality of purpose, the educator and the learner, which provides the only necessary bridge we need to form a learning community. That bridge is the desire to grow, to learn, to seek the truth, and to reach our potentials as human beings. We, the academic community, are the vessels of learning. We need to plot a course with our learners so we can share the journey of scholarship.

Learner-Focused Education and Strategic Planning: Final Comments

We began the discussion in this book by tying academic planning to strategic planning. We want to end this book on the same note. Strategic planning in colleges and universities is a complex process which attempts to align the institution with its most crucial environments. In higher education, those environments are most closely identified with the needs of the society that populates an institution's primary service area. Resource providers, employers, prospective learners, governmental regulators and the community in general all set an environment to which colleges and universities must be responsive. This is what the strategic plan should be keyed to, and fit.

Academic planning is the primary construct that makes the strategic plan work. The types, breadth, and quality of academic programming define the potential for success the college or university will be capable of achieving. As we have argued throughout this book, academic programming is a substantive, pervasive, and crucial activity that requires objective and dedicated efforts to create a meaningful and relevant academic direction. It must be able to count and direct resources; it must be capable of doing substantive service community and discipline research; and it must be capable of tying the strengths of the campus assets to the needs of the service community. Without a distinct tie between the academic planning process and the campus strategic planning process, neither process will be effective. On the other hand, when academic planning and strategic planning are inextricably tied together on a college or university campus, there can be little doubt that both can succeed. And society benefits as well.

ഔ Bibliography ଔ

About Teaching -- #47, (1995) A Newsletter of the Center for Teaching Effectiveness, January University of Delaware— http://www.udel.edu/pbl/cte/jan95-edit.html.

Ackoff, Russell L. (1994) *The Democratic Corporation: A Radical Perspective for Recreating Corporate America and Rediscovering Success.* New York: Oxford University Press.

Allen, David F. (1999) "Desire To Finish College: An Empirical Link between Motivation and Persistence." *Research in Higher Education* (August) Volume 40, Number 4, 461-85.

Allen, David F. (1984) *Student Evaluation of Summer Orientation, Learning, Advising, and Registration.* Wilmington, NC.: North Carolina University.

Anderes, Thomas K. (1996) "Connecting Academic Plans to Budgeting: Key Conditions for Success." In Nedwek, Brian P. (ed.) *Doing Academic Planning: Effective Tools for Decision Making.* Ann Arbor, Michigan: SCUP. 129-134.

Anketell, Dikip M. (1996) "Integrating Academic and Facilities Planning." In Nedwek, Brian P. (ed.) *Doing Academic Planning: Effective Tools for Decision Making.* Ann Arbor, Michigan: SCUP. 117-128.

Argyris, Chris (1982) *Reasoning, Learning and Action: Individual and Organizational.* San Francisco, CA.: Jossey-Bass Publishers.

Asher, Hanna and Maureen Lane-Maher (2002) "Spirituality in the Workplace – A Measure of Success?" *Journal of Behavioral and Applied Management* (Spring) Volume 3, Number 3, 191-205.

Astin, Alexander W. and Helen S. Astin (1999) *Meaning and Spirituality in the Lives of College Faculty: A Study of Values, Authenticity, and Stress.* Los Angeles, CA.: Higher Education Research Institute.

Atkinson, Maxine P. (2001) "The Scholarship of Teaching and Learning: Reconceptualizing Scholarship and Transforming the Academy." *Social Forces* (June) Volume 79, Number 4, 1217-29.

Atwell, Robert (2001) "The Only Way to Reform College Sports is to Embrace Commercialization." *The Chronicle of Higher Education* (July 13) Volume 47, Number 44, B20.

Avakian, A. Nancy (1994). "A Guide to Writing Learning Contracts." (Working Paper.) *The ERIC Database.* Accession Number ED088385; CHN HE005266 Clearinghouse Number.

Banta, Trudy W. (1999) *Assessment in Community Colleges: Setting the Standard for Higher Education?* Boulder, CO.: National Center for Higher Education Management Systems.

Barak, Robert J. (1982). *Program Review in Higher Education: Within and Without.* Boulder, CO: National Center for Higher Education Management Systems.

Barak, Robert J. and Barbara E. Breier (1990). *Successful Program Review: A Practical Guide to Evaluating Programs in Academic Settings.* San Francisco, Ca.: Jossey-Bass Publishers.

Barnard, Chester P. (1938). *The Functions of the Executive.* Cambridge, Mass.: Harvard University Press.

Barrows, H. S. (1996) "Problem-Based Learning in Medicine and Beyond: A Brief Overview." In Wilkerson, L. & Gijselaers, W. H. (ed.s) *Brining Problem-Based Learning to Higher Education: Theory and Practice. New Directors for Teaching and Learning.* Number 68. San Francisco: Jossey-Bass Publishers Inc., Pg.s 3-12.

Bear, John B. and Mariah Bear (1997). *Bears' Guide to Earning College Degrees Nontraditionally.* 12th Edition. Benicia, CA.: C & B Publishing.

Benoist, Howard (1986). "Planning and Academic Program Review." *Planning for Higher Education* Volume14, Number 2, 22-25.

Bernauer, James A. (1998) "Teaching for Measurable Outcomes." *Journal on Excellence in College Teaching* Volume 9, Number 2, 25-46.

Birnbaum, Robert (2000) *Management Fads in Higher Education: Where They Come From, What They Do, Why They Fail.* San Francisco, CA.: Jossey-Bass, Inc.

Blanchard, P. Nick and James W. Thacker (1999) *Effective Training: Systems, Strategies, and Practices.* Upper Saddle River, N.J.: Prentice Hall.

Block, Peter (1995) "Rediscovering Service: Weaning Higher Education from Its Factory Mentality." *Educational Record (Fall)* Volume 76, Number 4, 6-13.

Bogue, E. Grady and Robert L. Saunders (1992) *The Evidence for Quality: Strengthening the Tests of Academic and Administrative Effectiveness.* San Francisco, CA.: Jossey-Bass Publishers.

Bok, Derek (1982) *Beyond the Ivory Tower. Social Responsibilities of the Modern University.* Cambridge, MA.: Harvard University Press.

Bonnen, James T. (1968) "Overcoming the Constraints of the Present University System." Chicago, Ill.: *Symposium on the University and the Transformation of Social and Political Institutions,* May 15.

Bowditch, James L. and Anthony F. Buono (2001) *A Primer on Organizational Behavior.* 5th Edition. New York: Joh Wiley & Sons, Inc.

Boy, Angelo V. and Gerald J. Pine (1982) *Client-Centered Counseling: A Renewal.* Boston, Mass.: Allyn and Bacon, Inc..

Boyatzis, Richard E. (1982) *The Competent Manager: A Model for Effective Performance.* New York: John Wiley & Sons.

Boyer, Carol M. and Darrell R. Lewis (1986) "Faculty Consulting and Supplemental Income." *ERIC Digest.* Washington, DC.: Association for the Study of Higher Education.

Bradburn, Ellen M. and David G. Hurst (2001) "Community College Transfer Rates to 4-Year Institutions Using Alternative Definitions of Transfer." *Education Statistics Quarterly* (Fall) Volume 3, Number 3, 119-25.

Bradley, A. Paul, jr. (1975) "A Role For Faculty in Contract Learning: Toward A Theory of Nontraditional Faculty Development." Chicago, Illinois. *30th National Conference on Higher Education,* March 23-26.

Brewster, Kingman, jr. (1968) "The Report of the President. Yale University: 1967-68." New Haven, CT.: Yale University.

Brown, L. David (1983) *Managing Conflict at Organizational Interfaces.* Reading, Mass.: Addison-Wesley Publishing Company.

Browne, Murray (1991) "Cosmopolitans as Heralds of a Vitalized Faculty Role." *Academe* (Sept.-Oct.) Volume 77, Number 5, 19-22.

Campbell, Donald T. and Julian C. Stanley (1963) "Experimental and Quasi-Experimental Designs in Research on Teaching." In N.L. Gage (ed.) *Handbook of Research on Teaching,* 171-246. Chicago, Ill.: Rand McNally.

Cardinal, Bradley J. (1990a) "An Old Wine in a New Bottle: Opportunities for Physical Educators to Package and Deliver It, not Just Stomp Grapes." Reno, NV: *Annual Conference of the Western College Physical Education Society*, October 17-19.

Cardinal, Bradley J. (1990b) "Justifying and Developing a Comprehensive Wellness-Fitness Institute on a University Campus." *Eastern Washington University.* Cheney, Wash.: Eastern Washington University.

Carnegie Foundation for the Advancement of Teaching (1990) *Campus Life: In Search of Community.* Princeton, N.J.: Princeton University Press.

Carpella University (2002) http://www.capellauniversity.edu/aspscripts/news/pressroom/ overview.asp, 8/29/02.

Carroll, Stephen J., Frank T. Paine, and John M. Ivancevich (1972) "The Relative Effectiveness of Training Methods-Expert Opinion and Research." *Personnel Psychology* Volume 33, 495-509.

Chamberlin, W. Sean (2001) "Face-to-Face vs. Cyberspace: Finding the Middle Ground." *Syllabus* Volume 15, Number 5, 10-11.

Chandler, A. D. (1962) *Strategy and Structure: Chapters in the History of the American Industrial Enterprise.* Cambridge, MA: MIT Press.

Cobb, Lawrence E., William J. Stone, Lori J. Anonsen, and Diane A. Klein (2000) "The Influence of Goal Setting on Exercise Adherence." *Journal of Health Education* (Sept.-Oct.) Volume 31, Number 5, 277-81.

Collins, Valerie-Hawkes (1991) "The Faculty Role in Governance: A Historical Analysis of the Influence of The American Association of University Professors and the Middle States Association on Academic Decision Making." Memphis, TN.: *Annual Meeting of the Association for the Study of Higher Education*, October 31 - November 3.

Conrad, Clifton F. and Richard W. Wilson (1986) "Academic Program Reviews." *ERIC Digest.* Washington, DC.: Association for the Study of Higher Education.

Cope, Robert and George Delaney (1991) "Academic Program Review: A Market Strategy Perspective." *Journal of Marketing for Higher Education* Volume 3, Number 2, 63-86.

Cordeiro, Wiilaim P. and Ashish Vaidya (2002). "Lessons Learned from Strategic Planning" *Planning for Higher Education* (Summer) Volume 30, Number 4, 24-31.

Cunningham, Alisa F. and Jamie P. Merisotis (2002) "National Models of College Costs and Prices." *Planning for Higher Education* Volume 30, Number 3, 15-26.

Dalton, Jon C. (2001) "Career and Calling: Finding a Place for the Spirit in Work and Community." *New Directions for Student Services* (Fall) Number 95, 17-25.

Dart, Barry and Boulton-Lewis, Gillian (1998) *Teaching and Learning in Higher Education.* Victoria, Australia: Australian Council for Educational Research.

David, E. E., jr. (1982) "The University-Academic Connection in Research: Corporate Purposes and Social Responsibilities." New York: *New York City Bar Association*, April 21.

Davila, Evelyn M. (1985) "Today's Urban University Students: Part 2." A Case Study of Hunter College. Final Report on the Urban University Study." *College Entrance Examination Board.* New York: College Board Publications.

Davis, Todd M. and Patricia-Hillman Murrell (1993) "Turning Teaching into Learning. The Role of Student Responsibility in the Collegiate Experience." *ASHE-ERIC Higher Education Report No. 8.* Washington, DC.: Association for the Study of Higher Education.

Debus, Richard C. (1975) "Cost Analysis for Contract Learning." Chicago, Illinois: *30th National Conference on Higher Education*, March 23-26.

Dittrich, John E. (1988) *The General Manager and Strategy Formulation: Objectives, Missions, Strategies, Policies.* New York: John Wiley & Sons.

Dolence, Micahel G., Daniel J. Rowley, and Herman D. Lujan (1997) *Working Toward Strategic Change: A Step-by-Step Guide to the Planning Process.* San Francisco, CA.: Jossey-Bass Publishers.

Dolence, M. G. and Norris, D. M. (1995) *Transforming Higher Education.* Ann Arbor, MI.: Society for College and University Planning.

Dubin, Robert (1969) *Theory Building.* New York: The Free Press.

DuBrin, Andrew J. (2003) *Essentials of Management.* 6th Edition. Mason, OH.: South-Western .

Dunlap, Joanna C. (1997) "Preparing Students for Lifelong Learning: A Review of Instructional Methodologies." Albuquerque, NM.: *Proceedings of Selected Research and Development Presentations at the 1997 National Convention of the Association for Educational Communications and Technology*, February 14-18.

Dyer, William G. (1977) *Team Building: Issues and Alternatives.* Reading, Mass.: Addison-Wesley Publishing Company.

Ecker, Martha (1994) "Using Program Reviews for the Evaluation of Pedagogy." San Juan, PR: *The Conference on Current Collegiate Faculty Evaluation Practices and Procedures of the Center for Educational Development and Assessment*, November 7-8.

Ehrlich, Thomas (1997) *"Civil Learning: Democracy and Education Revisited." Educational Record* Volume 78 (Summer/Fall), p. 56-65.

Ewell, Peter T. (1983) "Program Reviews, Inputs and Outcomes NCHEMS Monograph 5." Boulder, CO.: *National Center for Higher Education Management Systems.*

Fickes, Michael (1999) "Outfitting Campus Fitness Centers." *College Planning and Management* (July) Volume 2, Number 7, 38-40.

Fields, Joseph C. (1993) *Total Quality for Schools: A Suggestion for American Education.* Milwaukee, WI.:ASQC Quality Press.

Finkle S.l. & Torp L.L., (1995) *Introductory Documents.* Aurora, Ill: Center for Problem Based Learning, Illinois Math & Science Academy.

Fisher, Ronald J. and John J. Andrews (1976) "The Impact of Self-Selection and Reference Group Identification in a University Living-Learning Center" *Social Behavior and Personality* Volume 4, Number 2, 209-18.

Fitzpatrick, Margaret M. (1988) "Social Responsibility in Higher Education." *NASPA-Journal* (Winter) Volume 25, Number 3, 191-94.

French, Wendell C. and Cecil H. Bell, Jr. (1999) *Organization Development: Behavioral Science Interventions for Organization Improvement.* 6th Edition. Upper Saddle River, N.J.: Prentice-Hall, Inc..

Fujishin, Randy (2001) *Creating Effective Groups: The Art of Small Group Communication.* San Francisco, CA.: Acada Books.

Galbraith, Jay (2002) *Designing Organizations: An Executive Guide to Strategy, Structure and Process.* New and Revised. San Francisco, CA.: Jossey-Bass, Inc.

Galbraith, Jay (1977) *Organization Design.* Reading, Mass.: Addison-Wesley Publishing Company.

Galbraith, Jay (1973) *Designing Complex Organizations.* Reading, Mass.: Addison-Wesley Publishing Company.

Geraghty, Mary (1996) "A New Kind of Student Union Aims To Meet Academic and Social Needs." *Chronicle of Higher Education* (November 29) Volume 43, Number 14, A39-A40.

Gibbons, M., Limoges, C., Nowotny, H., Schwartzman, S., Scott, P., & Trow, M. (1994) *The New Production of Knowledge: The Dynamics of Science and Research in Contemporary Socieities.* London: Sage.

Goodchild, Lester F. (1986) "Changes in the Professoriate, the Curriculum, and the Aim of Higher Education from the Middle Ages to the Modern Era." San Antonio, TX.: *Annual Meeting of the Association for the Study of Higher Education,* February 20-23.

Goral, Tim (2001) "What Students Want (And What You Can Do About It)." *Matrix* October, 20-23.

Guffey, J. Stephen; Larry C. Rampp, and Mitchell M. Masters (1998) "A paradigm shift in teaching the academically unprepared student: building a case for an andragogical methodology." *College Student Journal (September)* Volume 32, Number 3, 423-9.

Hall, James W. and Richard F. Bonnabeau (1993) "Empire State College." *New Directions for Higher Education* (Summer) Number 82, 55-66.

Harkavy, Ira and John Puckett (1992) "Universities and the Inner Cities." *Planning for Higher Education* (Summer) Volume 20, Number 4, 27-33.

Harris, April L. (1998) *Special Events: Planning for Success.* 2nd Edition. Washington, DC.: Council for Advancement and Support of Education.

Harris, Shanette M. and Michael T. Nettles (1991) "Racial Differences in Student Experiences and Attitudes." *New Directions for Student Services* (Winter) Number 56, 25-38.

Harrison, E. Frank (1987) *The Managerial Decision-Making Process.* 3rd Edition. Boston, Mass.: Houghton Mifflin Company.

Harvard University, Office of the President (1993) "The President's Report 1991-1993." Cambridge, Mass.: Harvard University.

Hawkes, Ellen G. and Patricia Y. Pisaneschi (1992) "Academic Excellence for Adults: Improving the Teaching/Learning Process through Outcomes Assessment." San Diego, CA.: *National University Conference on Lifelong Learning: Meeting the Higher Education Needs of Adult Learners,* February 14.

Hawkins, Brian L. (1999) "Foreward" in Diana G. Oblinger and Richard N. Katz (1999) *Renewing Administration: Preparing Colleges ands Universities for the 21st Century (Eds.).* Bolton, Mass.: Anker Publishing Company, Inc.

Haworth, Jennifer G. and Clifton F. Conrad (1997) *Emblems of Quality in Higher Education: Developing and Sustaining High-Quality Programs.* Needham Heights, MA: Allyn & Bacon.

Hayes, Maurice B., and Yvonne-L. Newsome-Hales (1978) "Pragmatic Approach for Academic Program Planning and Evaluation." *Education* (Summer) Volume 98, Number 4, 415-9.

Hersey, Paul and Kenneth H. Blanchard (1993) *Management of Organizational Behavior: Utilizing Human Resources.* 6th Edition. Englewood Cliffs, N.J.: Prentice Hall, Inc.

Herzberg, Frederick W. (1968) "One More Time: How Do You Motivate Employees?" *Harvard Business Review* Volume 46, Number 1, 53-62.

Heydinger, Richard B. (1980a) "Academic Program Planning Reconsidered." *New Directions for Institutional Research (Number 28) Academic Planning for the 1980s* Volume 7, Number 4, 97-109.

Heydinger, Richard B. (1980b) "Introduction: Academic Program Planning in Perspective." *New Directions for Institutional Research (Number 28) Academic Planning for the 1980s* Volume 7, Number 4, 1-8.

Higgerson, Mary Lou and Susan S. Rehwaldt (1993) *Complexities of Higher Education Administration: Case Studies & Issues.* Bolton, Mass.: Anker Publishing Company, Inc.

Hirschman, Albert O. (1970) *Exit, Voice and Loyalty: Responses to Decline in Firms, Organizations, and States.* Cambridge, Mass.: Harvard University Press.

Hitt, M. A. (1998) "Presidential Address: Twenty-First-Century Organizations: Business Firms, Business Schools, and the Academy." *The Academy of Management Review* 23 (2). Pg.s 218-224.

Hofer, Charles W., Edwin A. Murray, Jr., Ram Charan, and Robert A. Pitts (1984) *Strategic Management: A Casebook in Policy and Planning.* 2nd Edition. New York: West Publishing Company.

Hollander, Elizabeth L. and John Saltmarsh (2000) "The Engaged University." *Academe* (Jluy-August) Volume 86, Number 4, 29-32.

Higgerson, Mary Lou and Susan S. Rehwaldt (1993) *Complexities of Higher Education Administration: Case Studies & Issues.* Bolton, Mass.: Anker Publishing Company, Inc.

Homans, George C. (1950) *The Human Group.* New York: Harcourt, Brace & World.

Hoerner, John Martin, jr. (1998) "Emerging Information Technologies, Psychological Type, and Learning Styles: Evaluating Competing Methodologies for Teaching Television Lighting." Las Vegas, NV: *44th Annual Convention of the Research Division of the Broadcast Education Association,* April 15-18.

Hu, Shouping and Don Hossler (1998) "The Linkage of Student Price Sensitivity with Preferences to Postsecondary Institutions." Miami, FL: *Annual Meeting of the Association for the Study of Higher Education,* November 5-8.

Huebner, Dwayne (1995) "Education and Spirituality." *An Interdisciplinary Journal of Curriculum Studies* Volume 11, Number 2, 13-34.

Huff, A. S. (2000) "Presidential Address: Changes in Organizational Knowledge Production." *The Academy of Management Review* 25 (2). Pg.s 288-293.

Hugenberg, Lawrence W. (1997) "Assessment of Learning and Program Review: Data for Continuous Improvement." Chicago, IL: *83rd Annual Meeting of the National Communication Association,* November 19-23.

Hunger, David J. and Thomas L. Wheelan (2000) *Strategic Management.* 7th Edition. Upper Saddle River, N.J.: Prentice-Hall.

Ihlanfeldt, William (1980) *Achieving Optimal Enrollments and Tuition Revenues.* San Francisco, CA.: Jossey-Bass.

International Assembly for Collegiate Business Education (IACBE) (2002) *Accreditation Manual.* Overland Park, Kansas: IACBE.

Janis, Irving L. (1983) "Groupthink." In *Organizational Behavior and Management: A Contingency Approach.* Henry L. Tosi (ed.). Boston, Mass.: PWS-Kent Publishing Company, 195-202.

Kaplan, Robert S. and David P. Norton (1996) "Using the Balanced Scorecard as a Strategic Management System." *Harvard Business Review* (January-February) Volume 74, Issue 1, 75-86.

Katz, Daniel and Robert L. Kahn (1966) *The Social Psychology of Organizing.* New York: John Wiley & Sons, Inc.

Katz, Richard N. and Diana G. Oblinger (1999) "Renewal as an Institutional Imperative" in *Renewing Administration: Preparing Colleges and Universities for the 21st Century.* Diana G. Oblinger and Richard N. Katz (eds.), 302-314.

Keene State College (1998) "Report to New England Association of Schools & Colleges, Inc." (Working Paper.) *The ERIC Database.* Accession Number ED436993; CHN Clearinghouse Number HE032611.

Keith, Novella Z. and Nelson W. Keith (1994) "Backing into Community: A Reconceptualization of Equity and Assessment in Higher Education." New Orleans, LA: *Annual Meeting of the American Educational Research Association,* April 4-8.

Keller, George (1999) "The Emerging Third Stage in Higher Education Planning." *Planning for Higher Education* Volume 28, Number 2, 1-7.

Keller, George, 1983 *Academic Strategy.* Baltimore, Md.: Johns Hopkins University Press.

Kember, D. & Gow, L. (1994) "Orientations to Teaching and Their Effect on the Quality of Student Learning." *Journal of Higher Education.* V. 65 (1). January/February, Pg.s 58-74.

Kerr, Steven (1975) "On the Folly of Rewarding A, While Hoping for B." *Academy of Management Journal* Volume 18, 769-83.

Kerstetter, Deborah L. and Georgia M. Kovich (1997) "An Involvement Profile of Division I Women's Basketball Spectators." *Journal of Sport Management* (July) Volume 11, Number 3, 234-49.

Kezar, Adrianna J. (2000) "Faculty: ERIC Trends, 1999-2000." Washington, DC.: ERIC Clearinghouse on Higher Education.

Kezar, Adrianna J. (1999) "Higher Education Trends (1997-1999): Faculty. ERIC-HE Trends." Washington, DC.: ERIC Clearinghouse on Higher Education.

Kieft, Raymond (1976) "Pressure Point On Campus: Academic Program Planning and Resource Allocation in Conflict with the Bargaining Table." (Working Paper.) *The ERIC Database.* Accession Number ED126840; CHN Clearinghouse Number HE008162.

Kiker, B.F. (1971) *Investment in Human Capital* (Ed.). Columbia, S.C.: University of South Carolina Press.

Klein, Thomas A., Patsy F. Scott, and Joseph L. Clark (2001) "A Fresh Look at Market Segments in Higher Education." *Planning for Higher Education* Volume 30, Number 1, 5-19.

Kotler, Phillip and Karen F.A. Fox (1995) *Strategic Marketing for Educational Institutions.* 2nd Edition. Englewood Cliffs, N.J.: Prentice-Hall, Inc.

Kotter, John P. (1978) *Organizational Dynamics: Diagnosis and Intervention.* Reading, Mass.: Addison-Wesley Publishing Company.

Kramer, Howard C. (1985) "Advising and Faculty Development: The Institution's View." New York: ERIC Database.

Krank, H. Mark (2001) "Commentary: learning styles and higher education: a tool of inclusion or exclusion?." *Journal of College Reading and Learning (Fall)* Volume 32, Number 1, 58-9.

Kreps, Gary L. (1998) "The Power of Story To Personalize, Enrich, and Humanize Communication Education: My Own Story about Having Fun Spinning Tales, and Illustrating Key Points in the Classroom." New York, NY: *Annual Meeting of the National Communication Association,* November 21-24.

Kushner, Remigia (1994) "A Model for a Mission." Vail, CO: 51st National Council of Professors of Educational Administration, August 11-16.

Lawrence, Paul R. and Jay W. Lorsch (1969) *Developing Organizations: Diagnosis and Action.*

Lehmann, Timothy (1975) "Educational Outcomes from Contract Learning at Empire State College." Chicago, Illinois: *30th National Conference on Higher Education,* March 23-26.

Lester, Stan (2002) "An Introduction to Phenomenological Research." http://www.devmts.demon.co.uk/resmethy.htm, 8/30/02.

Lewis, Ralph G. and Douglas H. Smith (1994) *Total Quality in Higher Education.* Delray Beach, Florida: St. Lucie Press.

Lewin, Kurt (1951) *Field Theory in Social Science.* New York: Harper.

Lewis, Ralph G. and Douglas H. Smith (1994) *Total Quality in Higher Education*. Delray Beach, Florida: St. Lucie Press.

Lindblom, Charles E. (1959) "The Science of Muddling Through." *Public Administration Review* (Spring) Volume 19, 79-88.

Long, Durward (1980) "Linking Academic Planning and Budgeting." In Micek, Sidney S. (ed.) *Integrating Academic Planning and Budgeting in a Rapidly Changing Environment: Process and Technical Issues.* Boulder, Colorado: NCHEMS. 29-40.

Long Island University & Southampton College Federation of Teachers (2000) *Draft Agreement: September 1st, 2000 – August 31st, 2001.* Greenville, N.Y.: Long Island University.

Love, Patrick and Donna Talbot (1999) "Defining Spiritual Development: A Missing Consideration for Student Affairs." *NASPA Journal* (Fall) Volume 37, Number 1, 361-76.

Luthans, Fred (1998) *Organizational Behavior.* 8th Edition. New York: Irwin McGraw-Hill.

Lynton, Ernest A. and Sandra E. Elman (1987) *New Priorities for the University. Meeting Society's Needs for Applied Knowledge and Competent Individuals.* San Francisco, CA.: Jossey-Bass Publishers.

Lyons, Joseph (1965) *A Primer of Experimental Psychology.* New York: Harper & Row.

Maslow, Abraham H. (1943) "A Theory of Human Motivation." *Psychological Review* (July), 370-396.

Mathews, William E. (1993) "The Missing Element in Higher Education." *Journal for Quality Participation* Volume 16, Issue 1, 102-108.

McClenney, Byron N. (1980) *Management for Productivity.* Washington, DC: American Association of Community and Junior Colleges.

McClung, Steven (2001) "College Radio Station Web Sites: Perceptions of Value and Use." *Journalism and Mass Communication Educator* (Spring) Volume 56, Number 1, 62-73.

McCorkle, D. et.al (1999) "Undergraduate Marketing Students, Group Projects, and Teamwork: The Good, The Bad, and The Ugly?" *Journal of Marketing Education*, 21(2), Pg.s 106-117.

McGregor, Douglas (1960) *The Human Side of Enterprise.* New York: McGraw-Hill Book Company, Inc.

McKee, James P., Sharon L. Kiser, and Russ Lea (1999) "Transforming Research Administration." In Diana G. Oblinger and Ricahrd N. Katz (1999) *Renewing Administration: Preparing Colleges and Universities for the 21st Century (Eds.)*. Bolton, Mass.: Anker Publishing Company, Inc.

Mets, Lisa A. (1995) "Program Review in Academic Departments." *New Directions for Institutional Research* (Summer) Number 86, 19-36.

Middaugh, Michael F. (2002) "Faculty Productivity: Different Strategies for Different Audiences." *Planning for Higher Education* Volume 30, Number 3, 34-43.

Middle States Association of Colleges and Schools (1996) *Framework for Outcomes Assessment*. 2nd Edition. Philadelphia, PA.: Commission on Higher Education.

Miles, Raymond C. and Charles C. Snow (1984) "Fit, Failure, and the Hall of Fame." *California Management Review* Volume 26, Number 3, 10-28.

Milter, R. G. & Stinson, J. E. (1996) "Educating leaders for the new competitive environment." In Gijselaers, W. H. et al (ed.s) *Educational Innovation in Economics and Business Administration*. Dortdrecht: Kluwer Academic Publishers.

Mintzberg, Henry (1994) *The Rise and Fall of Strategic Planning*. New York: The Free Press.

Mintzberg, Henry (1987) "Concept I: Five P's for Strategy." *California Management Review* Volume 30, Number 1, 11-24.

Mintzberg, Henry (1975) "The Manager's Job: Folklore and Fact." *Harvard Business Review* (July-August) Volume 53, Issue 4, 49-63.

Mintzberg, Henry, Jospeh Lampel, James B. Quinn, and Sumantra Ghoshal (2003) *The Strategy Process: Concepts, Contexts, Cases*. 4th Edition. Upper Saddle River, N.J.: Prentice-Hall.

Misanchuk, Melanie, Tiffany Anderson, Joni Crancr, Pam Eddy, and Carol L. Smith (2000) "Strategies for Creating and Supporting a Community of Learners." Denver, CO: *Proceedings of Selected Research and Development Papers Presented at the 23rd National Convention of the Association for Educational Communications and Technology* Volumes 1-2, October 25-28.

Moore-Jansen, Cathy (1997) "What Difference Does It Make? One Study of Student Background and the Evaluation of Library Instruction." *Research Strategies* (Winter) Volume 15, Number 1, 26-38.

Mosher, Frederick C. (1982) *Democracy and the Public Service.* 2nd Edition. Oxford: Oxford University Press.

Morrison, J. L., Renfro, W. L., & Boucher, W. I. 1984 *Futures Research and the Strategic Planning Process: Implications for Higher Education.* Washington, D. C.: ASHE-ERIC.

Mourier, Pierre and Martin Smith (2001) *Conquering Organizational Change: How to Succeed Where Most Companies Fail.* Atlanta, GA.: CEP Press.

Nader, Ralph and Donald Ross (1971) *Action for a Change: A Student's Manual for Public Interest Organizing.* New York: Grossman Publishers.

Nedwek, Brian P. (1996) *Doing Academic Planning: Effective Tools for Decision Making (Ed.).* Ann Arbor, MI.: Society for College and University Planning.

Nielsen, Robert M. and Irwin H. Polishook (1986) "Academic Reform and the Faculty." *Chronicle of Higher Education* (June 18) Volume 32, Number 16, 27.

Nowacki, Steven (1977) "Student Affairs as Perceived Through Abraham Maslow's Hierarchy of Needs." Albuquerque, NM: *Annual Meeting of the National Association of Student Personnel Administrators,* November.

Nutt, Paul C. (1992) *Managing Planned Change.* New York: Macmillan Publishing Company.

Odiorne, George S. (1965) *Management by Objectives: A System of Managerial Leadership.* New York: Pitman Publishing Corporation.

Olagunju, Amos O. (1981) "Direct Assessment and Treatment of Attrition and Retention Problems." Washington, D.C.: *U.S. Department of Education.*

Pascarella, E. T. and Terenzini, P. T. (1991) *How College Affects Students.* San Francisco, CA.: Jossey-Bass Inc., Publishers.

Pearce, Jack A. II and Richard B. Robinson Jr. (2000) *Formulation, Implementation and Control of Competitive Strategy.* 7th Edition. New York: Irwin McGraw-Hill.

Peters, Thomas J. and Robert H. Waterman Jr. (1982) *In Search of Excellence: Lessons from America's Best-Run Companies.* New York: Harper & Row.

Peterson, Marvin W. and Derek S. Vaughan (2001) "A Multidimensional Strategy for Student Assessment." *Planning for Higher Education* (Winter) Volume 30, Number 2, 13-27.

Pfeffer, Jeffrey and Gerald R. Salancik (1978) *The External Control of Organizations: A Resource Dependence Perspective.* New York: Harper and Row.

Pfeffer, Jeffrey (1977) "Usefulness of the Concept," in Goodman, P.S. and Pennings, J. M. (ed.s) *New Perspectives in Organizational Effectiveness.* San Francisco, CA: Jossey-Bass Inc., Publishers.

Pearce, John A., II and Richard B Robinson, Jr. (2000) *Strategic Management: Formulatiom, Implementation, and Control.* New York: Irwin McGraw-Hill.

Pinder, Craig C. (1984) *Work Motivation: Theory, Issues and Applications.* Glenview, Ill.: Scott, Foresman and Company.

Porter, Micahel E. (1985) *Competitive Advantage: Creating and Sustaining Superior Performance.* New York: The Free Press.

Powers, Susan M. and Jennie Mitchell (1997) "Student Perceptions and Performance in a Virtual Classroom Environment." Chicago, IL: *Annual Meeting of the American Educational Research Association,* March 24-28.

Pratt, Daniel D. (1997) "Reconceptualizing the Evaluation of Teaching in Higher Education." *Higher Education (July)* Volume 34, Number 1, 23-44.

Pressman, Jeffrey L. and Aaron Wildavsky (1973) *Implementation.* 2nd Edition, Expanded. Berkeley, CA.: University of California Press.

Pride, William M. and O.C. Ferrell (2003) *Marketing Concepts and Strategies.* 12th Edition. Boston, Mass.: Houghton Mifflin Company.

Queeney, Donna S. (1996) "A Learning Society: Creating an America that Encourages Learning throughout Life." *Kellogg Commission of the National Association of State Colleges and Land Grant Universities,* Washington, DC.

Residential College Task Force (1998) "The Residential Nexus: A Focus on Student Learning. Setting New Directions by Making New Connections. In-Class Instruction/Out-of-Class Learning." Columbus, OH: Association of College and University Housing Officers-International.

Rogers, Carl R. (1969) *Freedom to Learn.* Columbus, OH.: Charles E. Merrill.

Rogers, Judy L. and Michael E. Dantley (2001) "Invoking the Spiritual in Campus Life and Leadership." *Journal of College Student Development* (Nov./Dec.) Volume 42, Number 6, 589-603.

Rose, Amy D. (1987) "Individualized Higher Education and Empowerment: The Potential and the Pitfalls." Washington, DC: *Annual Meeting of the American Association of Adult and Continuing Education,* October.

Rotter, James B. (1990) "Internal versus External Control of Reinforcement: A Case Study of a Variable." *American Psychologist* Volume 45, 489-493.

Rowley, Daniel J. (1998) Interview with top administrators at the University of the Highlands and Islands, Inverness, Scotland. March 18, 1998.

Rowley, Daniel J. and Herbert Sherman (2002) "Implementing the Strategic Plan." *Planning for Higher Education* (Summer) Volume 30, Number 4, 5-14.

Rowley, Daniel J. and Herbert Sherman (2001) *From Strategy to Change: Implementing the Plan in Higher Education.* San Francisco, CA.: Jossey-Bass, Inc.

Rowley, Daniel J., Herman D. Lujan, and Michael G. Dolence (1998) *Strategic Choices for the Academy: How Demand for Lifelong Learning Will Re-Create Higher Education.* San Francisco, CA.: Jossey-Bass, Inc.

Rowley, Daniel J., Herman D. Lujan, and Michael G. Dolence (1997) *Strategic Change in Colleges and Universities: Planning to Survive and Prosper.* San Francisco, CA: Jossey-Bass, Inc.

Sacken, Donal M. (1992) "Raise High the Drawbridge, Provost!" *Educational Record* (Summer) Volume 73, Number 3, 38-43.

Satterlee, Brian (1992) "Program Review and Evaluation: A Survey of Contemporary Literature." *The ERIC Database.* Accession Number ED356261; CHN Clearinghouse Number TM019686.

Saunders, P. and Werner, K. (2002) "Finding the Right Blend for Effective Learning: A Pilot Study," on the Western Michigan University webpage, http://www.wmich.edu/teachlearn/new/blended.htm.

Schein, Edgar H. (1987) *Process Consultation: Lessons for Managers and Consultants,* vol. 2. Reading, Mass.: Addison-Wesley Publishing Company.

Schilling, Karen Maitland and Karl L. Schilling (1998) "Proclaiming and Sustaining Excellence: Assessment as a Faculty Role." *ASHE-ERIC Higher Education Report* Volume 26, Number 3.

Selingo, Jeffrey (2001) "Las Vegas Leaders Want 2-year College to Start Intercollegiate Sports Program." *The Chronicle of Higher Education* (Oct. 9) Volume 45, Number 7, A53-A54.

Senge, Peter M. (1990) *The Fifth Discipline: The Art and Practice of the Learning Organization.* New York: Doubleday.

Serow, Robert C. (2000) "Research and Teaching at a Research University." *Higher Education* (December) Volume 40, Number 4, 449-63.

Seymour, Daniel T. and Jonathan D. Fife (1988) "Developing Academic Programs: The Climate for Innovation." *ASHE-ERIC Higher Education Report No. 3,* Washington, DC.: Association for the Study of Higher Education.

Sherman, Herbert (1991) *The Strategic Management Process: Readings, Cases and Exercises.* Needham Heights, MA.: Ginn Press.

Sherman, Herbert (1984) "A Model of Communication Processing in Organizations." In Edward D. Bewayo, Jeffrey Cross, Eileen Kaplan, Carl Rodrigues and Herbert Sherman (1984) *Management Process and Organizational Behavior: Selected Readings (Eds.).* Lexington, Mass.: Ginn Custom Publishing.

Sherr, L. A. and Lozier, G. G. (1991) "'Total Quality Management in Higher Education," in Sherr L. A. and Lozier, G. G. (ed.s) *Total Quality Management in Higher Education – New Directions for Institutional Research No. 71.* San Francisco, CA.: Jossey-Bass Inc., Publishers.

Shirley, R. C. (1988) "Strategic Planning. An Overview." *New Directions for Higher Education.* No. 64, Winter. Pg.s.. 5-14.

Simon, Herbert A. (1976) *Administrative Behavior: A Study of Decision-Making Processes in Administrative Organizations.* 3rd Edition. New York: The Free Press.

Skolnik, Michael L. (1989) "How Academic Program Review Can Foster Intellectual Conformity and Stifle Diversity of Thought and Method." *Journal of Higher Education* (Nov.-Dec.) Volume 60, Number 6, 619-43.

Slater, Stephen F. and John C. Narver (1995) "Market orientation and the learning organization." *Journal of Marketing* Volume 59, Issue 3, 63-74.

Smith, Craig. O. and Robert F. Bourgault (1976) "Teaching Failure Analysis: Two Approaches." *Engineering Education (January)* Volume 66, Number 4, 332-333.

Smith, Kimberley-Robles (2000) "Great Expectations: Or, Where Do They Get These Ideas?" *Reference and User Services Quarterly* (Fall) Volume 40, Number 1, 27-31.

Sonwalker, Nishikant (2001) "The Sharpe Edge of the Cube: Pedagogical Driven Instructional Design for Online Education." *Syllabus* Volume 15, Number 5, 12-21.

Southampton College of Long Island University (2002) *Middle States Decennial Self-Study.*   Southampton, N.Y.: Southampton College.

Southampton College of Long Island University (2001) *Undergraduate and Graduate Bulletin 2001-2003.*   Southampton, N.Y.: Southampton College.

Southampton College Federation of Teachers (2000) *Draft Agreement: September 1st, 2000 – August 31st, 2001.*   Greenville, N.Y.: Long Island University.

Spaulding, W. B. (1991) "Revitalizing Medical Education." *McMaster Medical School in the Early Years, 1965-1974.* Philadelphia: Decker.

Stephens, Jason M.,   Anne Colby, Tom Ehrlich, and Elizabeth Beaumont (2000) "Higher Education and the Development of Moral and Civic Responsibility: Vision and Practice in Three Contexts."   New Orleans, LA.: *Annual Meeting of the American Educational Research Association*, April 24-28.

Strosnider, Kim (1997) "Testing High-Tech Concepts for the Bookstore of the Future."   *Chronicle of Higher Education* (Oct. 31) Volume 44, Number 10, A49-A51.

Sturdivant, Frederick D. and Heidi Vernon-Wortzel (1990) *Business and Society: A Managerial Approach.*   4th Editon. Homewood, Ill: Irwin.

Swope, Suzanne C. (1994) "The approaching value-added education." *Educational Record* Volume 75 (Summer), 17-18.

Taylor, Frederick W. (1947) *Scientific Management.* New York: Harper & Brothers Publishers.

Thompson, James D. (1967) *Organizations in Action.* New York: McGraw-Hill.

Tisdell, Elizabeth J. (2001) "Spirituality in Adult and Higher Education."   *ERIC Digest.*   Columbus, OH.: ERIC Clearinghouse on Adult, Career, and Vocational Education.

Trippe, Anthony (2001) "Extensive UOP Program Brings (and) Keeps Faculty UP to Speed." *Distance Education Report* (September) Volume 5, Number 17, 4.

Trout, Paul A. (1997) "What the Numbers Mean: Providing a Context for Numerical Student Evaluations of Courses." *Change* (Sept.-Oct.) Volume 29, Number 5, 24-30.

Union Institute -The Graduate College (1999) "Adjunct Handbook: Guidelines for Adjunct Professors." Cincinnati, OH.: The Union Institute.

VanWagoner, Randall J. (2001) *A Framework for Academic Planning: Engaging Faculty in Strategic Dialogue.* Omaha, NE.: Metropolitan Community College.

Votruba, James C. (1996) "The University's Social Covenant: A Vision for the Future." *Adult Learning* (Jan.-Feb.) Volume 7, Number 3, 28-29.

Walker, Orville C., Jr., Harper W. Boyd, Jr., and Jean-Claude Larreche (1999) *Marketing Strategy: Planning and Implementation.* 3rd Edition. New York: Irwin McGraw-Hill.

Walton, Ricahrd E. (1969) *Interpersonal Peacemaking: Confrontations and Third Party Consultation.* Reading, Mass.: Addison-Wesley Publishing Company.

Warren, Jonathan R. (1982) "The Faculty Role in Educational Excellence." Kingston, RI: *National Commission on Excellence in Education*, August 27-28.

Webbcr, Ross A. (1979) *Management: Basic Elements of Managing Organizations.* Revised Edition. Homewood, Ill.: Richard D. Irwin, Inc..

Weick. Karl E. (1979) *The Social Psychology of Organizing.* 2nd Edition. Reading, Mass.: Addison-Wesley Publishing Company.

Wick, Calhoun W. and Lu Stanton Leon (1993) *The Learning Edge: How Smart Managers and Smart Companies Stay Ahead.* New York: McGraw-Hill, Inc.

Wilkerson, L. & Gijselaers, W. H. (1996) "Concluding Comments." In Wilkerson, L. & Gijselaers, W. H. (ed.s) *Bringing Problem-Based Learning to Higher Education: Theory and Practice.* . *New Directors for Teaching and Learning.* Number 68. San Francisco: Jossey-Bass Publishers Inc., Pg.s 101-104.

Wolfc, Alan (2002) "Faith and Diversity in American Religion." *The Chronicle of Higher Education* (Feb. 8) Volume 48, Number 22, B7-B10.

Yao, Esther-Lee (1983) "Chinese Students in American Universities." *Texas Tech Journal of Education* (Winter) Volume 10, Number 1, 35-42.

Yin, Robert K., Karen A. Heald, and Mary E. Vogel (1977) *Tinkering with the System: Technological Innovations in State and Local Services.* Lexington, Mass.: Lexington Books.

Zeegers, Petrus J. (2001) "Approaches to learning in science: a longitudinal study." *The British Journal of Educational Psychology (March)* Volume 71, Part 1, 115-32.

http://achieve.phoenix.edu/

http://sg.motorola.com/inside/mu/aboutus.htm (July 30, 2002)

http://www.aahe.org/FFRR/principles_brochure2.htm (July 30, 2002)

http://www.aaup.org/issues/workplace/facdo.htm (July 30, 2002)

http://www.berkeleycollege.edu/Overview/BerkeleyWay.htm (July 30, 2002).

http://www.dc.edu/mission.shtml (July 30, 2002)

http://www.touro.ru/main.php?trg=2

http://www.tui.edu/About/indenx.html (July 30, 2002).

Daniel James Rowley is a Professor of Management and Chair of the Management Department at the Monfort College of Business at the University of Northern Colorado. He is the lead author of three previous scholarly books on strategic planning and strategic management in colleges and universities; a workbook in the same series; a book on academic supervision; and a forthcoming textbook on business strategic management with Dr. Sherman. He is also the author of numerous articles and presentations on these subjects. He has presented papers and seminars and held workshops on academic strategic planning nationally and internationally. He has served as Editor and as Associate Editor of the *Journal of Behavioral and Applied Management,* and has published book reviews and article reviews in several different journals. He received his B.A. from the University of Colorado at Boulder; his MPA from the University of Denver; and his Ph.D. from the University of Colorado at Boulder as well. He lives in Greeley, Colorado with his wife, Barbara, and daughter, Rebecca.

Herbert Sherman is a Professor of Management at Southampton College - Long Island University where he teaches courses at the undergraduate and graduate level in strategic management, research methods, and business ethics. His academic interests include case writing (soley and with co-authors), strategic planning and implementation, academic planning, and change management. His most recent publications include co-authored work with Dr. Rowley in the areas of strategic management in higher education. He is currently the Editor of *the Journal of Behavioral and Applied Management* and is completing a textbook in strategic management with Dr. Rowley for South Western, a Division of Thompson Learning. Dr. Sherman received his B.A. in Political Science from City College of New York, his M.S. in Management Science from Polytechnic University, and his Ph.D. in Strategic Management from the Union Institute and University. He lives with his wife Amy, his daughter Melissa, while his son Seth is attending the University of Texas – Austin.